Surviving Your Thesis

Completing a research thesis is not easy. From choosing a supervisor and topic to staying motivated, each stage presents a different challenge and many students struggle through without identifying the skills needed to make the most of their time. *Surviving Your Thesis* is a wonderful new resource for all doctoral and masters level research students, exploring the challenges and complexities of successfully engaging in the research process and thesis writing, to offer an accessible and practical guide.

The text takes readers from the very early stages of choosing to do a thesis through to the final stages of examination and publication. Chapters cover:

- Choosing and working with a supervisor
- Developing a research proposal
- Motivating yourself
- Choosing the right research method
- Responding to criticism
- Advice from the examiners
- Preparing work for publication.

The case examples and advice offered will appeal to researchers, supervisors and writers working in a variety of disciplines. The book addresses the questions all novice researchers face, and also includes chapters on cross-cultural issues and international study, making this text highly relevant for students studying abroad.

Surviving Your Thesis is a practical and informal guide to minimizing the difficulties of completing a thesis. No research student should be without it.

Suzan Burton is a Senior Lecturer in Management at the Macquarie Graduate School of Management, Macquarie University.

Peter Steane is Professor of Management at the Macquarie Graduate School of Management, Macquarie University.

Surviving Your Thesis

Edited by
Suzan Burton and
Peter Steane

Routledge
Taylor & Francis Group

LONDON AND NEW YORK

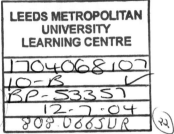
First published 2004
by Routledge
11 New Fetter Lane, London EC4P 4EE

Simultaneously published in the USA and Canada
by Routledge
29 West 35th Street, New York, NY 10001

Routledge is an imprint of the Taylor & Francis Group

© 2004 Suzan Burton and Peter Steane editorial matter
and selection; individual chapters, the contributors

Typeset in Perpetua and Bell Gothic by
Florence Production Ltd, Stoodleigh, Devon
Printed and bound in Great Britain by
TJ International, Padstow, Cornwall

British Library Cataloguing in Publication Data
A catalogue record for this book is available from the
British Library

Library of Congress Cataloging in Publication Data
Surviving your thesis / edited by Suzan Burton, Peter Steane.
        p. cm.
    Include bibliographical references and index.
    1. Dissertations, Academic.   I. Burton, Suzan.   II. Steane,
Peter.
    LB2369.S89 2004
    808′.02–dc22   2003021059

ISBN 0–415–32221–9 (hbk)
ISBN 0–415–32222–7 (pbk)

Contents

CONTENTS

Illustrations

FIGURES

TABLES

BOXES

Notes on contributors

TONY ADAMS is the General Manager of the Macquarie University International Office.

PETER BERGQUIST is Emeritus Professor of Biology and a past Deputy Vice-Chancellor (Research). He is currently Director of the Macquarie University Biotechnology Research. He is a noted international scholar in biotechnology.

PETER BURGESS is the Manager of the Macquarie International Offshore Program Group.

SUZAN BURTON has received numerous nominations and awards for MBA and doctoral teaching. She teaches quantitative methodology and marketing at Macquarie Graduate School of Management, Macquarie University.

YVON DUFOUR is a past Director of the DBA programme at Macquarie Graduate School of Management, Macquarie University. He teaches and researches in the field of strategy.

RICHARD DUNFORD is a Professor of Management and Deputy Dean of the Macquarie Graduate School of Management, Macquarie University.

ROB GRAY is a Professor and Director of the Centre for Social and Environment Accounting Research at Glasgow University. He is editor of *Social and Environmental Accounting* journal and serves on ten editorial boards. He was editor and joint editor of *British Accounting Review* for thirteen years.

JAMES GUTHRIE is a Professor of Accounting at the Macquarie Graduate School of Management. He is Australasian editor of the *Journal of Intellectual Capital*, serves on eighteen journal editorial boards and advises governments on public sector management and budgeting accounting matters.

JOHN MATHEWS is a Professor of Management and the Director of Research of the Macquarie Graduate School of Management, Macquarie University. He has been conducting major research programmes into the Asia-Pacific business arena and developmental strategies. His most recent books include *Tiger Technology* (2000) and *Dragon Multinational* (2002).

PAUL NESBIT has practised as a psychologist and currently teaches and researches in human resource management at Macquarie Graduate School of Management, Macquarie University.

RUTH NEUMANN is Associate Professor of Higher Education and Management and Higher Education Policy Adviser in the Vice-Chancellor's Office at Macquarie University. She has completed a national study of Australian doctoral education for the Commonwealth Department of Education, Science and Training. She consults to the United Nations and the Malaysian government on human resource development in education and training.

LEE PARKER is Professor and Associate Dean of Research in the School of Commerce at the University of Adelaide. He teaches qualitative methodology in doctoral programmes and is on the editorial board of twenty academic journals.

PETER STEANE is a Professor of Macquarie Graduate School of Management, Macquarie University. He is Director of Corporate and Executive Education (International) and Deputy Director of International Programmes. He teaches on doctoral and MBA programmes in ethics and strategy. He sits on the editorial boards of three academic journals.

YIMING TANG is the Director of the DBA programme and teaches international marketing, marketing management and market research at Macquarie Graduate School of Management, Macquarie University. He is also the co-ordinator of MGSM's China Study Tour programme. Dr Tang's research has focused on key issues in the field of marketing development in China, including market orientation and its impact on business performance, guanxi and relationship marketing and value chain management.

Introduction: Resilience in doing a thesis

PETER STEANE AND SUZAN BURTON

This is a book about capacity. In particular, it's about increasing your capacity to complete a thesis. It's about the practical skills of starting, doing and completing a research thesis. We don't believe that successful postgraduate students have unique or particular skills; completing a thesis relies on the ability to seek out and listen to good advice, to structure and develop a coherent and well planned project, good writing skills and the drive to achieve a difficult goal. These skills can be learned and improved by anyone. They can be used to sustain you in your project and can collectively provide the resilience sometimes necessary to adapt to, and overcome, setbacks in the task of completing a thesis.

This book arose from two sources. First, it grew out of our experience in teaching on structured doctoral and masters' programmes offered by Macquarie Graduate School of Management in Australia and Asia. From running these courses, we knew there was a range of skills that research students often needed, and we also knew that the existing books of advice for research students didn't offer the sort of practical, step-by-step advice that many students wanted. Second, the book arose from discussions between the editors, and the realization that we wanted to capture the resilience that we learnt to enable us to survive when we were doctoral students, and now (years later) to try to pass on that resilience to our doctoral students in our teaching and supervision. As a result, we chose to collect the advice from a range of experts in different areas of doing research, to compile what we believe is a comprehensive overview of the skills and tasks that are important in any dissertation project.

Resilience is the ability to bounce back after setbacks and to remain focused on a goal, yet to be adaptable enough to modify how the goal is to be achieved. There is increasing evidence that people who are resilient are more successful in life, because they are better able to cope with setbacks. Resilience is an apt quality for a person to develop if they seek to complete a postgraduate research programme, because in the course of doing research many challenges and problems will emerge, as well as opportunities. Challenges and problems may be frustrating, but they shouldn't be seen as abnormalities in the process. They are, in fact, normal dimensions of undertaking research projects, which require of you an ability to continue and persevere. Some people claim they could never undertake a thesis, for whatever reason, because they see the task as too difficult. But there are others who do aspire to complete a thesis and, while it *is* arduous and demanding, find the very journey of completing a thesis a worthwhile experience, separate from the satisfaction of completing the thesis. As US President John F. Kennedy said in 1961, America was going to put a man on the moon, and do other hard things:

> not because they are easy, but because they are hard, because that goal will serve to organize and measure the best of our energies and skills, because that challenge is one that we are willing to accept, one we are unwilling to postpone, and one which we intend to win, and the others, too.

A thesis, like other challenging goals, because it *is* hard, and is a goal that not everyone can achieve, is a more worthwhile goal.

STRUCTURE OF THE BOOK

The stages of a thesis, and thus the parts of this book, can generally be divided into three broad levels: the preparatory, operational and submission levels. The preparatory level concerns topics important when first considering the task of doing a thesis. The operational level contains chapters pertaining to the actual time while undertaking your thesis. Finally, the submission level includes chapters written on topics relevant when reaching the final stages of your thesis prior to submission and/or publication.

At the preparatory level, Yvon Dufour offers reflective comments on the question all candidates must ask themselves – is this right for me to do? He distinguishes between course work and research degrees, as well as some of the qualities necessary to succeed in a research thesis. Peter Burgess and Tony Adams provide an international perspective on dissertations. They outline the practical concerns of undertaking postgraduate study, especially those raised by studying in another country and away from home, such as accommodation and support services. Suzan Burton and Peter Steane discuss the important task of choosing and working with a supervisor over the length of a thesis. They outline the different approaches to supervision and discuss how to develop and maintain a good professional relationship with this important person. The chapter discusses expectations of supervisors over the course of a thesis, and the implications for students. Richard Dunford provides an overview on the development of the research proposal. This is usually the first task undertaken in the thesis, and is critical in putting a structure around your idea or question of inquiry. Peter Steane contributes a chapter discussing ethical issues in research, and, in particular, fulfilling the ethical requirements of your university. The final chapter in this preparatory level is Ruth Neumann's on the resources that can be useful in postgraduate study. These include different resources – personal (scholarships and grants), academic (library and software) and other more general information – which can simplify your life as a research student. Ruth's chapter provides references for a variety of web sites, providing a wealth of valuable information for potential and current students.

The chapters within the operational level deal specifically with the basic skills and tasks necessary in successfully undertaking the thesis. Paul Nesbit's chapter deals with that important factor which will ensure resilience: motivation. A thesis is a major task, a major project, and motivation is critical in sustaining your effort. Paul discusses the nature of motivation and strategies to assist you in the task ahead. Yiming Tang writes an engaging chapter as a series of interrelated parables. Yiming draws on a tradition that will be familiar to Asian readers, of using short stories to convey a fundamental message. By means of a series of stories he conveys a strong sense of the qualities that are critical for research students: determination, persistence, focus and patience, all coupled with the ability to choose the right goal and the right supervisor. The chapter on the literature review by Peter Steane looks at what a critical review of a field of knowledge is meant to be. It addresses skills in structuring the review in order to recognize gaps in the theory and build coherence, in order to proceed to data collection. Suzan Burton's chapter on quantitative research methodology covers the design of survey instruments, the management of data and the reporting of these data. An overview of the qualitative approach to research methodology is provided by Lee Parker's chapter, including a rich resource profile of qualitative theorists. Suzan Burton and Peter Steane contribute a chapter on the skills involved in writing the thesis, and strategies for improving your writing. This is particularly relevant, because writing is usually the prime medium you will use to convince examiners. Suzan and Peter provide another chapter on the common problems encountered while undertaking a thesis. These can vary from communication problems with your supervisor to 'writer's block'. They suggest possible reasons for these problems and strategies for overcoming them.

The final submission level contains chapters that are most relevant when the end of the thesis is approaching – or at least when you can see the light at the end of the tunnel. Peter Bergquist's chapter deals with the expectations of universities and examiners, and how to plan to ensure your thesis will pass their scrutiny in the examination process. John Mathews contributes a chapter on how to respond to criticism of your thesis. He deals with feedback from examiners and reviewers and also covers the delicate topic of examiners' advice to 'revise and resubmit' and the psychological challenge that presents candidates. John suggests strategies on how to approach addressing the examiners' criticisms in order to complete the examination phase satisfactorily. James Guthrie *et al.* contribute a chapter on the skill of redesigning your thesis for publication. Such publication may be in academic or professional journals, or in the form of a book. The chapter gives an overview of planning your work for publication: targeting a journal, identifying the audience, clarity of writing and the review process.

These three levels of preparatory, operational and submission themes provide a useful structure for the book. The contributors have generally taken an informal tone to provide you with fundamental skills and advice in the research exercise. While the chapters outline the authors' best advice on their topic, no one can prepare you for the unexpected difficulties that are likely to be encountered. This is where the skill of resilience comes in. Knowledge of what needs to be done at every step, and of the resources which will help you achieve each step, puts you in a far better position to adapt your proposal in a more flexible way or to adjust your work due to changed resources at your disposal.

COMMON THEMES

There are some common themes that recur in the book. Different authors reinforce these themes in their own way. The editors have chosen the three themes of momentum, focus and communication to focus on.

The theme of momentum appears in chapters that are linked with the discipline of the effort required of you as well as keeping your motivational energy sustained. There is reference to the importance of actually starting to write, to knowing when you have read enough and your ideas are adequately formed, and to not holding back unnecessarily or when to do so would be unwarranted. It is momentum that enables resilience to manifest itself. There will be times when motivation wanes or unexpected obstacles present, but it will be your commitment to study and reflection that will make you resilient.

A second theme is focus. The importance of focus appears in every chapter of the book, be it focus on choosing a supervisor, focus on specific methods or focus on anticipating and satisfying the examiners' expectations. This emphasis on focus illustrates the need to read and think carefully about your task. It is the refinement of thinking that assists coherence and builds a firm foundation for sustained effort. Deciding whether the thesis is the right course of action for you, preparing your research proposal and preparing your literature review, to name a few, are all essential tasks that rely upon focused thought.

Another theme is communication. Communication is important at the personal level of relating to a supervisor and in establishing a professional relationship with other academics. Superior communication skills are also required if you are performing a human subject study, in how you explain and seek involvement from your sample or interviewees or case organizations. Communication is also the core of the skill of writing well, so that your thesis coherently demonstrates your contribution to knowledge. You will be required to demonstrate good communication skills to your supervisor, examiners and readership when published. Communicating proficiently in the medium of writing and argument is crucial to the successful completion of the thesis.

Despite its optimistic title *Surviving Your Thesis* can't guarantee that you will succeed. However, the book will give you a much better understanding of what is required to succeed, strategies to increase your chance of succeeding, and advice on how to achieve and maintain the resilience needed to survive the almost inevitable setbacks. If it was easy, and everyone could do it, would you really value the qualification so much? We wish you luck with your thesis, and we hope that you do, indeed, survive, and graduate, and look back in wonder at your own survival – at your own resilience.

Part I

Preparation for the thesis
and the early stages

Chapter 1

Is a thesis right for you?

YVON DUFOUR

> One does not set out in search of new lands without being willing to be alone on an empty sea.
>
> (André Gide)

Enrolling in a research thesis is not a decision that should be taken lightly. This chapter discusses some of the factors that all students should consider before they make the decision to invest so much of their time and money (in fees, or in lost salary) in undertaking a research degree. Perhaps by the time you read this you will already have enrolled, and you may think that any advice contained in the chapter will be too late. If you have already started a thesis, and encountered some of the inevitable hurdles, asking yourself 'Is a thesis right for me?' can be a very challenging question, in case the answer seems to be 'Maybe not' or even 'No!' There are no clear-cut indicators of who are likely to be the best research students at the start of their studies. Even the most experienced academics find it hard to predict which students will succeed and who will fail. However, this chapter discusses some of the skills and personal attributes that can make success more likely. If you haven't yet enrolled, you should consider whether you possess, or can develop, those skills. If you have already started, identifying the characteristics most consistent with success can help you determine what you need to work on to make success in your thesis more likely.

WHAT DOES A THESIS INVOLVE?

There are significant differences between the sort of thesis written for a doctorate (for example, a PhD or a DBA) and one written in partial fulfilment of the requirements for a master's degree. In the UK many universities make a distinction between a 'thesis' for a master's degree and a 'dissertation' for a doctorate. But in many countries the terms are used interchangeably, so this book uses the term 'thesis' in the broadest sense, for both masters' and doctoral theses. The first term, 'thesis', places the emphasis on the proposition to be maintained or established whereas the second, 'dissertation', puts the focus on the book-length detailed discourse needed in order to maintain or prove the thesis. Together, they show what is expected in a thesis by any student, whether at master's or doctoral level: that the thesis will contain an in-depth investigation of a specific and important research topic, providing an original contribution to knowledge, presented in a lengthy written document which summarizes the contribution of the thesis. The difference between a master's and a doctoral thesis, then, is not in the format itself, but in the significance and the level of contribution.

There are further distinctions within and between quantitative and qualitative theses, between faculties, between academic divisions and disciplines, and between universities and countries. To paraphrase Professor Andrew Pettigrew, a noted organizational scholar, such distinctions result from the rich and dynamic interactions between the contexts in which the research is conducted, the processes used by the researchers and the contents of the research itself. However, despite these differences, all research shares the common element of requiring substantial time and effort, drawing on particular skills that few people in the community possess. If it was easy to complete a thesis, lots of people would do it, and the degree wouldn't be so valuable.

IS A THESIS RIGHT FOR YOU?

There is a common saying that there are only two things in life that are certain: death and taxes. One of the frustrations of research study is that no one can be certain when they start that they will successfully complete a thesis. Finishing a research degree can be a very rewarding personal experience. It shows that you have triumphed in the ultimate form of study by understanding the nature of an important and specific problem, that you have defined hypotheses or questions for investigation, and used an appropriate method to collect data to test your hypotheses and to interpret your results. It can be the beginning of a challenging and rewarding career, helping you to master important investigative skills that are the essence of academia, but also valuable in many jobs outside academia and research.

However, not everyone does succeed in finishing a thesis. In fact, one of the difficult aspects of doing a degree by research is to survive the inevitable and numerous ups and downs of research for months or years, without the certainty that you will ever complete. There is also the possibility that, even if you do complete, the degree may not even improve your career prospects. Graduates with higher research degrees cannot always expect to find a career related to the research on which they spent so much time and effort. The high personal costs involved in failing to complete, and the uncertain gains that result from completion, mean that potential research students should always carefully consider whether enrolling in a research degree is the right choice for them.

Some people apply for a research degree without seriously thinking about what it really involves. Many candidates who have been highly successful in under-graduate and postgraduate course work find, to their surprise and frustration, that the skills required of a research student are very difficult from the skills required for coursework study. Formal courses usually provide students with structure, regular feedback and a high probability of completion if sufficient effort is made. Success under this system, while providing a good indicator of intellectual ability, does not guarantee that a student has the high level of self-discipline, self-motivation and determination that is required to write a thesis. Do you think that you possess these skills? It is worth reflecting on whether you can initiate study, reading and data collection, as well as sustain your momentum without frequent and clear feedback, and in the face of almost inevitable setbacks, disappointments and frustration.

Research methodology textbooks often give an idealized view of research as being a sequential process of bite-size tasks. In truth, various research activities often run concurrently, involving many false starts, wasted time and abandoned work. For example, for most students, even the choice of a dissertation topic itself is not easy, requiring reading, discussion, reformulation of initial ideas and abandonment of early work as the topic changes or becomes clearer. The final topic is rarely the same as the one first undertaken, resulting instead from an extended process incrementally driven by a combined search for scientific rigour, opportunism and pragmatism. Ask yourself whether you can work with elements of complexity, confusion and frustration in your life, without the certainty that you will ever complete your research degree.

It is generally accepted that the aim of a thesis is to make a distinctive and original contribution to knowledge and/or practice. Developing new knowledge or new practice is more like a marathon than a sprint. It is not necessarily the brightest students who are successful in completing a thesis, but more often those with unwavering patience and perseverance, who cope well with uncertainty and without regular feedback. In contrast to coursework degrees, there are usually few rewards and limited feedback as you complete each step of the thesis. The focus is not so much on the quantity of your effort, although that is important, as on the quality of your contribution. You can't count up the course credits as a sign of clear progress towards completion, as you might with a coursework degree. You can't ever be certain that you have done enough until you eventually receive a final feedback from your examiners, years after you started your research.

Different chapters of this book address the different skills and tasks required to complete a thesis successfully. Perhaps the most important skill, however, is the ability to discipline yourself to carry out a long and unstructured process, success-fully drawing on and synthesizing existing research, adding to that research, and integrating your results within that research to establish your original contribution.

Consider whether you can set realistic targets and challenges for yourself. Is your time management good? Can you break a major research topic into its smaller components? You might find yourself having to make a trade-off between the magnitude of your research contribution and the pragmatics of finishing the thesis. Are you pragmatic? Are you prepared to abandon work which you have done, and/or which interests you, to get your thesis finished in time, if necessary?

Assuming that you believe that you have the motivation, persistence and time management skills to organize a complex task and to continue during the setbacks and difficulties of a thesis, the major challenge of a thesis is to learn how to conduct in-depth research, to report and discuss your findings in a scientific and rigorous way. If you have no experience of conducting and writing up research from your previous study, you will need to develop these skills to achieve the rigorous standards that will be expected by examiners. Many universities will require research students to undertake course work to give you some mastery of basic research skills. However, even the very best courses can never teach you all that you will need to know for your particular research. You will need to put a substantial amount of time and effort into ensuring that you are using the right research method and interpreting your results in a way that will be acceptable to your examiners. Any university library will contain past theses that you will be able to look through. Reading through some of them can help to show you the strengths and weaknesses of successful theses. No thesis is perfect: any thesis you look at could always be improved. But by the end of your thesis you will need enough knowledge and self-confidence to state and defend your own thesis, as well as to live with its weaknesses.

The next critical skill in successfully completing a thesis is the ability to write: clearly, correctly and in a style which meets the rigorous standards of the academic and scientific community. Academic writing, like good business writing, requires you to be impartial, to justify assertions, to be clear when an opinion is expressed, and to present and develop a complex argument in a form which is comprehensible and acceptable to an educated and informed audience. Few people find that this sort of writing comes easily. It is even harder if you intend to complete a thesis in a language that is not your native tongue. If you know that you are not a good writer, your thesis will be a much more difficult and frustrating task. This doesn't mean that it is impossible, but it should serve as a warning that you will need to put substantial time into developing your writing skills.

Most people who have completed a thesis will probably tell you that it is a long, reclusive and at times lonely and daunting journey of discovery – not only about the research subject itself, but also about yourself. Embarking on a research degree involves a substantial investment of money, time and resources. But the most significant resource required is the enormous emotional and intellectual energy that needs to be invested in order to achieve your goal of successful submission.

Successfully completing your research degree establishes you as one of a community of scholars who have all gone through the same process of researching and writing in accordance with well established customs of the discipline of research and the reporting of findings. Good research is also about discovering something new. But discovering something new is usually only a small part of a thesis. Most people do not make major discoveries in their thesis: only a handful of people publish their thesis and even fewer get any fame from it. A thesis, like genius, is sometimes said to be 95 per cent perspiration and 5 per cent inspiration. Discovering something innovative or contributing something new to knowledge lies in the 5 per cent inspiration. Discovering that 5 per cent of inspiration requires a commitment to the arduous and mundane task of research – the 95 per cent perspiration.

The title of this chapter could easily have been 'Is a thesis right for me?' The latter captures the spirit of a research degree thesis. The ultimate responsibility for the outcome belongs with the candidate alone. This does not mean that other people, such as your supervisor, will not have a significant impact on the process and content of your thesis. It does mean that at the end of the day you, and you alone, will be responsible for addressing the research question or hypothesis and for ensuring the quality of the final contents of your thesis. Think carefully about whether you are ready to take on that responsibility.

CONCLUSION

This chapter raises a number of questions for you to consider to help decide whether you are prepared to take on the effort of a thesis. A research degree is an immense challenge, but can also be a very rewarding experience. Some people do it for the challenge, others for interest and others for the pragmatic reasons of career advancement. I finish with some advice for you: reflect on your levels of self-discipline and self-motivation; on your record of commitment to challenges thrown at you, and how you manage your time and balance the complex demands of study, work and social life. Such a process is important because it will help you to answer the fundamental question of this chapter, 'Is a thesis right for you?' As I said earlier, no one can be sure of the answer to that question when they start, but carefully considering the challenges involved, and whether you think you can meet those challenges, is likely to provide some insight into the degree of investment required to successfully negotiate the journey of a research degree.

Chapter 2

An international perspective on postgraduate research degree studies

TONY ADAMS AND PETER BURGESS

> Travel is fatal to prejudice, bigotry, and narrow-mindedness, and many of our people need it sorely on these accounts. Broad, wholesome, charitable views of men and things cannot be acquired by vegetating in one little corner of earth all one's lifetime.
>
> (Mark Twain)

This chapter addresses issues that particularly concern candidates intending to enrol in postgraduate research degrees in a foreign country. The chapter reviews some of the key differences and similarities in higher degree offerings in different countries including the United States, the United Kingdom and Australia, and the implications for prospective students. Other factors influencing the decision to study in another culture, such as visa, cultural and financial issues are also discussed, to enable prospective research students to better understand the options that are available, and the factors that should be considered when choosing to enrol in a research degree in another country.

A BEGINNING

Education is an accepted means to upward mobility and is acknowledged as a priority for virtually all sectors of the global community. Studying in an English-speaking country is often seen as an attractive option for foreign students, because qualifications from particular countries often have higher prestige and at the same time offer students the opportunity to experience a different culture and simultaneously develop their language skills. The combined effects of a high-prestige degree, providing advanced knowledge, good language skills and broader cultural experience typically result in excellent career prospects in the home country, opening the door to good jobs and comparatively higher wages. Another influence underpinning much of the extensive demand for foreign postgraduate qualifications is the limited availability of appropriate research degree places in some countries' tertiary education institutions. For these reasons, a growing number of prospective students are willing and able to pay for the advantages of foreign research degrees. These factors combine to create a high demand for foreign qualifications, with the result that there is often intense competition for places at the better universities, and the process of deciding where to study can be a difficult one, requiring substantial research and time to decide which universities offer the best match for your interests and skills.

In some cases, the choice of a degree and university will be influenced by the extent to which it is recognized in the student's home country. In Singapore, for example, individual Ministries are responsible for the recognition of foreign degrees, and employment opportunities within such Ministries are conditional on this recognition. However, such restrictions do not seem to influence foreign degree choice in circumstances where career opportunities are sought in the private sector.

The decision to enrol in a foreign postgraduate research degree is therefore not as simple as it might first seem. The choice can be influenced by a range of factors: destination preference; discipline orientation; university reputation, recognition and ranking; entry requirements; duration and timing of the course; language of instruction; host government visa regulations and requirements; fees, scholarships and the cost of living abroad; research and employment opportunities during and after study; student facilities and resources; library resources; the academic environment, such as the university's level of internationalization; access to appropriate accommodation, and general safety and security issues.

Whilst such choice criteria are readily identifiable, the ultimate decision as to where to study and with whom is often outside the control of the candidate. The difference between what a prospective candidate would like to do and what is available to them can be poles apart. It is this distinction that first confronts most intending candidates when they start the initial search for preferred options. As a result, it's a good idea to consider a range of programmes at the start, rather than limiting yourself to one university, or even one country. By gathering information about a range of options, in the best case, you may discover a course that suits you much better than the one you first considered. In the worst case, if you consider a range of options and still return to your first choice, you will be able to be more confident that it is, in fact, the best option for you.

The need to fulfil specific programme requirements can further complicate your choice of university or the timing of your application. For many universities, admission of international students will depend on satisfactory performance on standard grading tests, such as the Graduate Management Admission Test (GMAT) or the International English Language Test S (IELTS). These tests may be offered only in certain locations at specific times, such as at the beginning of each academic year. Depending on their prior qualifications and the degree they are enrolling in, students may sometimes have to attain an interim award in the lead up to the sought research degree qualification. This interim award is often used as an exit strategy for students who have satisfactorily passed the required study but who have not achieved the standard that is required to progress to the next level of study.

Given such entry requirements, the range of suitable courses often narrows, and an alternative option can become the preferred choice. This is where careful planning comes into play. In deciding what universities and programmes might be acceptable, you will need to consider issues such as what you can afford, what are then the best available options and which of these options maximizes the particular benefits you are seeking.

DEGREE OF DEGREES

Even after being accepted, your suitability for a research degree sometimes needs to be demonstrated, for example by passing a prerequisite certification with satisfactory grades and/or by passing a written examination. It is often only after a student satisfies such initial requirements that the actual research dissertation can commence. For example, from an initial group of forty students starting a US PhD degree programme, as few as 50 per cent of the cohort might proceed to the dissertation, the others having been excluded for non performance or having decided that the programme was too difficult. In such circumstances, alternative qualifications, such as a Master of Arts (MA) or Master of Philosophy (MPhil) degree may be available to a student who completes the coursework component of the programme and/or preliminary research but who is excluded or chooses not to proceed to the dissertation.

Once they have started their research work, candidates will typically be required to continue to demonstrate satisfactory progress, for example by presenting a seminar paper or by showing adequate progress since the last review. In addition, there may be major hurdles, such as a formal written and/or oral presentation of the planned dissertation proposal to a committee of academics, which has to be judged as satisfactory to allow continuation of the thesis. In investigating a research degree, you should ensure that you know what examinations or hurdles you will need to pass along the way, and whether there are acceptable exit strategies if you don't surmount these hurdles.

This variation in entry, coursework and examination requirements stems partly from the fact that there is not one commonly accepted format for the components of a PhD or master's degree, and there can be wide variation between different countries. For example, the US PhD degree is generally a mixture of course work and dissertation, and most universities encourage the completion of all requirements for the PhD within a five-year period. Outside the US, most doctorates don't involve the same level of course work. For example, in Australia only professional doctorates such as a Doctor of Business Administration (DBA) or Doctor of Education (EdD) normally combine a mixture of course work and thesis, and are thus more similar to US doctoral programs. Most Australian and British research degrees have minimal coursework requirements. Instead, they generally require the candidate to undertake a major research project leading to a thesis of 80,000 words or more, usually presented in English, and completed over a period of three to five years of study. In most cases, however, it is recognized that the exact amount of time needed to complete a research thesis will depend on the student, the topic selected, the amount of data collection involved, the complexity of the analysis and the many other problems that can be encountered whilst conducting a piece of original research.

Assessment criteria for theses also tend to be different in American universities, compared with British or Australian research degrees. The thesis component of an American degree is normally examined by a committee of experienced researchers from within the student's university. Examination of British or Australian theses almost invariably requires external assessment, using a majority of examiners (two, or possibly three) from outside the university of study.

APPLICATION, ACCEPTANCE AND ENTRY

The application process for a research degree generally varies by institution and country. For master's level entry, it can require a twelve to eighteen-month lead time, with students entering at certain academic calendar dates to fit in with the prescribed coursework requirements. Four years of undergraduate study are considered normal as a prerequisite for entry into a postgraduate research degree. The application process is often more difficult, though not impossible, for students whose previous qualification was a three-year bachelor's or honours degree.

Admission to a PhD programme will vary with the particular programme, but if there is no course work involved, PhD students can often be admitted at any time during the year, since their admission does not have to fit in with scheduled course work. Nevertheless, there can be advantages in starting at the beginning of the academic year. Most universities offer a variety of social events and general orientation and information sessions for new students, and these are most likely to be available at the beginning of the academic year. In addition, settling into a new country and making new friends can often be easier when there are other students in a similar situation. The main disadvantage of starting at the same time as most other students can be in finding suitable accommodation, since the influx of new students at the start of the year puts the greatest pressure on the available student accommodation at this time. For a research student with some flexibility of starting date, this can suggest that starting about one month before the beginning of the academic year can capture dual advantages, by first providing a greater

17

choice of accommodation, and second by allowing access to all information sessions and social activities at the beginning of the academic year.

Obtaining a student visa can be time-consuming and difficult depending on the intended country of study. For example, the student visa regime in the United States has been tightened as a result of national security concerns. This may impact on the ability of even the best students from some countries to gain entry to a US research degree programme. For students hoping to study in Australia, the regulations vary depending on their home country, but may require a score of six or more on the IELTS English language test, plus pre-visa checks on health, character and evidence of ability to pay the fees and support themselves and any dependants, as shown by the provision of six consecutive months of bank statements.

International research students in Australia also need to fulfil a number of particular requirements: undertake an approved full-time course of study; obtain health cover; pay international student fees (currently set at approximately A$15,000 per annum for a PhD); comply with student employment restrictions that set a maximum ceiling of twenty hours' work per week; meet satisfactory progress targets and achieve a minimum English-language IELTS result of 6.0 or better. For the student with a spouse or dependent children there will be other costs, because accompanying children will be required to pay school fees of approximately A$5,000 per annum, and spouses are normally not permitted to work. While scholarship schemes and work opportunities within academic departments are often available, the arrangements are not as systematic in Australian universities as they are in the US.

Within the US there are over 4,000 universities and colleges, of which only about 400 offer doctoral degree programmes. Competition to get into US research programmes is consequently very high, with only the best students being selected. This competitive environment reflects a US PhD system that is designed to produce graduates for the general community but, in particular, to produce the next generation of highly qualified US research academics. Many research departments, particularly in areas such as science, mathematics, engineering and economics, would not exist without the large number of high-quality international students they attract. This means that there can be generous scholarships for the very best foreign students, but fees and costs will be high for those without scholarship support. Tuition fees can be up to US$24,000 per year, with additional living costs of around US$15,000 per year.

In many cases, successful applicants in public US universities will be offered lower 'in state' tuition and employment in a tutorial or other assistant role. In addition to lower or waived fees, students in these employment arrangements may also receive a small amount of money as a stipend. However, even these arrangements will not normally be sufficient to cover all the costs of living and studying in another country. Consequently, unless applicants have a scholarship, they should ensure that they have sources of funding to cover all student fees and living costs, independent of any likely university income. Student visas in the US do not allow unrestricted work rights off campus, so students should not expect to cover their costs by working in the community.

The UK system is basically the same as the Australian and American tertiary education models. The UK has a similar fee-based system, with fees ranging from £7,000 to £15,000 sterling per annum, and a variety of scholarships exist for the best students. You can expect to have to budget for up to £10,000 per year for living expenses in the UK. International students in the UK usually have the ability to work for a limited number of hours, similar to conditions in Australia.

Prospective students in Australia and the UK will often be asked to submit a potential research proposal with their application, though the final research area is usually finalized after admission and acceptance of the student. While the actual research topic may change, the initial proposal can be important in influencing a student's admission. It demonstrates your writing ability, your ability to identify a worthwhile research topic and your ability to propose a suitable research methodology. A badly written, poorly thought out proposal is unlikely to be considered favourably by any academic who reads it, so it is important to put substantial effort into the proposal, and into any other written components of your application, because your writing skills will often be judged as a key indicator of your ability to write an English-language thesis. For most research degrees however, student admission occurs before the final determination, preparation and approval of the research proposal. During this preparatory stage, which normally takes around six months, academic supervision arrangements will be finalized and the student may undertake formal research training. Many students find this a challenging and often difficult period, as they must also cope with a new culture, learning style and language. It can be a lonely time, in which progress often seems slow.

If the prospect of living and studying abroad for several years seems to be financially or personally challenging, there may be the opportunity to remain in your home country for a major part of your enrolment. Many foreign universities, particularly those outside the US which don't include a substantial component of course work, may allow students to complete part or all of their studies in their home country, usually with the appointment of a local supervisor. These external or offshore research programmes may require a period on campus each year but will usually mean that a student visa is not required, as the programme will be undertaken outside the host country. The student can often continue working part-time, decreasing the financial stress of study, and avoiding the potential loneliness of studying in another country and culture. The degree can also be completed in either full-time or part-time mode, in contrast to the full-time mode required by most student visas.

19

RANKINGS

Large US universities typically have very high levels of funding, and as a result, can often support intensive research and specialization in a number of areas, and as a result, the best American universities are usually ranked as the best in the world. The large number of universities in the US, however, means that there are substantial differences in quality between programmes and specializations at different universities. American universities are ranked by specialist publications such as the *Peterson's Guide to Graduate and Professional Programs*, available from major educational booksellers worldwide. These publications can be a useful resource for checking the reputation and specializations of potential universities.

Australian and UK universities have similar educational standards to US universities, with the major differences being in the degree of specialization available and in the depth of their programmes. Most Western universities, even the smallest, will have major national and international research strengths in particular areas. The web site www.hero.ac.uk/rae/ contains government rankings of British universities by discipline for each university. There is no national ranking scheme in Australia, although the results of audits of universities undertaken by the Australian Universities Quality Agency are available on-line (www.auqa. edu.au). *The Good Universities Guide*, a privately published book, rates Australian universities on a wide range of activities.

THE APPLICATION PROCESS

North American universities generally do not employ overseas agents to support recruitment, although university representatives may attend specialist education fairs in Asia and Europe. Candidates will therefore generally need to apply direct to the preferred tertiary institution. Further information can be obtained from the US Educational Advising Centers (http://apps.collegeboard.com).

The British Council represents UK universities worldwide through a network of offices and carries out a range of recruitment activities (www.british council.org/education/). Australian universities are represented outside Australia by IDP Education Australia, which has offices in many countries and regions. The IDP web site (www.idp.edu.au) provides extensive information about studying in Australia. Application to Australian universities can be made direct to the university or via an agent. Agents are located in most of the major student markets, and will generally represent a number of universities in different countries and/or those that have different specializations and academic strengths. University web sites will contain details of their appointed agents. In addition to admission and academic programme advice, these agents can provide information on applicable living costs, visa requirements, pastoral care and pre-departure considerations. Depending on the home country, agents may charge a fee for these services. Staff from many universities also regularly visit major source countries to take part in education fairs, conduct information sessions and/or conduct interviews with potential applicants. Attending these sessions can be a valuable way to get information about potential programmes and to get a feeling for the universities' focus and approach, and to ask detailed questions about studying in that country.

In addition to university agents, the Australian government operates Australian Education Centres (http://aei.dest.gov.au) throughout Asia, and Australian universities operate the Australian Education Office in Washington DC. These offices do not recruit students, but provide information and resources on Australian education. Australian embassies and consulates also provide education information about studying in Australia, such as visa requirements and details of Australian government research scholarships and aid programmes.

Many British universities also use agents and attend the education fairs that are held regularly throughout the world. The best advice that can be given to potential candidates is to undertake your own research on preferred universities by accessing university web sites to identify those with appropriate research strengths, and then identify and contact academics from within your target discipline area. Most academic staff will be able to advise as to the likelihood of an application being successful and, more important, whether there is a good match of research interests between what you want to study and the ability of the university to supervise you.

High-quality doctoral programmes that welcome international students will obviously be available in many countries. The Internet is an excellent source for collecting information on research degree opportunities and application requirements and processes. For example, the Association of Universities and Colleges of Canada (www.aucc.ca) provides information about Canadian institutions and www.mynzed.com information about New Zealand universities. Further information about studying in other countries can be readily obtained using the search engine Google (www.google.com).

FREQUENTLY ASKED QUESTIONS

How many international students are admitted to postgraduate research programmes?

Competition is very tough for entry into higher degree research programmes. Only the best students will gain admission and only the best of these will receive scholarships and other financial support. In the US, research students are generally inducted into a coursework component of the programme as part of a class group. In Australia and the UK, an academic department may admit a group of students at the one time, or it may accept individual students throughout the year when supervision is available. At PhD level in Australia and the UK, where supervision usually depends largely on one or two academics per student, admission may depend less on the potential number of places than on the ability of the university to provide a suitable supervisor in the area you wish to study. In both these countries the majority of local research students are likely to be studying part-time, so international students may find themselves working alone, or in small research groups with supervisory support.

What financial support (scholarships, fellowships, teaching assistantships) is available?

Limited numbers of scholarships are available at most universities, but are generally limited to the best research candidates. Various government scholarship or loan schemes are also available for each country and these can be readily researched through the various web sites listed for that country. Work is often available for research students in the department in which they are studying as a teaching or research assistant. However, competition for these places is often quite high among research students, and students with very good English skills will usually find it easier to get work.

Must applicants take the GMAT or an equivalent entry examination?

This will depend on the university, although the use of grading tests like the GMAT (Graduate Management Admission Test) is particularly common in the US and the UK.

Do foreign students need to take a language test like IELTS or TOEFL?

For English-speaking countries, all applicants who have not completed their undergraduate degree in English will generally need to take the IELTS or TOEFL language test and achieve an acceptable score. This score may also be a prerequisite to obtaining a student visa to the country of choice. In Australia students from some developing countries are required to obtain an IELTS score of 6.0 or above to be eligible for a student visa. However, this score will not always be sufficient to obtain university entry, as some universities will accept only students with a minimum score of 6.5 on the IELTS test, or an equivalent score from TOEFL or a similar test.

How is admission decided?

In general, admission to a postgraduate research degree requires satisfactory completion of an honours or a four-year bachelor's degree with the equivalent of first-class honours. Alternative entry requirements can include a master's degree by research or course work with a significant research component, or a combination of another approved qualification and research and work experience. Other primary admission factors are likely to include:

Graduate Record Examination (GRE) or an alternative such as GMAT. Applicants will sometimes need to submit scores on the aptitude portion of the GRE. In some cases, applicants may substitute scores on the GMAT test. The scores of successful applicants on each of the three components of the GRE typically fall within the following percentile ranges:

- Verbal   70–81
- Quantitative 70–99
- Analytical   70–92.

An application statement that includes personal details, prior academic record, objectives and expected outcomes.

Transcripts of academic record:

- *Admission requirements* (MA). Honours degree with a minimum B+ average. Successful applicants will often have an A average.
- *Admission requirements* (PhD). MA degree with a minimum B+ average; however, almost all successful applicants have an A average. Many PhD students are also promoted from the MA programme, and sometimes students who apply to the PhD programme are instead admitted to an MA and then promoted if their academic performance is satisfactory.

Interview. Many universities will arrange interviews for prospective students in their home country to determine students' suitability for study. These interviews may be conducted by university staff or by their representatives in their major student 'markets'.

References. A number of references, or letters of recommendation, are usually requested to establish independent character references regarding the candidate's academic, personal and professional ability, commitment and ambitions. They form an important part of the selection criteria, so it is worth putting substantial thought into who should be your referees. For a research student, academics who know the student and their academic ability are probably the most important referees. In particular, a reference showing aptitude for research is likely to be more influential than a reference which discusses performance in previous course work.

Application fee. This will depend on the university and may cost up to the equivalent of US$100.

Statement of purpose. Applications will sometimes request a 'statement of purpose' from the student, or a similar summary of their aims. This statement is normally presented as a written essay that addresses the purpose of study, the student's particular research interests, qualifications and experience, plans for the future, outcomes sought and the reason/s for selecting the particular university of choice.

As mentioned previously, admission to most programmes, particularly at the better universities, is very competitive. GRE scores within the above ranges do not necessarily ensure admission. Each applicant's ability and potential for further study are assessed at both the departmental level and by a programme-wide admissions committee. Although the academic record and test scores are important factors in the admission process, other relevant factors, in particular any demonstrated ability to conduct publishable research, will be taken into consideration.

Does the university accept transfer students from other universities?

Approval of student transfer between tertiary institutions is dependent on the nature of the transfer, complementarity of research interests and degree offerings, and particular university policy. Whilst factors such as the academic standing of the institution of prior study and a student's academic record will often assist transfer arrangements, recognition of previous academic research should not be assumed to count towards advanced standing in the new programme. In particular, if a student wants to transfer after starting the research component of a thesis, a transfer is likely to be successful only if the target university can provide a suitable supervisor. Even if a suitable supervisor is available, transferring to another supervisor within the same or a different university will nearly always delay progress, as the suggestions and interests of the new supervisor will need to be accommodated.

Will the university provide any indication of the likelihood of offering financial assistance prior to commencement?

Candidates would be unwise to commence their programme without first receiving formal notification from the university that they have qualified for financial assistance, if this is necessary for them to enrol. Similarly, hoping to secure sufficient income to meet programme costs and/or living expenses from paid employment in the community is not always an option. Many countries impose strict conditions on foreign student visas that effectively limit the option of paid employment.

Does the university consider applications outside the specified application dates?

This will depend on the nature of the degree and the university. In research degrees with little or no course work, such as those often offered in Australia and the UK, research student applications will often be accepted and processed throughout the year. For other courses, even within the same university, applications may be required to be submitted by a certain date to allow commencement in the following year. In US-style research degrees involving substantial course work it is likely that there will be fixed application and start dates. Details for each course and university are likely to be available on the university's web site.

How important is the academic supervisor?

The issues involved in targeting a particular supervisor are discussed in greater detail in Chapter 3, but in the British and Australian systems, applicants will generally have to match the preferred research area with the university's ability to supervise within a very specific research area. This means that part of the preliminary investigation in targeting a university should involve finding universities, departments and individual members of faculty that are working in the area of the proposed research. This may involve discussions with faculty at a home university, surveying the research literature and researching university research web sites. Contacting particular academic departments can provide information on research capabilities and strengths and help to identify the institutions that best match a candidate's research needs and supervision requirements. Direct contact with a university can also assist in the application process, by revealing or clarifying information that may not be apparent from standard application information.

In US-style research degrees, applicants will undertake coursework programmes over a period of up to two or three years, and during this time there will be ample opportunity to search out the various research options and available supervisors. At the appropriate time, students will be allocated a research supervisor who will support them throughout their programme. They will then become a member of a research group studying alongside other students and academic staff within the selected discipline area.

Do I get research training?

Most universities provide formal and/or informal research training, often as part of the development of the research proposal. In the US-style degree, this research training will usually form part of the coursework component.

Can I do a foreign doctorate without leaving home?

Many universities offer PhDs that can be partly or completely carried out without leaving home. With the benefit of on-line access to library databases, and regular contact with the supervisor by e-mail, teleconferencing and/or phone calls, physical attendance at a university is less important than ever before. Depending on the university, enrolment from another country may require a period on campus each year. Students will generally also require some form of local supervision, in addition to their supervisor in the university of enrolment.

LEARNING GAPS

The educational background of a postgraduate international student is often inadequate to prepare them for what faces them in the foreign learning environment. In some instances, candidates will have graduated from a school of undergraduate experience that has an authoritarian teaching style. It may also be the case that there has been no questioning or discussion permitted in what are often overcrowded classrooms, with very limited library and laboratory resources available. Learning in this context is usually the result of observation, memory and replication. In contrast, the Western education environment, particularly for research students, is based on a learning style that requires independent research and analysis, and argument based on critical thinking and participation.

The challenge for a foreign postgraduate research student is therefore to bridge such education gaps as quickly as possible, and, without coursework support, this can be difficult in the early stages of adjustment. Language is of course the other key issue for most international students. Even with a good score on a test such as IELTS, students can experience difficulties in understanding colloquial speech, and in making themself understood. In addition, learning to read critically, identify relevant information and synthesize key arguments, difficult skills for many research students, can be even more challenging in a second language. Beginning right from the proposal preparation stage, specific linguistic skills will be required. Supervisors do not see it as their role to teach English, and can sometimes become frustrated with a student who writes badly. However, admitting that these skills present a challenge is often the first step in beginning to acquire them. Most universities offer a range of services for international students, such as courses in academic writing, and may also offer academic preparation programmes that cover a mixture of English language and related academic skills.

STUDENT SERVICES

Most universities provide a number of services and programmes for international students. Prospective students will often be notified of these services, but searching the university web site can reveal the full array of services available to students. Typical services will include the following.

Pre-arrival information

This will include information on how to prepare for campus life as well as information on the new living environment, average living costs, enrolment procedures, visa requirements, ability to work, getting to the university for the first time, finding accommodation and suchlike.

Orientation

Most universities will have an orientation period that may last from a day to a week. During the orientation period a variety of presentations are likely to cover aspects that are particularly relevant to international students, such as living in the environment, opening a bank account, employment regulations and conditions. Other sessions which are also relevant for local students will cover issues such as settling into the university, an introduction to university services such as the library and health services, university tours, and social events to help meet new friends and colleagues. Attendance at orientation sessions can be particularly useful in decreasing loneliness, by offering the chance to meet other new students.

English-language instruction

For applicants from non-English-speaking backgrounds, pre-specified levels on language tests such as the TOEFL or IELTS will need to be met in order to gain entry to the university. However, many students find that meeting the minimum level for such tests does not adequately prepare them for the rigorous demands of researching and writing a thesis in English. Many universities conduct English language and academic preparation courses, or can advise on specialist providers of these courses. The international and research offices may also provide specialist advisers, and many universities offer specialist courses and advice on writing a thesis in English.

Social opportunities

Universities typically have a variety of sporting and social clubs and societies to assist students to become part of the university community. Often these are country-based such as a Malaysian Students' Association. The university union and the international office may also provide a variety of social activities to help new students settle in.

Accommodation

Accommodation is usually available for graduate students in university-owned or leased apartments and dormitories. Most universities will also have a central housing office that can place students in dormitories or apartments or help students to find shared or off-campus accommodation. Whatever the arrangement, students will need to pay for the cost of this accommodation. Consequently, it is advisable for students to arrive a few weeks before they need to start courses or research work to give them the best opportunity to find accommodation that suits their particular needs.

Health insurance, health and welfare services

Health insurance may be required by some countries or by particular universities to ensure that you can meet any health care costs. Universities will generally provide a comprehensive range of health and welfare facilities, including medical, counselling, employment and academic advice services.

Immigration, taxation and employment issues

Before committing to a research programme in an overseas university, applicants must first ensure that they understand the immigration and employment regulations. Getting good-quality visa advice before leaving home is very important. Questions that all candidates should have answers to include:

- What is the duration of the visa?
- What are the work permit regulations?
- When is it permissible to leave and return?
- Are there academic requirements that impact on retaining the student visa?

In Australia, for example, students are permitted to work up to twenty hours per week during the term period. Prospective candidates need to understand the visa rules and the way that they work. For example, if a student works twenty-one hours in one week and nineteen hours in the next during an academic semester in Australia, then the student is in breach of the visa regulations and may be deported. Candidates also need to understand the tax rates, the effect of tax on their take-home pay, and know how and when to complete a tax return to recover any possible taxes. In the US many students work as teaching assistants, but may find that most of the salary will go towards payment of their tuition fees unless they also have an arrangement to waive these fees.

Many students hope to stay and work in the host country after their research degree is completed, and in most countries a degree, particularly a research degree, will help an application for residence. If you are considering this, you should ensure that you understand the relevant immigration regulations. Permanent residence applications are likely to be more difficult, even with a research degree, if your host country does not have a need for skills in your research area. In addition, particularly in a period of global security concerns, immigration regulations can sometimes change quite suddenly, so skills that are required at one time may be less valuable for residence applications several years later.

Research facilities

University departments have a serious commitment to both teaching and research on a wide range of theoretical, empirical and applied topics. To support such research, most Western universities' libraries hold millions of volumes and thousands of serials in open stacks with study space available to graduate students. Research students, in particular, will often have access to resources that are not available to undergraduate students. Increasingly, universities are providing extensive on-line access to journals and databases, which means that a student can obtain access to these from home. In addition, many departments maintain their own libraries and computer laboratories for student use and there are generally many other computing facilities available on campus.

CONCLUSION

This chapter has reviewed the multiple factors involved in selecting and applying for a postgraduate research programme and foreign university. It can be seen that the investigation and decision processes leading to the choice of, and entry into, a higher research degree in a foreign country are complex, and the ultimate choice of a particular programme is often determined by a mixture of controllable and uncontrollable factors. However, by engaging in substantial research, and by systematically reviewing the particular features of different programmes, prospective research students should be better able to make informed decisions, and to identify and target the programmes which have the best chance of providing them with a rewarding, and ultimately successful, research programme.

REFERENCES

Ashenden, D., Ramsay, G. and West, L. (2003) *The Good Universities Guide,* Melbourne: Hobsons Australia.

Graduate and Professional Programs an Overview 2003 (2004) Princeton: Peterson's.

Chapter 3

Choosing and working with a supervisor

SUZAN BURTON AND PETER STEANE

> You know, both of us will probably cry before this is over.
> (Supervisor to incoming doctoral student)

The selection of a supervisor is one of the most important steps in starting a post-graduate thesis. Effectively managing your relationship with that supervisor is then a critical component of a successful candidature. There will be few, if any, people who will understand and share with you the trials and successes of the research journey in the way that your supervisor will. On the other hand, both the student and the supervisor can become frustrated and unhappy with the other's perceived and/or actual shortcomings. In the worst cases, the relationship can deteriorate to the extent that it damages the student's thesis.

This chapter aims to help you identify the factors that you should consider in choosing and working with a supervisor. The choice of supervisor is, for many students, the first critical decision in undertaking a thesis. The right supervisor can help you to produce a better thesis, and do it faster, while providing you with valuable experience and contacts. Choosing the wrong supervisor will add further tensions to the usual stresses of a thesis, and in the most extreme cases can result in students dropping out or restarting on a new topic with another supervisor, causing a substantial delay in completion. So choosing the right supervisor is obviously important. But how do you tell who will be the 'right' supervisor for you? The same academic might be a fantastic mentor and supporter to one student and the 'supervisor from hell' for another student. In this chapter we discuss three fundamental issues in the student/supervisor relationship: appropriate expectations, how to choose the right supervisor for you, and how to work most effectively with your supervisor. We discuss some of the ways to work out whether a potential supervisor will be right for you, how to make yourself attractive to a potential supervisor, and how to manage the relationship with a supervisor once you are working together. The chapter concludes with a discussion of the codes of supervisory practice that exist in some universities, and what these mean for you as a student.

APPROACHES TO SUPERVISION: BE CLEAR ABOUT EXPECTATIONS

Styles of supervision will vary across disciplines and across universities. For example, in the science disciplines much research is conducted in laboratories, often working in close proximity with the supervisor and/or on related work. The work of research students in science is often one part of a supervisor's own research work, perhaps funded in full or in part by the supervisor's grants. All these factors mean that supervisor/student relationships in the sciences tend to be very close. In contrast, research students in the arts or social sciences are often working on a research topic of their own choosing, which may be only peripherally related to the supervisor's own research interests. This can be a particularly important issue for students doing professional doctorates, such as a Doctor of Business Administration, where the student enters the programme with a clear idea of the area that they are interested in researching. Many of these research students work primarily at home, with less frequent contact with the supervisor, usually during formal meetings, resulting in a more distant student/supervisor relationship. It's useful to understand these differences in supervision patterns, because otherwise students can become frustrated when they see friends in other disciplines receiving a much more directed style of supervision, which can sometimes appear very attractive to students who are having difficulty with their thesis. Common patterns and differences in supervision resulting from these differences in discipline areas are summarized in Table 3.1.

In the arts or social science disciplines, most students have a clear idea of their topic area before they apply to a university. In these areas, it is also common for universities to review a student's application, and if it is accepted, to then appoint a supervisor. This process of appointing students to supervisors is sometimes a university or departmental policy, in order to share the load of research students around. Even if your university has a policy of appointing supervisors to students, you can usually still influence the process. You can investigate the faculty at the

Table 3.1 Comparison of supervision issues across disciplines

	Arts/Social science	Science
Supervision style	General advice, then 'hands-off'	General and specific advice given. Close mentoring
Meetings	Irregular and infrequent	Regular and frequent
Joint publications	Generally uncommon, but increasing	Generally common, and increasing
Mentorship	Uncommon	More common

department you are applying for and suggest a supervisor who you think may be a good match for your research topic and personality. If the university appoints a supervisor for you it is still possible to change supervisors, but it is always better to do so early in the thesis, before you have committed substantial time working on the agenda of, or under the direction of, one supervisor.

If you don't have a clear research topic, it is important to see a supervisor or potential supervisor both as a 'sounding board' for your ideas and plans for research and also as a resource. Your research will hopefully provide mutual benefits, and the supervisor can help you to identify research areas that will increase these mutual benefits. The supervisor is likely to bring particular knowledge and expertise to issues and topics that you may wish to study. They may be able to facilitate access to research sites, or to potential subjects, through their professional and academic reputation and contacts. In the sciences this can mean links with teams in clinical trials and access to laboratories and equipment. In the social sciences it may mean access to data sources or contacts with experts in the relevant field. Finding out what resources, if any, a supervisor can provide can be an important factor in helping you to decide whether to study with a particular person. For the supervisor, an active research student can be a welcome addition to their own research interests, and can also provide a source of joint publications.

CHOOSING A SUPERVISOR

The selection of an appropriate supervisor depends on a number of criteria, both professional and personal. On a professional basis, you should certainly aim for a supervisor with research interests related to your topic area. Generally, you should consider faculty who actively engage in research, because you want to work with someone who has a research profile and has demonstrated expertise. You can assess a potential supervisor's research activity by searching for and assessing their publications, paying particular attention to recent publications, which are likely to be the best indicator of current activity. On a personal level, we suggest you should consider people who are accessible and with sufficient interpersonal ability to interact with you honestly, but also diplomatically, about your research. This section discusses a range of factors that will help you identify who might be a good supervisor for you, how to target a particular supervisor, and how to make yourself attractive to a potential supervisor so that they are willing to take you on.

How do supervisors choose students?

The supervisor will nearly always have the ultimate choice about whether they agree to take a particular research student. While you are trying to choose the supervisor who will be right for you, academics are trying to identify students whom they are prepared to work with. So part of your process of choosing the right supervisor should consist of making yourself appear to be a 'good' student. To that end, it is helpful to think about how supervisors choose students, and ways in which you can try and convince potential supervisors that you are the sort of student that they want to supervise.

Supervising students is, for most academics, extremely time-consuming. They don't usually get paid any extra to supervise students, and generally do so because they hope to develop their own research and/or career, by working with a bright student, who, they hope, will have the potential to become a valuable colleague. If the student drops out, this usually means that the academic has invested a lot of time for little or no return – time that they could have spent on their own research, or on consulting, or perhaps with their family, or doing something else they enjoy.

When a student applies to a university without stating that they have the support of a particular academic, their application will usually be passed to academics working in the particular field, to see if they are interested in supervising this student. At some universities, academics will be expected to supervise a certain number of students, so there is often an incentive for the academic to take on a certain number of students. In almost every university, however, academics have a choice as to which students (if any) they take on each year, and a student who drops out can reflect badly on the academic, so the academic is likely to be keen to choose students who have the highest possibility of succeeding. This usually means the students who they think have the greatest probability of writing a high-quality thesis, and also those who are working in an area in which the academic is interested. So supervisors will naturally be more attracted to you and your topic if you can show that you are very likely to succeed, and also if you are prepared to work in an area that interests them.

Topic or supervisor?

Let's assume that you are in the fortunate position of having a choice of possible supervisors. You can choose to target the supervisor who you think will be best, which may mean agreeing to work in an area that they are interested in supervising. If you already have a topic that you are keen to research, you may be able to convince your preferred supervisor to take you on in that area. However, if your topic is particularly unusual or specialized, you may need to find a supervisor who will agree to supervise a thesis in that area. So choose your supervisor first, and agree on a topic with them later, or should you choose your topic, and then find a supervisor for the thesis?

The answer as to whether you should choose your topic or supervisor first (as with most answers in research) is 'it depends'. It depends on how attractive you think your topic will be to a supervisor, on how much help you think you will need with your thesis, and on why you are doing a thesis. If you are a very good student, with substantial research experience, a supervisor may be prepared to take you on to research an area that the supervisor isn't interested in and/or doesn't know much about. However, the cost to you is likely to be that it will be harder for the supervisor to add value to your thesis, because they won't know the area as well as you. You are likely to be doing much more of the thesis on your own, because any supervisor will be less help in an area that they don't know well. This can mean a more difficult, frustrating and riskier thesis for you. It doesn't mean it's impossible, just harder. But for most people, working in an area in which the supervisor has some interest and knowledge is an easier and safer option. Your supervisor is then more likely to be interested in your research, and thus more likely, and more able, to make useful suggestions.

There is one school of thought that the topic of your thesis is largely irrelevant if you are doing a PhD and planning to be an academic. This view is based on the belief of some academics that the single most important factor in influencing a PhD graduate's first employer is the calibre of their supervisor. Your supervisor's reputation can thus be very important; if they have a high standing within their academic area, a recommendation from them will be more influential, and their contacts and your association with them can help you to obtain a position in a first-rate institution. There can also be disadvantages in working with an established academic (see the discussion on p. 32, 'Experienced or new supervisor?'). However, as a general rule, if you have the chance to work with an academic who has an excellent reputation, it is likely to reflect well on you, and possibly help you in the first few years of an academic career.

How do I approach an academic to ask them to supervise me?

There's no one right approach, but the most effective way is probably to first obtain some information about the potential supervisor's research interests, and then try and talk to them in order to find out whether they are likely to be interested in supervising you and your topic. Many academics (and certainly the more established supervisors) receive frequent approaches from potential students, so you should do some research first, and remember, your aim is to impress the academic. If you can get someone, like another academic, or one of their existing students, to introduce you or mention your name, this can be an effective way of bringing yourself to the attention of the academic. Once you know something about the academic and their research interests, a brief phone call or an e-mail can establish whether they are taking on any students, and if so, whether they have any interest in your area. If the academic is interested, most will then ask you to prepare something in writing (which gives them some idea of your writing and thinking skills) and/or agree to meet you.

Your first introduction to your supervisor and your first meeting with them can be a stressful time. You want to make a good impression and also to gauge whether there is likely to be a good rapport between the two of you. Box 3.1 provides a checklist of things to think about before and after that meeting. Other suggestions for negotiating the foundations of a good relationship follow. These are intended to offer some advice based on the authors' experience, but they are by no means exhaustive.

- *Investigate the academic's research area.* If you know what they appear to be interested in, you are in a better position to demonstrate how your proposed research can add to their own research. It also shows that you are serious about your proposal, and about approaching this academic, because you have taken the trouble to relate your proposed research to their work. A proposal which is clearly related to the academic's area of research is almost certain to get greater attention and consideration.
- *Send a research proposal beforehand* to demonstrate you have thought long and hard about the area you want to study. It doesn't have to be long: perhaps a few pages, indicating the area that you want to research, a justification of why the research is worth doing, a brief discussion of what you think are the key references in the area, and a general plan of the research project. This sends a clear message that you are serious and will be an active partner in the research relationship
- At your meeting, you should ask *what expectations they would have* of you, in terms of timelines for meetings and for submitting drafts or final work. By getting some idea of their expectations early, you can avoid problems later. If the supervisor says that they would expect to meet you every three months, and you know that you work best in a close relationship with frequent discussion of ideas, that supervisor is unlikely to be right for you.
- *State what you want out of the relationship*, such as constructive criticism, clear direction, access, and so forth. If you understand your learning style (for example, you know that you work well to deadlines) then tell them what style or method of supervision you respond to.
- *Get a feel for your reaction to the academic.* While it can be hard to be objective at a first meeting, especially since you are likely to be nervous, if you feel uncomfortable talking to the potential supervisor, and they seem unwilling to listen to your ideas, it may be a clear warning that you won't be able to have a close working relationship.

Establishing honest and blunt expectations is always hard work. But the intensity and loneliness of the research path of reading, thinking, data collection, writing and rewriting will be much easier if you have a supervisor who will give

Box 3.1
CHECKLIST: YOUR SUPERVISOR AND YOU

Before meeting a potential supervisor

- Do I know what areas their past and recent research is in? ☐
- Do I know how many students they have successfully supervised before? Do I know how many have dropped out? ☐
- Do I have a clear, brief summary of the area that I am interested in researching? ☐
- Do I have brief answers to the following questions likely to be asked of me by the potential supervisor:
  - *Why do you want to do a thesis?* ☐
  - *Why do you want to do a thesis with me?* ☐
  - *How will you balance the demands of study/work/family life?* ☐
  - *What is your experience with research?* ☐
- Have I checked the university web site and/or research office to find out what scholarships, if any, are available? ☐
- Have I found out about the possibility of teaching or research work (if this is important to me)? ☐
- Does the university require co-supervision? If so, do I have ideas about who I would like as a co-supervisor? ☐
- Even if the university does not require co-supervision, would that be desirable? ☐

After meeting the potential supervisor

- Have the supervisor and I agreed (in general terms) on a research area and methodology? ☐
- What resources (e.g. equipment, subject payment) might I need for the planned methodology? Is there funding available to meet these projected costs? ☐
- Have we discussed what course work, if any, I would need to do for the thesis? ☐
- Do I have a clear idea of how often I would meet with the supervisor? ☐
- Do I have a clear idea of the amount of feedback I can expect from the supervisor? ☐
- Is the supervisor planning extended absences from the university during my enrolment? If so, what would be the arrangements for my supervision during that time? ☐

- Are they willing to give me the name of a past student who I can talk to? ☐
- Do I know what needs to be done next to submit my thesis and/or scholarship application? ☐

Once you and the supervisor have agreed to work together

- Do you have an agreed schedule for regular meetings and/or delivery of work? ☐
- Have you discussed how you will submit work (hard copy or e-mail?), how often you will submit work, and the feedback that the supervisor will provide? ☐
- Do you know what sort of turn-round time you can expect from the supervisor? ☐
- Do you have a rough timetable for the thesis, with a projected completion date? ☐
- Do you have a date and agenda for the next meeting, and/or agreed date to submit the next piece of work? ☐

you specific, honest and timely feedback and advice. You can never be sure in advance whether the supervisor will do this, but at the first meeting, and in your early interactions, you are trying to get clues as to whether a potential supervisor will be someone who gives you useful feedback and with whom you can work. You should also be trying to find out whether they might be the kind of supervisor that you should avoid: someone who will criticize everything you do, someone who will be too busy to meet you or give you too little critical feedback, instead agreeing with everything you say.

After the first meeting with a potential supervisor, it's always a good idea to send an e-mail or phone them to thank them for their time. (Remember, you are trying to impress them!) This is also a good time to follow up on, or clarify, any questions that you didn't get answered at the first meeting. (See Box 3.1.) Your e-mail or phone call should also tell the supervisor what you intend to do, and indicate your expected time frame for action. If the meeting went well, you might promise to provide them with any information that they requested, and tell them when you expect to submit your application. If the meeting didn't go well, and you want time to think about whether this person is likely to be the right supervisor for you, you can tell them that you need time to consider a major step like enrolling in a thesis. Whatever your decision, remember that, even if you decide not to work with the academic, you may be working with their colleagues, or they may eventually be an examiner of your thesis, so you have nothing to gain, and possibly a lot to lose, by being unprofessional in your dealings with them.

What is likely to impress a potential supervisor?

- *Your research background* is probably the single most important factor in persuading an academic to take you on. You should be prepared to demonstrate why you are likely to succeed at research. Lack of a research background won't necessarily bar you from either a master's degree or a doctorate, but it means you will be less attractive to the supervisor, and you may need to do research course work before you start on your thesis.
- *Your previous academic background* is important, though less critical than your research background. However, all else being equal, most supervisors will prefer a student with a very good academic record. If you can provide academic references showing evidence of your ability, it can help to distinguish you from other candidates. If you don't have a good record, you will need to work harder to impress in other areas.
- *Writing skills* are critical for any thesis. Supervisors are generally less keen to accept a student who may demand constant micro-supervision of basic spelling and grammar. If English (or the language of your thesis) is not your first language, you should be prepared to put particular effort into your written work, to indicate that you have the ability to complete the thesis.

What doesn't impress a potential supervisor?

- An approach to a supervisor (by e-mail or phone) that does not appear to be a personal request is unlikely to be successful. Many students will first approach a potential supervisor with a very general inquiry, which can suggest that the candidate is simultaneously approaching many other potential supervisors. This sort of shotgun approach is unlikely to result in interest from any academic. When you first contact the supervisor (by phone, e-mail or letter) you should tell them why you are approaching them, such as because of their expertise in your area of interest, or because of your previous experience with them, etc.
- Organizing scholarships, visas, applications or similar administrative material is not the supervisor's role. A request to a potential supervisor for information about these matters is likely to suggest that you are lazy

and/or disorganized. You can usually find out information about these matters from the university. Try the postgraduate, international or research offices of the university. See also Chapter 6, 'Resource issues in undertaking postgraduate research'.

One supervisor or two?

Some universities have a policy that all students must have more than one supervisor, in order to ensure that supervision continues if a supervisor leaves, and/or to provide extra input for the student. Even if it isn't the policy of your university, it may be worth requesting co-supervision, particularly if your thesis spans more than one area. For example, one supervisor may be an expert in your research area, and the other in the methodology.

Having two supervisors can provide advantages, by giving you more feedback and input. However, it can also result in disadvantages. Co-supervision usually results in only partial credit for any one academic, so co-supervisors may not be prepared to spend as much time with you as they would if they were the sole supervisor. In the worst case, co-supervision may mean that neither supervisor takes responsibility for you, so you may get less input from two supervisors than you would with one. Sometimes two supervisors will disagree about what should be done, and you can spend a lot of time trying to satisfy both. In the worst cases, if the supervisors don't get on, and have different views, you can find yourself being told to do different things by each supervisor.

For these reasons, if your university's policy is to have co-supervision, or if you are considering co-supervision, you should discuss with both potential supervisors what they see as their role. For example, will one be deemed to be the principal supervisor? Will you have joint meetings (which will always be harder to arrange)? It's also a good idea to ask around to try and find out whether the co-supervisors get on: if they have a reputation for criticizing each other, it is unlikely that they will be able to co-operate on your thesis. The worst disasters in co-supervision usually arise when the supervisors disagree, and the student gets caught up in their argument. The best case for joint supervision is when the supervisors already have a record of working together in research, because co-operation in supervision is then much more likely.

Experienced or new supervisor?

Students often think that a more established academic, with a record of graduating students, will be a better supervisor than a new academic, who may not possess a track record of successful completions. As discussed above, working with an academic with an excellent reputation has some advantages, because their reputation is likely to reflect well on you, and they are likely to have useful

39

contacts in the academic world, which, if they are prepared to use them to promote you, can be very useful if you are planning a career in academia. More senior academics, and/or established researchers, are also more likely to have access to funding sources. If they can use these to support you, it is likely to make your life and thesis much easier.

However, working with very experienced supervisors can also have disadvantages. While established academics may have successfully supervised more students, they are often busier, and/or less willing to spend time with new students. In addition, a record of successfully graduating research students may also include a record of students who have dropped out. Don't assume that because they have got a lot of students through that *you* will also be successful, unless you know that they have never had a student drop out!

Newer academics may not have a record of successful supervision, but because the whole process of supervision is more novel for them, they tend to be more interested in their students' research, and so may be prepared to spend more time with their students. They will also often provide much more, and better, feedback than experienced supervisors. Successfully graduating research students is important for the career of less established academics, so they are typically prepared to put extra effort in to making sure that their students graduate. In addition, they are often more up to date with the literature and new methodologies, because it will have been less time since their own doctorate. In contrast, one student who drops out probably isn't terribly important for an established professor, who may put less effort into helping you if you are having problems with your thesis.

Supervisor/student fit

Before approaching a supervisor, it's a good idea to try and find out (tactfully and diplomatically) what their record is: how many of their students have graduated? More important, how many have dropped out? How long, on average, do their students take to graduate? Where are they working? If you can talk to current or past students about the supervisor's style, it can give you a very good indication of whether you are likely to be able to work successfully with the supervisor. Ask the student what their experience was of supervision. Did the supervisor provide feedback or make suggestions? Did the supervisor take their students to conferences and introduce the student to their academic colleagues? If the supervisor has a group of students, are they treated equally, or did the supervisor have favourites?

When you talk to the supervisor, you should try and get a feel for what their supervision style will be. If you don't have a clear idea about what you want to research, does the supervisor have suggestions? If the supervisor doesn't suggest a specific research topic to you, and suggests that you start your thesis and work out the topic later, warning bells should sound that your thesis will not be completed quickly. A supervisor who has an established research programme, and/or who suggests a specific research topic, is likely to be one who is more interested, and more involved, in your thesis.

When you are hoping that a supervisor will take you on, it's easy to ignore warning signs that the person will not be a good supervisor for you. Most students underestimate problems in advance, and, if they are warned that the supervisor has a poor record, are likely to think that it won't happen to them ('because I'm smarter than the other students who had problems'). You probably aren't. Most of the problems that have been experienced by other students probably can, and may, be experienced by you. Before agreeing to work with a supervisor, you should ask yourself whether you could work with this person. Consider how your relationship with the supervisor is likely to go when you are under stress, when you have had a sleepless night, and when they criticize your work. After meeting the supervisor, and if possible after meeting some of their current or past students, you should think carefully about the advantages and disadvantages of working with this person. If you have doubts, or hear warnings from other students or academics, take some time and consider your choice very carefully. A thesis takes too much time to be conducted with a supervisor who constantly makes your life difficult (and some do!).

Once you have chosen, or been assigned to, a supervisor your aim should be to make the most of the relationship so you can most effectively and efficiently use them to help you complete your thesis in the fastest reasonable time, while maintaining a good relationship. The next section discusses strategies for managing the relationship with your supervisor, so you can increase your chances of a successful and timely thesis completion.

WORKING WITH THE SUPERVISOR

Once you and the supervisor have agreed to work together, it's important to try and ensure that you get maximum value out of the relationship. However, keen your supervisor is, your thesis is more important to you than it is to them, so the more efficiently you can work with your supervisor the more you will get out of them. If you treat your supervisor like a boss at work whom you want to please, and aim to cause them the least possible irritation, you are likely to have a much more profitable relationship. This may strike you as unreasonable, because you might hope that the supervisor will put equal effort into the relationship, but they may not. Sometimes supervisors are unreasonable, immature and lacking in empathy with the pressures of study. Whatever your supervisor is like, you will get more out of them if you manage the relationship very carefully. Simply put, the more they feel you are worth the effort, and the easier that you are to work with, the more you are likely to get out of them.

There are many things that both help and hinder a good working relationship between a student and a supervisor. Knowing what characterizes a 'good' student in the eyes of the supervisor, and recognizing the student behaviours that supervisors generally hate, can help you to ensure that you are in the first category!

Things that supervisors generally like

- *Students who point out the main areas that they want feedback on.* For example, you might have been working on the literature review and are now working on the methodology. It may be helpful for the supervisor to look at both together, but giving detailed feedback on both chapters will take them a lot of time. You are likely to get more useful feedback if you submit both chapters but clearly target the supervisor's attention, for example by telling them that you have submitted the literature review for their background information, but that at this stage, you really want feedback on the methodology.

- *Students who have ideas and opinions, and can justify them on the basis of a critical understanding of both the literature and the research.* Ideas and opinions are common in postgraduate study. What is less common, however, is opinions based on previous research. If you can justify your opinions to your supervisor on the relevant basis of the literature, then you will be judged to be a much better student, and are more likely to receive your supervisor's time and useful feedback. The further on you are in your thesis, the more you should have mastered the relevant literature. If you can justify your opinions on the strength of prior research, and/or by logical deduction, then you are likely to impress your supervisor (and your examiners).

- *Well organized students who seem to value the supervisor's time.* You should view your supervisor as you would a high-value consultant, and you should value their time accordingly. For example providing a simple written agenda for each meeting with a supervisor can be a very useful way of maximizing the benefit from your meeting time. A simple agenda might include a report on activity since the last meeting, a list of particular issues that you want their feedback on, and your plans for the interval before the next meeting. If you want feedback on a written document, make sure that it is provided to the supervisor with enough time for them to read it before the meeting. Finally, establishing a date, time and targets for your next meeting can be an effective way of both committing a supervisor's time and motivating yourself to agreed milestones.

Things that supervisors generally hate

- *Students who submit a second draft of a chapter that doesn't address issues that the supervisor identified in a previous draft.* If you haven't had time to address previous feedback, say so. If you think a suggested change was unnecessary, say why. *Never* ignore previous feedback if you want the supervisor to continue giving feedback. This does not mean you must always accept the feedback. Remember, it is *your* thesis. But feedback is an opportunity to discuss the areas that you and your supervisor agree and disagree on. If your supervisor doesn't like something, they may be wrong, and you may be able to demonstrate to them that they are wrong. However, the fact that they don't like something may be a clue that examiners will share the supervisor's opinion, so you might need to express your ideas in a clearer, or more convincing, way. Using word-processing features such as 'track changes' can demonstrate to the supervisor how a draft has been altered since their last comments.

- *Students who submit a long chapter two hours before a meeting and expect feedback on the chapter.* You may think that your supervisor has time to review your work, but they may have other plans for the time before the meeting. You should find out how long your supervisor generally wants to read your work before you can expect feedback, so you can give them adequate time.

- *Students who submit poorly written work, which hasn't been spell- or grammar-checked and that doesn't appear to have been proof-read.* You should always assume that your supervisor's time is valuable (because they certainly do). If you submit poor work and early drafts, it will be difficult for them to give good feedback, and they will probably be tired of you before you have developed a good draft. Sometimes you may want to give a supervisor a very early draft, to get them to look at something specific in the draft. In that case, you should tell them clearly what you expect, rather than appear lazy. For example: 'I've given you a very early version of the results so you can see what I am thinking. What I am interested in is your opinion on my interpretation of the results of hypothesis 3.' This avoids wasting the supervisor's time in reviewing an early draft and, more important for you, protects you from them thinking that you are sloppy and submit poor work. Alternatively, you might summarize an intended argument in bullet points so you can get feedback on the argument before you take the time to develop a complete argument.

- *Students who ask complex questions without appearing to have done any work themselves.* Supervisors, especially those who are generous with their time, sometimes find that they are frequently interrupted in their own work by

43

students asking questions. If you are lucky enough to have a supervisor who gives you help, make sure you do some work yourself first. For example, if you are having problems with your methodology and ask your supervisor a fairly basic question, without appearing to have done any work yourself, you won't create a good impression. If, in contrast, you tell your supervisor that you are having problems in a specific area, tell them what references and sources you have already consulted without success, and then ask for suggestions, you are likely to obtain a much more sympathetic and helpful response.

To summarize, just as students have expectations of their supervisor, supervisors will have expectations of their students. First, they will expect an increasing level of independence and initiative through the period of the thesis. This means you need to be active and motivated enough to develop your reading and research, rather than expecting a supervisor to tell you what to do. Second, supervisors expect candidates to write clear and coherent work. They do not expect to receive poorly developed drafts. Third, supervisors expect a reasonable level of work and progress. The best way for you to fulfil these expectations is to agree, and deliver on, the milestones and targets for your thesis.

CODES OF SUPERVISORY PRACTICE

Despite the best intentions, tensions will usually arise at some stage during a supervisor/student relationship. Given the stress placed on both the student and the supervisor to complete a thesis successfully, it would perhaps be unusual if problems didn't arise. Most of these problems, like problems in any relationship, are not serious, and they will sometimes resolve spontaneously, or can be solved with discussion. In Chapter 13, 'Common problems and potential solutions', we discuss strategies for dealing with a range of problems, including problems with the supervisor.

If you do have problems with your supervisor (and even if you don't), a useful resource to help you understand what's expected of your supervisor can be the university's code of supervisory practice. Many universities have established these codes of practice to enhance the supervision process, partly by ensuring that the expectations of both student and supervisor are reasonable. The codes usually provide the university's expectations and standards for both the supervisor and the research student. Areas covered in a code are illustrated in Box 3.2.

Codes of practice are an important means of establishing clear levels of responsibility and quality standards in the supervisor/student relationship. They are an excellent starting point for you in clarifying what the university expects of both you and your supervisor, and some of the formal mechanisms that monitor your progress, and that can be called on if serious problems arise.

Box 3.2
WHAT'S IN A CODE OF SUPERVISORY PRACTICE?

- Requirements for a research degree. This outlines the standards expected for the completion of a thesis.
- Policy and procedures for progress reports, where the level and intensity of formal reporting processes are outlined.
- Roles and responsibilities of the department you are enrolled in. This is helpful to gauge the administrative support available to you as a student.
- Roles and responsibilities of the supervisor, where the assistance, level of contact and quality goals are outlined.
- Many codes also include a section where the roles and responsibilities of research students are specified. This is an important indication of the standards expected as a condition of candidature.
- Grievance procedures, outlining the available procedures to address, and hopefully resolve, problems, if they arise.

CONCLUSION

Choosing the right supervisor, and working effectively with that person, is one of the most important factors in ensuring timely success in your thesis. However, no supervisor or student is perfect, and problems can arise in any supervisor/ student relationship. Ideally, the supervisor will put as much effort as you into developing an effective relationship, and will guide you towards a successful thesis completion in a reasonable time. In the end, however, it is your thesis, and your supervisor is imperfect, and will have many other demands on their time. By learning to use the supervisor's time most efficiently, you will be able to extract most value from the relationship, and hopefully develop what will be a long-lasting research partnership.

FURTHER READING

Phillips, E. and Pugh, D. (1993) *How to Get a PhD*, Buckingham: Open University Press.

Chapter 4

Developing a research proposal

RICHARD DUNFORD

> Want to make God laugh? Tell Him you've got plans.
>
> (Anon.)

Most prescriptions for the research process describe it as a series of sequential steps, beginning with the identification of a research problem or question, then moving (via a review of the existing literature) to a statement of a conceptual model, data collection and finally to analysis and a conclusion. However, this is a somewhat idealized statement of the process. In reality, the process is often much less clear, because research is a learning and iterative process in which 'later steps' clarify 'earlier steps', allowing the latter to be modified or at least stated more clearly. For example, the specific focus of the research will often be fine-tuned in the process of carrying out the research, leading to a rephrasing of the topic in later drafts.

None the less, there are still good reasons for beginning the research process with a formal statement of intent – a formal research proposal – which specifies the proposed 'journey', at least as it appears at this initial stage. Formally outlining the proposed research forces you to clarify your thinking, and to consider whether what you are doing is sufficiently justified, and whether your proposed method is feasible. In addition, a proposal summarizes and communicates your proposed contribution to others, so that they can see clearly what you are doing and, as a result, are better able to give you feedback.

This chapter is structured in two parts. It begins with a rationale for the research proposal, then proceeds with the major part of the chapter on the different key elements of a proposal.

RESEARCH PROPOSALS: WHY BOTHER?

Research proposals have several functions.

'Reality check'

Writing a research proposal is a valuable way of finding out whether the 'great idea' in your head sounds as good once it has been committed to paper. A piece of poetry constructed as part of a night of committed socializing may seem an insightful comment on the human condition when read at 2.00 am; its contribution to great literature is often less obvious after a good night's sleep. In a comparable fashion, research ideas that exist just as ideas in our heads can lull us into a false sense of the importance of, or originality of, or need for, or viability of, the proposed research. Committing ideas to paper is good discipline. Seeing what one proposes in black and white can provide a rather confronting form of 'reality check'.

Research students' proposals are typically designed to be read by their supervisor and/or by a committee. However, you shouldn't assume that the only, or even most important, audience for the proposal is the reader. The person that it must make the most sense to is you. While others may have the capacity to approve and/or fund what you are proposing, this approval process is rather pointless unless you know what it is that you are intending to do. Ultimately, it is your time that is most at stake, and you don't want to unnecessarily spend time (years, in the case of a thesis) on a poorly thought out research proposal. You are the one with the most to gain by developing a research proposal that clarifies your thinking and facilitates the research. Because of this the 'reality check' aspect of a proposal should not be underestimated.

'It gets you started'

Nobel Laureate Albert Szent-Gyorti tells the story of a group of soldiers lost in the European Alps. A soldier discovers a mountain map in his gear and, using it, leads the others down the mountain to safety. Only then is it discovered that it is a map of the wrong mountain. The point is that despite the map subsequently being shown to be the wrong one, the existence of a map gave the soldiers the confidence to venture into the unknown. It got them started. Once started, they made decisions when confronted by choices. Without the map they might not have begun the journey. In similar vein a research proposal should be treated not as a set of decisions 'cast in stone' but as a statement of direction and general intent which helps initiate the research process. That the proposal may subsequently bear little resemblance to the finished product does not diminish the value of the proposal because of the vital role that it played in the initiation of the research.

'No choice'

Most researchers are required to produce a research proposal of some form. That is, they have no choice in the matter. For example, university-based researchers are typically required to get ethics clearance for any research that they intend to carry out. This will commonly involve the submission of some form of research proposal to a body such as the university's Ethics Committee, even where the researcher is not making any request for funding. Postgraduate research students will typically be required to present a proposal (albeit a brief one) as part of the application process and a more substantial one later as a precursor to being given the 'go-ahead' to undertake the actual research. Similarly, researchers wishing to receive funds from some funding body will almost certainly be required to prepare a detailed proposal.

ELEMENTS OF A RESEARCH PROPOSAL

Most research institutions, whether universities or funding bodies such as those that dispense endowments or government funds, have specific requirements in terms of what information they require and the form (and length) in which it is to be submitted. It is important to check to see what the expectations are of the institution with which you are involved. Even if specific formal guidelines are not available, it may be that there is an informal expectation which can be identified through discussion with key people (e.g. your supervisor or a member of staff with some assigned responsibility for research students).

None the less, although the expectations of different institutions are likely to vary, there are some core elements that will be expected in most proposals:

- The topic/problem should be clearly stated.
- The objectives of the research should be clearly defined.
- The rationale of the research should be provided.
- The existing literature should be reviewed.
- The conceptual framework should be clear.
- The research methodology should be clearly described.
- A timetable and a budget (where relevant) should be provided.

There are also some other elements that it is wise for the researcher to address:

- The researcher's expertise and 'track record' and why the researcher is an appropriate person to undertake the research.
- Presentation and layout.

The chapter will address each of these elements in turn.

The topic/problem should be clearly stated

A proposal has many elements but there is nothing more fundamental than the need to express exactly what it is that you, the researcher, are proposing to research. Everything else is irrelevant if this intention is not clearly communicated.

Sourcing the topic

Research topics can come from many different sources. For example:

- A classic source for postgraduate students is a topic that has interested them as a result of exposure to that topic in their preceding years of study.
- For those who have undertaken some years of work prior to returning to formal study, their own experience may be a rich source of topics of interest.
- Reports of research, such as those published in peer-reviewed journals, will commonly conclude with a statement as to implications or suggestions for future research (e.g. still unanswered questions, unresolved debates, new ideas that have emerged as a result of the research, etc.).
- The media, both general and business/professional, may contain ideas for research, particularly that of an applied variety.
- Talking to practitioners can provide interesting insights into key issues – whether conceptual or immediately pragmatic – that may offer interesting research opportunities.
- Some research topics come to the attention of potential researchers because some funding body, either government or private-sector, makes it known – by public advertisement or by contacting select individuals or organizations – that it wishes to have research undertaken on a particular topic (and typically, is willing to pay).

From 'I'm interested in . . .' to a specific topic

It is common for a particular research project to first take form as an expressed interest in a particular phenomenon or practice of a fairly general nature. Thesis students, in particular, will often express a view that they are 'interested in' a generic topic such as international human resource management (HRM) or the management of not-for-profit organizations, or eco-tourism, etc. This situation possesses both 'good news' and 'bad news' aspects. The 'good news' is that an area of interest has been identified and that is not insignificant. The 'bad news' is that it is very difficult, if not impossible, to undertake a piece of research about a topic at such a high level of generality. Taking an example mentioned above,

49

international HRM is perhaps best thought of as an 'area of practice' or an 'area of research interest' rather than as a research topic *per se*. This is because within international HRM lie such diverse topics as:

- the relationship between HRM practices and business strategies in multinational corporations;
- the relationship between organizational culture and national culture;
- managing the reintegration of returning expatriates.

Much the same could be said of any topic that is an area of research interest. What this means is that, in putting a proposal together, the researcher needs to progress from 'I'm interested in . . .' to 'My research topic is . . .'.

A good proposal is one in which the area of research interest is refined into the form of a specific research topic or problem. However, in practice this step will sometimes not occur until after the literature review has occurred. This is because it is often not until the researcher becomes familiar with the literature in depth that they can decide what specific aspect of the interest area will form the focus of the research. Nevertheless, writing even a preliminary research proposal, perhaps one submitted to a potential supervisor, based on only a general understanding of the literature, will help you to clarify your thinking and to identify broad research questions and methodologies which can be specified in greater detail at a later date.

The objectives should be clearly defined

The proposal should clearly state the intended output of the research. Objectives may take many forms reflecting the diverse purposes of research. For example, Collis and Hussey (2003: 2) note the following as possible purposes of research:

- to review and synthesize existing knowledge;
- to investigate some existing situation or problem;
- to provide solutions to a problem;
- to explore and analyse more general issues;
- to construct or create a new procedure or system;
- to explain a new phenomenon;
- to generate new knowledge;
- a combination of any of the above.

Whichever of the above applies, the proposal should include as specific as possible a statement of the intended outcome of the research. For example, if the general interest area is 'innovation in organizations', the specific outcome that is sought from a proposed piece of research may be something like 'to be able to

Box 4.1
CHOOSING THE TITLE

It is important that the title should provide as accurate a description as possible of the content. While this does not have to be finally determined until the write-up process, it is none the less helpful to have a proposal title which helps the reader accurately gauge the intention of the researcher. Researchers will some-times be attracted to some colourful imagery which they see as more evocative than literal language. For example, I once undertook some research on the way in which corporations sought to control the introduction of new technology-based products in order that sales of existing products should not be detrimentally affected. In the course of the research I read an article on this phenomenon from early in the twentieth century in which the writer remarked that the avail-ability in the market of a particular new product was, from the point of view of some established companies, 'as welcome as a bomb thrower in the court of the Czar [of Russia]'. This historical imagery seemed to me to be so rich that I selected it for use in the title of a report on this research. Thus the title became 'As Welcome as a Bomb-thrower in the Court of the Czar: Tactics for Technology Suppression'. However, this was not a very good decision. Even though the part of the title after the colon was literal, the pre-colon part of the title caused confusion, as its significance was not clear. It was revealed only to those who persevered until two-thirds of the way through the report when the expression was cited and its origins revealed. I'm not trying to advocate the removal of all imagery from titles; indeed, the 'image: literal description of content' form can be rather attractive. But users of this form need to be careful not to fall into the trap that I did of selecting an image that is just a bit too obscure to be understood by the bulk of readers. Literary 'cleverness' has its place but can get in the way of clearly communicating one's intent. At the stage of a research proposal, I suggest you err on the side of a clear literal description of what it is that you intend to investigate.

identify whether the processes which produce innovation in the financial services sector are the same as those which produce innovation in the manufacturing sector.'

The rationale for the research should be provided

The rationale for the research is likely to be implicit in the discussion provided in the earlier stages of the proposal, but it should none the less be stated expli-citly. Whereas the 'objectives' section of the proposal answers the 'what' question

('What do you propose to do?'), the statement of rationale provides an answer to the 'why' question ('Why is this an issue worth investigating?'). It is important to address this issue because a research issue may be a passion of yours and you may also believe that 'only a fool' would not realize the importance of the topic. While I'm not suggesting that you should treat the readers of your proposal as fools, I do strongly advise you to start from the assumption that your readers may not see the 'blindingly obvious' and will need to be taken step by step through the logic of your argument. If the logic really is clear, this should be a simple exercise.

The rationale for undertaking a particular piece of research is usually based on it having the potential to answer some gap in our knowledge of the phenomenon under study. This gap may be primarily conceptual in nature, as in the case of an unresolved theoretical debate, or it may have emerged from a very practical concern, such as the high failure rate of organizational change programmes.

The literature should be reviewed

The literature on a topic may have several different functions within the research process. In some situations it is the source of an idea for a piece of research, when previous writers have identified issues needing further research. This is common, because one of the stylistic expectations in published reports of research is to include a statement about 'implications for research' in the concluding discussion. In other situations, the increasing familiarity with a particular topic that comes from immersing oneself in the literature means that the reader will arrive at his or her own interpretation of 'gaps' in the literature. Either of these situations provides a basis for citing existing literature in support of one's proposal.

Another important reason for citing the existing literature is to substantiate the claim – which may be implicit in a research proposal – that original research is needed to answer the specified question. If previous research has answered the question, then what we are facing is an information retrieval situation, not a research situation. In a number of commercial and government situations, people labelled researcher are not really involved in doing research in the way we use the term in this book. In the former situation, 'researchers' have the task of locating information and providing it for someone in the company or government. However, this is really information retrieval; it involves finding out what already exists. Genuine research is about investigating that which is not currently known. From this perspective, research is not needed if the answer already exists. So part of the goal of the research proposal is to show that your research is, indeed, original, or in other words will investigate a question which hasn't been addressed before.

The literature review also contextualizes the proposed study within what has already been done and shows the reader that your analysis is informed by your familiarity with existing knowledge on the topic. This adds credibility to your argument that original research is required to answer the issue that you have identified.

The proposal provides a particular challenge in regard to the review of the literature. Because of its length, it cannot be comprehensive. In fact, almost no literature review can be, unless the field of research is very new and disconnected from prior areas of research. Such a situation is unlikely, or at least extremely rare. As a result, the literature review in the proposal is likely to be substantially less comprehensive than the one that will appear in the final thesis or research document. In the proposal, it is important to focus on a relatively small number of sources from the literature, so their identity is important. Concentrate on those that seem to be the 'influential core'. In most fields of research there are a relatively small number of writers and/or journals that are regularly cited in research publications. In your proposal, when you have to deal succinctly with a range of issues, focus on sources that are most likely to be seen as authoritative, as that will add credibility to your argument.

Finally, don't be afraid to place your own interpretation on the existing literature. Just because others have 'mapped' the literature in a particular way, that need not be the way you present it. In fact, providing a new perspective on the existing literature can provide a useful contribution.

The conceptual framework should be clear

The notion of 'conceptual framework' often causes concern amongst those new to research because of uncertainty as to just what the term means. The student may assume that the conceptual framework has something to do with 'theory' but may be clear about little beyond that.

The significance of a conceptual framework may best be made clear by asking the question: can there be concept-free research? Consider the practical issue that was of concern to a colleague of mine: why do a significant number of major Information Technology (IT) projects fail to produce the outcomes expected of them? This very practical concern, none the less, had at its heart, the concept of 'outcome'. To be able to investigate the question, the concept of 'outcome' had to be 'operationalized', that is, defined in a particular way. Similarly, the notion of an 'IT project' had to be defined. For example, when was such a project defined as having come into existence? Was it something determined by the labelling of some IT activity as a 'project', or was it more an indication of the level of expenditure involved? Even the most practical of research questions involve some form of concept. So the conceptual framework should clarify the boundaries of the research, the usage of critical terms, and should clearly indicate the research, and hence the intellectual thinking, on which the study is based.

Most research is able to build upon the work of predecessors. Even where a piece of research is deemed to be 'original', this label is more likely to signal the investigation of a nuance, rather than something so original that there seems to be no connection with existing work. A review of relevant literature is likely to reveal some already existing body of writing and/or research that directly or indirectly proposes an explanation for the phenomenon in which you are interested. For example, if you are interested in the behaviour of people in organizations, there is a range of theories in areas such as motivation, stress and group dynamics that can provide the conceptual foundation for the research. Where developed theories exist, research often proceeds *deductively*, that is, by developing hypotheses based on the established theory. Such research involves hypothesis testing.

The role of hypotheses in research is an interesting one. Some writers on research methods treat hypotheses as a necessary part of research (e.g. Salkind 2000). However, this is an unnecessarily limited view of research. It fits well with a situation where there is an already well developed body of knowledge – that is, established theory from which hypotheses may be derived – but is less appropriate where the research is more concerned with developing our understanding of a relatively new field of study, that is, where the need is for theory building more than theory testing.

There are other situations where hypothesis testing may not be central to the research. In situations where a lot of hypothesis-based research has already established the relationship between certain variables, the greatest contribution may come from an intensive study of the dynamic of that relationship. Whereas the former relies on the study of a large number of situations – typically involving statistical analysis of data from a large number of instances – the latter is best advanced through the in-depth, 'rich' description of the processes in a small number of situations.

The research methodology should be clearly described

The terms 'method' and 'methodology' are often used interchangeably. Unfortunately, the latter is sometimes used as if it is simply a more sophisticated term than the former. When this happens it does disservice to the important distinction underlying the two terms. The two terms exist for good reason. *Method* refers to the means of data collection, whether it be experiment, survey, ethnography or interviews. It tells us how the data are to be collected. *Methodology*, on the other hand, involves what might be called 'the theory of the method', that is, why the chosen method is appropriate. It is important that the method is consistent with the nature of the research question, and that this is established in the research proposal.

Some research is based on the idea that 'the facts' exist in the world and they simply await accurate measurement. That is, the world has an objective reality that can be determined through accurate measurement. If there are multiple dimensions to this reality one needs a measurement tool based on multiple variables. With this approach, reality is believed to be more closely approximated as more variables are added, as long as each additional variable adds an additional percentage to the capturing of this objective reality. This position, sometimes termed *positivism*, is based on the view that the social sciences are much the same as the natural sciences, and that the role of the researcher is to capture as accurately as possible the nature of this external reality. Methods of data collection such as the experimental method (where some variables are held constant and others varied) and surveys (where data are analysed through statistical methods) are most associated with this approach. A positivist approach is therefore most likely to be associated with quantitative methods of data collection.

An alternative approach to research takes the view that the social sciences are different in that the actions of people, individually and collectively, are based on their constructions of the nature of the world in which they operate. That is, the actions of people are mediated via an interpretive process whereby the meanings people attribute to situations determine the actions that they take. This *interpretivist* approach lends itself to means of data collection such as interviews and to an in-depth focus on the data. It is likely to be investigated by the study of a small number of cases in depth, rather than by large-scale survey methods. An interpretivist approach is therefore most likely to be associated with qualitative methods of data collection.

From the point of view of an assessor of a research proposal, the key issues are that the proposer shows an awareness of the need for, and justification of, the selected method or methods of data collection and for the subsequent method of data analysis to be consistent with the nature of the question that is being asked.

A timetable and a budget (where relevant) should be provided

Almost everyone who begins a piece of research, especially if they have gone through the vetting process associated with entry to a graduate research programme, has the intellectual capacity to undertake and to complete the research. However, many research projects begun with the best of intentions do not reach completion. Sometimes this is due to factors beyond the researcher's control, such as the withdrawal of funding or the withdrawal of data access critical to the study. However, more often than not it is because the researcher just does not complete the research; sometimes they barely get started.

Research is as much a feat of tenacity as a matter of intellect. Tenacity involves two key dimensions – motivation and organization. Both are critical, but neither alone is likely to be sufficient. A proposal is not a great means of communicating motivation – although one's enthusiasm for the topic can be conveyed – but it can give the reader/assessor an indication as to the level of the proposer's awareness of the logistical aspects of completing a thesis. At the very least it is advisable

55

to include a timetable which shows the proposed stages in the thesis such that it will be completed within the required time. Even though there is every likelihood that some deviation from the plan will take place during the course of the research, it is still better to show that your research is being undertaken within a structure that acknowledges not just the intellectual context, but also the need to 'project-manage' the research.

The researcher's expertise and 'track record' (why the researcher is an appropriate person to undertake the research)

The weighting given to this aspect varies considerably between different situations, being less central in the case of most postgraduate students than if the proposal is part of a process of seeking substantial government or private sector funding. In some situations the track record of the proposer is given almost equal weighting with the rest of the proposal, because the funding body may need to be convinced, not just of the value of the topic, but also that the proposer has the necessary background and/or is best placed to carry out the research. This 'background' may comprise both knowledge and experience of the research area, track record in terms of delivering on promised outcomes and as a record of getting results published in good journals.

Another aspect of the track record is whether the proposer has solid grounds for believing that the proposed data collection method will work. For example, a study based on interviewing the CEOs of the 200 largest companies in the country may not be flawed in principle but could founder on the basis of access problems. The viability of such a method, in practice, may have a lot to do with the established links and profile of the proposer. While 'methodological appropriateness' is important, the practicability of the research will often ultimately depend on such 'real life' matters.

For these reasons, the issue of researcher credibility is worth addressing even if it is not explicitly listed as a necessary component in a particular proposal. Good research is likely to result from a match between the topic and the skills of the researcher. While some of the skills are technical in the sense of referring to specific research methods, others are based on academic study and/or knowledge of the research context. A good research proposal will not just identify a valuable area for research; it will also identify you as someone well positioned to carry out that research.

Presentation and layout of the proposal

Although it is the ideas in the proposal that constitute its core, a proposal is a means whereby the writer is seeking to convince the reader of the soundness of the proposition being put to him or her. As such, the style of presentation is not a peripheral matter; it is a central means whereby the clarity of the message can be either enhanced or obscured. The idea that the strength of the core argument in the proposal should be all that is evaluated may have some merit, but more realistically a proposal stands or falls on its ability to communicate the intent of the writer to the reader. The capacity of the reader to determine the intent of the writer is determined as much by the structure and coherence of the proposal as by the innate ideas that the proposal contains.

Attention should be given to such matters as making sure that there is a logical flow of argument through the document, that the hierarchy of headings is consistent and clear, that pages are numbered and that all sources cited in the proposal are appropriately referenced. Where the research involves a series of connections between different concepts, it is often a good idea to use diagrams to illustrate the connections, as it may be difficult to rely on the capacity of words alone to convey these connections. Often it is useful to give the proposal to a colleague or friend – not necessarily someone who knows the research area – because it is very difficult to do a good job of proof reading one's own work. Because you know what you intend to say, it is often difficult to see the omissions or ambiguities that are evident to others, and having someone else read the work can identify areas that need to be expressed more clearly, or in more detail.

PROPOSAL FORM AND LENGTH

As noted above, it is possible to identify in general terms the information that should go into a research proposal. However, in practice, you are likely to be preparing a particular proposal for a particular purpose and audience. Sometimes all that is expected is a preliminary proposal – something of around two to five pages – that describes the research in rather general terms. Proposals of this length will often be sufficient to form the basis of a decision by potential supervisors as to whether they are interested in, and/or appropriate supervisors for, the proposed research.

Such a proposal may identify an area of research interest rather than a specific research topic. At this stage it is also likely to be much more focused on the 'what' and the 'why' than on the 'how'. That is, at the preliminary proposal stage, the main task is to explain what you're interested in and why it is an issue worth researching. Unless this is established to a reasonable degree of clarity, addressing issues of method is somewhat premature.

Even once a full proposal of twenty to thirty pages has been completed, it is often useful to produce a very brief version of no more than a page or two in length. In many research projects there are times when a shorter version of the project is a useful document to have on hand. For example, if the research requires the co-operation of one or more organizations, such a document can be a convenient way of communicating the core elements of the research without the level of detail required by an academic audience. In producing an abbreviated proposal make sure that the language and content are suited to the purpose and the audience. If the prime motivation is to convince the organization to grant access, make sure that there is a 'selling point', for example, a clear statement of the benefits that the organization will derive from co-operating.

CONCLUSION

This chapter has provided an overview of the process necessary to develop a research proposal. It is important to explain clearly the reason for the proposed study, as this provides direction for your effort. I offer nine key elements in the actual structure of the proposal. Different universities are likely to vary their expectations of how your research proposal should be presented, as are the various disciplines. The time spent on developing a coherent proposal is time well spent in focusing your effort, and allows you to proceed with your actual research with more confidence.

REFERENCES AND FURTHER READING

Collis, J. and Hussey, R (2003) *Business Research*, Basingstoke: Palgrave.

Dawson, C. (2002) 'How to prepare a research proposal', in *Practical Research Methods*, Oxford: How-to Books.

Leedy, P.D. (1974) 'Writing the research proposal', in *Practical Research: Planning and Design*, 6th edn, Upper Saddle River NJ: Merrill.

Punch, K.F. (2000) *Developing Effective Research Proposals*, London: Sage.

Salkind, N.J. (2000) 'Writing a research proposal', in *Exploring Research*, Upper Saddle River NJ: Prentice Hall.

Walliman, N. (2001) 'Preparing the research proposal and starting to write', in *Your Research Project*, London: Sage.

Chapter 5

Ethical issues in research

PETER STEANE

Everything has been said before, but since nobody listens we have to keep going back and beginning all over again.

(André Gide)

One of the important considerations a research student must attend to is the ethics of their research. This is a necessity at both a professional level and at an administrative level. Either at masters or doctoral studies, there are expected standards about the appropriate structure and method and reporting of research. There are also expectations at most universities for researchers to justify and pay attention to ethical considerations, because the university is the formal entity from which you engage in the research. In essence, you are the public face of the university in the way you research and in how people perceive the research.

Research is a complex process in which a number of stakeholders are involved. These include; yourself as the researcher, and, depending on your research area, may include the participants constituting the sample group, the corporate entity of a case study, the university community commissioning the research, the supervisor(s) advising the researcher, the examiners who review the thesis and the readers who have access to the findings after the research is completed. This list constitutes but a few of the stakeholders, and reinforces that there are a range of interests and concerns that demand judiciousness on the part of the researcher.

Ideally, you should complete your thesis so that you and the university remain in good standing with the participants and your findings contribute to the advancement of knowledge or professional practice. Failure to design your research with ethical protocols can harm participants and result in misleading or biased results, and leave you exposed to the criticism of examiners. It can also expose the university's reputation to ridicule and damage. Unethical research can also expose a research or university or research institute to legal action in some countries.

This chapter outlines the fundamental issues involved in an ethical research process. It begins with a simple overview of ethical thinking and its link with the practice of research. Principles of ethical research are discussed, along with examples of ethical research problems. These basic principles are proposed as a starting point for developing proposals likely to satisfy university research ethics committees. The chapter concludes with an overview of the role of research protocols.

ETHICAL THINKING

In the Western tradition, the word 'ethics' is derived from the Greek *ethos*, and refers to character. It concerns itself with the moral dimension of what *ought* to be the right or good way to both operationalize the research process and report the findings. Ethics also concerns itself with processes and conclusions that are *just*, that is, legitimately give what is due or represent what is due to a participant, case study or point of view. Devising ethical protocols and research processes is a time-consuming part of the thesis, but a necessary one in building the researcher's credibility and balancing the divergent demands of multiple stakeholders.

I doubt there is an easy answer to determining the best means to practise justice in research. Both Aristotle (Book V of the *Nicomachaean Ethics*) and Aquinas under-stood justice as related to the distribution of some public gain. In research, this means you, as investigator, should ensure there is a net gain from the study being pursued. John Rawls called for a social contract approach to justice, based upon two principles: reciprocity and fairness. This emphasizes dimensions of equality in the relationships one has. In research, it would be expressed in principles where all participants are treated equally and by mechanisms to ensure views or data are not misrepresented. The principle of justice raises legitimate expectations that persons participating will receive an appropriate benefit arising from the research.

The principled approach to ethics derives from the philosophy of Emmanuel Kant (1724–1804), who defined actions as morally correct because of the reason and duty behind them, regardless of the context in which they were made. This approach has its source in the religious foundations of the 'golden rule' (do unto others as you would have them do unto you) and many other religious and spiritual philosophies, which suggest certain principles as binding duties. Essentially, the approach is based upon a *principle* or *rule* or *guide*. Kant claimed principles are 'maxims', that is, universal principles that can be applied everywhere. He saw *respect* and treating people as *ends* in themselves (rather than a *means* to an end) and thus as binding obligations to living the ethical life. Kant used a reflective test to gauge the ethics of a decision: an act is likely to be ethical if you are willing to have the act become a universal law. In the research context, such a view places an obligation on the researcher to treat participants with respect and to seek the truth in data analysis and reporting of findings.

The utilitarian approach to ethics derives from the philosophy of J.S. Mill (1806–73), who understood the good consequence as a prime factor in determining ethical worth. He saw the greatest utility of an action as creating the greatest happiness. Mill understood the golden rule of religious belief as promoting ethics because it was an ethic of utility: the greatest good of the greatest number. The focus is on outcomes, and as much as possible the overall good benefit of *all* stakeholders. According to utilitarians, a researcher's ethical obligation or duty in any situation is to act so that the outcome produces the greatest possible balance of good over evil.

It is very courageous to draw comparisons between Western and Eastern thinking about ethics, so the best that can be achieved is a very general guide. This is offered in this chapter because many postgraduate research scholars in European, Australian and American universities come from Asia, or alternatively study in Asia but in 'offshore' research programmes from a Western university. It is important for some understanding to be gained about the ethical expectations of research from the perspective of the degree-granting institution, because the ethical thinking of the university will be applied regardless of where it is studied.

Western culture generally regards thought as a separate function of a rational being. Eastern 'thinking' is more about *pondering* – fusing thinking, loving, feeling into some unity. The 'modern' Western approach dates back at least to the Renaissance and the Age of the Enlightenment and the superiority of reason. As a generalization, the Western mind proceeds in reasoning from the major premise to the minor premise, and then finally to a conclusion. Rationality dominates, and feeling is to be excluded in this so-called *scientific* exercise. In contrast, the Eastern person might proceed in reasoning from the assumption that nature and reality are rational, consistent and universal in scope. The mind, therefore, is not an object to control this but to *unwrap* the in-built laws for all mankind. The science of *I-ching* is based on relationship and coexistence and balance – hence the *yin–yang* of Eastern thought. A conclusion is not reached by the head, but by the whole psyche.

Hence, while Western and Eastern values may be similar, as a generalization, they emerge from different influences and from a different philosophical base. Using Chinese thinking again as an example, there are the philosophical perspectives of a humanist like Confucius, as well as the more structured legal perspectives of Han Fei Zi. What emerges are the common moral virtues of moral character, proper conduct, humanity, lifelong learning and balance in both work and relations with others. These virtues complement the ethical sentiments of the Western philosophical tradition.

Other sources of Eastern philosophy are based on the Buddhist Eightfold Path or Four Noble Truths, or the Sufi wisdom scriptures of Islam, or the Hindu writings of *Patanjuli*, and so forth. Much of Western ethical thinking is infused with the Judaeo-Christian scriptures. But there is a common thread in ethical thinking of benevolence, tolerance, honourable action, right relationships and truth. These are all sentiments incorporated in the ethical principles of university research ethics committees.

What does this mean for research? For the research student studying in a Western country or overseas research programme, it suggests that the ethical values of different traditions possess commonalities, except they derive from divergent roots. This means the ethical protocols can be developed along agreed lines of respect, privacy and honesty, but more likely the justification will reflect the philosophical thinking of the (Western) degree-granting institution.

RESEARCH AND ETHICAL ISSUES

There is an historical context to the increasing attention to ethics in research. The latter half of the twentieth century witnessed an increasing concern for formal ethical research guidelines. This came at the same time as the growing popularity and relevance of phenomenological research, otherwise known as qualitative research. The Nuremberg Code was developed after World War II, when the world had to come to terms with the medical experiments carried out by the Nazis, experiments of exposing soldiers to atomic blasts, and other questionable experiments resulting in substantial harm, or even death, to research subjects. The Nuremberg Code was an international effort to establish ethical guidelines for medical, scientific and social research. One of the primary principles that resulted from this process was that of *informed consent*. There appears, in today's twenty-first century, research activity that stretches the boundaries of ethical thinking. These include issues of medical research involving new drugs, the use of animals in research, embryonic and stem cell research, DNA profiling, protecting privacy in an Information Age, and so forth.

As a result of the Nuremberg Code, informed consent has become an essential part of research when there are human participants. Your research should ensure that people, as interview sample or as case interviewees, are informed of the study and its method and consent, either in writing or implicitly, to the dissemination of the findings. Such consent should not leave the participants willingly or unwillingly in a more vulnerable position.

Technology offers opportunities to engage in a whole range of projects that in the past were simply not available or possible. Databases for the collection and storage of information in quantitative and qualitative studies bring problems of security and unwarranted access that in the past were simply solved by a lock and key. Data can be manipulated far beyond the life of a project itself, raising potential problems of the invasion of privacy. Blood samples or human cell collections allow data at a later date to be reconfigured in genetic profiling. For example, many hospitals have for many years, as a course of normal procedure, taken blood samples from newborn babies for the noble intent of identifying and, if necessary, intervening in life-threatening illnesses. With advances in gene technology, such databases are a potentially excellent source of genetic research, even though the technology was not available for such research when blood sampling of newborn babies was commenced. This has led to ethical questions about access to data, and about the need for consent to data being collected. These are being debated at present and will continue to be debated as technology improves. Adequate ethical planning of research aims to try to address such challenging issues before they arise, rather than afterwards.

In some research, there are no participants and there is little chance to harm a person. For example, consider theoretical research in nuclear physics or the genetic manipulation of foodstuffs. This does not absolve such investigators from attention to ethics. Researchers also have an obligation to pursue the truth. Fraudulent or unethical research can damage university reputations and professional credibility. Ethical conduct in research is not a matter of etiquette but a question of the moral principles by which any researcher is guided. Even when no persons are studied, findings can be distorted, or double-dipping on submitting journal submissions can exist, indicating that there is a whole range of ethical dilemmas for researchers beyond the study of a person.

PRINCIPLES OF ETHICAL RESEARCH

There are values and principles that influence most research. Some overlap and can be subsumed under another category, but there is a pattern of consistency weaving through the language and practice. There is growing interest that the participants within your research project should know and agree to be involved, that your research findings will not harm them either physically or psychologically, and that your research design respect the integrity of the participants with confidentiality and anonymity if necessary. These values are provided as a guide for you to scrutinize your project and justify the judgements you will make. In the end, it is *your* thesis and it is *your* responsibility, as best as humanly possible, to adhere to these values. From these values, university research ethics committees select principles such as:

- informed consent
- honesty
- conflict of interest
- privacy
- nonmaleficence (principle of doing no harm).

This is not an exhaustive list, but gives an overview of some of the principles most universities expect research students to adhere to. You will be expected to

63

comply with such principles as best as humanly possible. Many universities will not allow the commencement of any data collection until the university research ethics committee is satisfied with your research plans. This is important, because from the very outset you should be aware of the impact such requirements will have on your research project. Any modifications you have to make to satisfy the university can have a carry-on effect in different ways: the sample, the cases, data collection, methodology, analysis, reporting and publication.

Each of these principles is discussed below in an effort to further explain the issues involved and to assist you in the design of your research project.

Informed consent

Research scientists who are used to stating formal hypotheses and deductive reasoning can be shocked at the range of ethical issues confronting the qualitative researcher. Informed consent derives from respect for the right of people to possess control over their lives. This means choosing whether to involve themselves in a pilot study or questionnaire or focus group or interview programme with full knowledge of any potential advantage or disadvantages to participants. Ask yourself if you have accommodated the possibility of someone withdrawing from your project and how you will deal with this in the final analysis and reporting? There are different ways to enhance informed consent, such as providing information to participants or a summary of the research aims. It could include an explanation of the research process and how findings will be used and reported, with details of disclosure and/or assurances of confidentiality, an option to withdraw, and (for some universities) grievance procedures.

Generally, informed consent is accepted by many scientists as implicitly given by participants upon the return of a completed survey instrument. Qualitative researchers involved in ethnographic research have to be particularly vigilant in their research when it can include observation, participation and immersion. The design and continuation of the study outlined in Box 5.1, despite its obvious ethical problems, illustrate an extreme example of the problem that ethical research should avoid. The study breached fundamental principles in ethics. Not only was there no informed consent, but there was also a long-term disregard for the dignity of persons, as Kant would advise, as ends in themselves.

A common mechanism for establishing informed consent is to obtain a signed university pro-forma consent form from a participant. As stated, for many universities, a returned questionnaire usually suffices for those involved in more statistical methodologies. But the use of consent forms is highly contested among qualitative researchers. While it may appease university research ethics committees, who may require it for administrative approval for you to proceed, it does not deal with the complexity surrounding grounded theory, ethnography or action research. While informed consent is often a requirement to proceed,

Box 5.1
THE TUSKEGEE SYPHILIS STUDY

One famous case in the United States involved both unethical research and scientific misconduct (Byrne 2001). It is known as the Tuskegee syphilis study and began in 1932. The study spanned forty years with the aim of documenting the natural course of syphilis in adult African-American men. Participants were not informed about the purpose or procedures of the research. The death rate of participants with syphilis was twice as high for participants in the control group, yet the researchers did not treat them, despite the fact that penicillin was available as an effective treatment. Key stakeholders within the medical profession (such as doctors, nurses, medical foundations and national medical organizations) knew about the research for many years and yet the study continued. In 1972 the study was terminated after it was reported in a newspaper.

it is advisable to familiarize yourself with the university regulations and discuss the matter thoroughly with the research ethics committee or your supervisor. This will place you in the best position to proceed so that, as best as humanly possible, most or all of the ethical principles are adhered to.

Honesty

In many Western countries, participation is considered part of the social obligation. People commonly allow themselves to be interviewed or surveyed at no cost to the researcher. Sometimes market researchers approach people in the street or home for opinions in return for enrolment in a lottery or some token prize. But research at the masters or doctoral level generally does not involve payment. As such, it is incumbent upon your professionalism to be honest and not to coerce or trick someone into participating in research. Deception can be when subjects do not realize they are participating in research, as well as where no effort to gain informed consent is undertaken. In this case, there is also a breach of privacy, where behaviour is recorded and used without knowledge. (Box 5.2.)

There are instances where deception in research is defensible, such as in cases of low frequency of events or because of some negative emotional association with what is being studied, for example, shame or dishonour (Sieber 1992: 65). What you have to be able to do is always justify your research, not only to university research ethics committees but also to an examiner who may raise a question about its propriety. As researcher you may have to balance partial deception with respect for the participants and the requirement not to harm them. You must

65

Box 5.2
DECEPTION AS PARTICIPATION

Investigators set up an elaborate laboratory in a brothel. As clients arrived, they were secretly given LSD. The behavioural results of the drug were filmed with a hidden camera. The subjects were never debriefed. One subject committed suicide while under the influence of LSD.

Source: Sieber (1992)

ensure privacy where appropriate in order not to harm, and you must show benefi-cence in the sense that the study, although using deception, results in some greater good to society.

Conflict of interest

The problem of conflict of interest is that it negates the integrity of a decision or process. In business, such conflict is described as a breach of the obligation to remain objective and without bias in relation to stakeholders. Conflict of interest in research raises questions of power and reliance, along with benefit and trust.

Morin *et al.* (2002) give a good example of how conflict of interest can be managed in the expansion of interaction between medical research and for-profit corporations in recent years. They advise biotechnology and pharmaceutical companies are becoming either active or passive partners in clinical research trials and creating problems of research independence. Substantial funding and clinical resources are made available to researchers in private, non-profit and public fields. University graduate programmes are not immune from such developments.

Pharmaceutical companies are sometimes active in enrolling both doctors and patients with incentives. This will often raise a conflict of interest concern because pharmaceutical companies have a vested interest in positive trial out-comes. Also, doctors may have a vested interest in enrolling patients. Such conflict can compromise the research integrity as well as the safety of research subjects. It raises a number of questions:

- the role of a research scientist
- the integrity of the informed consent process
- the risks and potential benefits of such research
- the treatment in such trials of patients/participants.

One way to assist in resolving some of the conflict issues is appropriate dis-closure such as revealing relationships and support arrangements as part of the informed consent process. There is no foolproof way of completely resolving conflicts of interest, because at the end of the day, research relies upon the integrity of the investigator. Protocols are often self-regulatory, but along with disclosure procedures are a good first step in avoiding or resolving dilemmas of this nature.

Privacy

Privacy and confidentiality are often used synonymously and are central ethical concerns in research. Confidentiality is the management of data to prevent participants' identities from being linked to their responses. Privacy is violated if data are collected or disseminated without participants' knowledge. A researcher can protect research participants' privacy by ensuring anonymity or confidentiality. Anonymity exists when participants in the research cannot be identified or, in some cases, linked to the actual data or responses.

One way to ensure the anonymity of participants is to develop codes that remove identifying links between the data and the person responding. Anonymity is sometimes a feature of the research design, such as questionnaires with anonymous returns. But in qualitative research, ensuring anonymity is sometimes more difficult. Interview transcripts need to be structured in such a way as to protect the data from outside access, and also to remove any identifying features. In order to ensure privacy is respected, a researcher should keep questionnaires, tape recordings and interview transcripts in a safe place, under lock and key, and not in or near the research site. If using coding keys for interviewees, keep this file separate from the actual raw data files. Cases like Joe's (Box 5.3) illustrate

Box 5.3
MANAGEMENT OF DATA

Joe is a doctoral student researching work satisfaction and leadership styles. He works for a company whose CEO is supportive of his research and has allowed Joe permission to use the company as one of his case studies. Joe keeps most of his data at home, except he also keeps a second copy of the interview transcripts for his own company in his work office. Over the course of months, he gathers significant data on this topic. In the course of interviews of employees within Joe's company, there is general disquiet about the CEO. Many people are openly critical of management and express clear dissatisfaction with their work lives. Joe is very happy with the data he is collecting.

What dangers do you see in Joe's management of the data? How would privacy be ensured?

that it is easy to be deluded by the exciting nature of data being collected to the detriment of upholding the privacy of respondents or subjects. In Joe's case he runs the risk of his data being accessed, and the opinions of interviewees being revealed.

Nonmaleficence

The researcher is obligated to avoid harming anyone in their study. One of the most important ethical aspects of research is the principle of *nonmaleficence:* to manipulate a person in the interview process through cajoling or leading questions treats them with minimal respect. In the tradition of Kant, every human being has intrinsic worth and basic dignity. The obligation is to respect that dignity and treat others as ends rather than as means to our ends. This means you need to respect the dignity of participants or questionnaire respondents in different ways: honouring privacy, honest research and by being mindful of the effects of your findings on participants' reputations, relationships, happiness and lives.

Ellsberg and Heise (2002) report a case of one Indian researcher who wanted to study wives who were admitted to hospital after having been burned by their husbands in disputes about dowries. However, the researcher could not guarantee the safety of the women who were to be involved in the study, so it was decided not to proceed with the research for fear that it would put women at risk. This case illustrates that a research project that cannot reasonably guarantee that no harm will come to those who participate is potentially unethical.

Research should be based on *beneficence*, that is, fostering greater good than harm. Beneficence refers to your obligation, as researcher, to consider the longer-term interests of those being studied. It means ensuring that your shorter-term goal of collecting data does not blind you to the consequences once you have finished, reported and published your findings in the thesis. You need to consider whether the findings will result in shame or embarrassment to any stakeholder. Researchers also have an ethical obligation to maximize possible benefits as much as humanly possible. Even though much of this refers to research involving human subjects, it also pertains to the research design, methodology and reporting of inanimate data if it can potentially be harmful to stakeholders, such as society generally.

ESTABLISHING A RESEARCH PROTOCOL

A protocol is a statement of your intent in the research, together with the plan of how you will carry it out in a way that honours the ethical principles stated by your university. These principles may include all or some of the principles covered in this chapter: informed consent, honesty, conflict of interest, privacy and nonmaleficence. Your university may, of course, include principles beyond these. It is your responsibility to familiarize yourself with the ethical research policies of your institution in preparing a protocol and ethics application to proceed with the data collection.

The protocol is your audit trail of how you will manage the research process and comply with ethical principles. It is meant to outline your steps to ensure that privacy is maintained, that harm is minimized and that informed consent is realized. You may not expect problems such as breaches of privacy, and you may not intend to harm anyone. But the protocol is a plan of action where you undertake an assessment of likely or potential problems. Included in this plan are the protocols or procedures for how to stop or minimize such problems from occurring. If problems do eventuate, the university research ethics committee will want to be convinced that you are in the best position possible to respond immediately. Many universities require research protocols also to include information about grievance procedures in case a participant or stakeholder complains. The university will want to ensure such grievances are avoided, and your protocol or ethics application is one way of assuring them of this.

It is usually a good idea for a researcher to establish an ethics protocol as part of the research project. Sieber (1992) offers a good overview of how ethics protocols can be established. Generally, a research protocol establishes your credibility as an ethical researcher, by establishing your project as one that is proceeding after reflection about what ethical principles are important. These ethical principles may vary, depending on the type of research you are undertaking. You do not wish your research to be perceived as an impulsive and haphazard exercise. You do want your research to be perceived as attentive to the interests of stakeholders. Your credentials as an ethical researcher are also established by the clarity of your research design, and by the proactive and rigorous manner to minimize problems occurring, or to stop them occurring in the first place.

Many countries have highly regarded institutions responsible for overseeing the ethical conduct of human research. For example in Australia, the National Health and Medical Research Council (NHMRC) sets out the ethical principles that apply to clinical research. Such committees provide guidelines for researchers and assist university human research ethics committees in their approval and monitoring of research protocols. It is prudent to familiarize yourself with the various regulatory bodies, at national or disciplinary or university level, in order to assist you in understanding the particular ethical issues at stake in *your* research, and in advising you on how best to develop both ethics approval applications and ethical research protocols.

CONCLUSION

In summary, research is full of ethical considerations. As the prime investigator, you are responsible for ensuring your research design and implementation comply

69

with all the ethical standards of your university. As well, you will want to ensure your research findings stand up to scrutiny when presented and published.

FURTHER READING

Byrne, M. (2001) 'The concept of informed consent in qualitative research', *Association of Operating Room Nurses (AORN) Journal* 74 (3): 401–3.

DeLorme, D., Zinkhan, G. and French, W. (2001) 'Ethics and the Internet: issues associated with qualitative research', *Journal of Business Ethics*, 33 (4): 271–86.

Ellsberg, M. and Heise, L. (2002) 'Bearing witness: ethics in domestic violence research', *Lancet*, 359 (9317): 1599–604.

Morin, K., Rakatansky, H., Riddick, F. and Morse, L. (2002) 'Managing conflicts of interest in the conduct of clinical trials', *Journal of the American Medical Association*, 287 (1): 78–84.

Sieber, J. (1992) *Planning Ethically Responsible Research: A Guide for Students and Internal Review Boards*, New York: Sage.

Van den Hoonaard, W. (2001) 'Is research ethics a moral panic?' *Canadian Review of Sociology and Anthropology*, 38 (1): 19–36.

Chapter 6

Resource issues in undertaking postgraduate research

RUTH NEUMANN

> He who chooses the beginning of a road chooses the place it leads to. It is the means that determine the end.
>
> (Harry Emerson Fosdick)

Resources can be critical in achieving timely and successful thesis completion. While most prospective students are strongly focused on decisions about their research topic and the selection of appropriate supervisor/s, resource matters often do not feature strongly in their decision making. However, on deciding to pursue a research degree, serious consideration should be given to the resource support available at different universities.

In the context of this chapter, resources encompass a wide range of financial and non-financial support structures and opportunities provided by the government as well as by each university and its departments. They include scholarships to undertake postgraduate study, funds to support research activities and conference attendance, the availability of space, equipment and technical support, as well as courses covering specific aspects of the research process. Added to these is the variety of technical and organizational tools on hand to facilitate the research process. These tools, which include software programs, can provide assistance in sourcing information, recording and managing your information, through to the development of personal organization and time management skills. While no one of these resources on its own, or collectively, can guarantee a successful thesis completion, they can make an important difference to understanding and managing the research process.

This chapter provides an overview of the type and range of resources available, where to locate them, and an assessment of their usefulness to assist in your research. The emphasis is very much on providing an overview and alerting you to what is possible. It is important to note that in this realm the detail changes often, so directions are pointed and examples of web sites and material are offered, but continual changes mean that you are likely to find further useful information by searching the Internet.

In selecting the scope of issues to discuss, I have drawn heavily on a recently completed study of the doctoral education experience in Australian universities (Neumann 2003). This study interviewed 130 doctoral students, experienced supervisors and university managers and included a specific section on resource issues and their role in the research process. Many of the suggestions offered and examples given are drawn from this study. Much of the discussion in this chapter is particularly relevant to Australia, since it is one of the most common destinations for international students. However, the advice, examples and suggestions are pertinent not just to Australia but to many Western, in particular English-speaking, countries, where the trends and patterns in postgraduate research study over the past decades are very similar.

The chapter begins with an overview of important financial aspects, then considers courses and information sources to assist with the different aspects of the research process, and, finally, points to some personal organization and management considerations.

RESOURCE CONSIDERATIONS: FINANCIAL

Time

Time is the most precious resource for research students. A research degree spans several years; in Australia and the UK, for example, three or four years of full time study should be allowed for a doctorate, but many students take longer. Part-time students may take eight to ten years before completing a doctorate.

Research is not like course work, where comparatively neatly allocated bundles of time are organized for study sessions and for the completion of assignments which have been determined by a lecturer. Research means that students need to generate questions, ideas and the momentum for their study themselves. These activities do not fit into neat, bounded time packages. Further, undertaking research also includes attendance at seminars and conferences and active participation in the department's research culture. Thus research creates a different demand for, and use of, time. Inevitably research students find that the research process forms a considerable part of their lives, and, typically also of their family's life.

Adequate financial support to undertake research over a period of several years is thus an imperative. Money buys time free from the competing demands of work, family and other life stresses. The majority of students undertake research degrees as full-time students, though this varies considerably across the different fields of study and depends on the individual situation. International students on student visas, for example, are required to study full-time. Students in professional fields such as law, management and commerce sometimes find it difficult to stay 'outside' the profession for long periods, even if their topic is situated within the practice context. In deciding whether to study full-time or part-time, important decisions relating to career advancement and salary maintenance therefore come into play. Studying part-time is a common way to decrease financial pressure and maintain a career. However, many part-time students feel particular time pressure in undertaking research, especially when writing up the thesis while working full-time.

Thus, whether studying full-time or part-time, the issues of time and money are inextricably linked and are *the* main resource issues for students. In undertaking a research degree all students need to be able to ensure that the research is able to take priority. This means that wherever possible work, family and social commitments are able to take a back seat for a period of some years. The long-term support of family, friends and colleagues is essential. Sufficient income, particularly if researching full-time, is also a clear necessity. Notions of impoverished students sacrificing themselves in the quest for knowledge are romantic and hard to sustain in the twenty-first century.

Funding research student places

In undertaking a research degree, it is important to understand how research student places are funded in universities, in order to make an assessment of the cost implications for you. Until recently, many governments carried a substantial portion or all of the tuition and supervision costs of postgraduate research student places. However, in many countries there is a growing trend to full-fee postgraduate research study. This means that increasingly students have to pay full tuition fees as set by each university and also support their own living costs. The number of full-fee research places is growing but there is considerable variation across the different fields of study and universities.

In Australian universities, Australian postgraduate research students may either receive a government-supported RTS (Research Training Scheme) place or they may be full-fee-paying. There are also government-supported scholarships for international students to study in Australia, and international students may also come to Australia as full-fee-paying students. Universities receive a quota of fee-exempt places (known as RTS places) from the government, and these are available to local postgraduate research students. As these places are fee-exempt, they are also HECS (Higher Education Contribution Scheme) so postgraduate research students, unlike undergraduate students, do not incur a HECS debt. However, RTS places are limited and the number that a university has available will vary from semester to semester. If there are more applicants than places available, then allocation is competitive. For further information and updates of changes regarding HECS and RTS places see the Department of

73

Education, Science and Training (DEST) web site: www.dest.gov.au/highered/research/rts.htm.

While many schemes such as an RTS place means no fees, they do not provide a living allowance, and as a result local students who wish to study full-time need to obtain a scholarship or find other methods of supporting themselves during their degree. International students usually need to look for other means of financial support in order to 'buy' a research place.

Scholarships

Scholarships typically provide a stipend, usually with fortnightly payments, and a waiver of tuition fees (apart from Student Service Fees charged by the institution) and are available for a specified length of time, usually with limited possibilities of an extension.

Most scholarships are awarded on academic merit and are available for full-time study, or sometimes in very specific circumstances for part-time study. For example, such circumstances might include a medical condition or heavy carer commitments but do not include work commitments. Students on a scholarship are usually permitted to take on only limited part-time work to supplement their income. Some people suspend their scholarship if they need to work more hours, and then continue to work on their research part-time.

A useful search engine for information on postgraduate scholarships for Australians or for people who want to study in Australia is JASON. This site lists scholarships and relevant links for Australian students wishing to study at home or abroad, and for international students wishing to study in Australia. Students can enter details about themselves and their funding requirements, and call up a list of applicable scholarships. It can be found at www.jason.unimelb.edu.au.

The Australian government also maintains a web page with information on government scholarships, as well as links to scholarships offered by international agencies for Australians to study in other countries. There are also links to the scholarship page of each Australian university: www.dest.gov.au/highered/scholarships.htm#AustralianUniversityScholarships.

Australian Postgraduate Award

Many countries offer their citizens scholarships to undertake advanced study and research. In Australia the major scholarship for Australian students is the Australian Postgraduate Award (APA). Applications for an APA are made direct to a university. Each university is allocated a specific number of APAs based on institutional research performance, and student selection is then determined by the university. An advantage of this scholarship is that if students elect to change university during the course of their candidature, then the scholarship is transferable (though technically at the discretion of the home institution). The stipend is tax-exempt and indexed annually. For 2003 the base rate stipend for full-time students is A$18,009. For more information see the DEST web site: www.dest. gov.au/highered/research/apa.htm.

APA (Industry)

APAIs are Australian government scholarships that fund collaborative projects between university researchers and industry partners (IPs). A scholarship related to a particular project is advertised, and a current or potential full-time postgraduate research student is selected to participate in the project.

There are several advantages in an APAI scholarship compared with the APA award. It provides a higher stipend than the APA award and the industry partner contributes extra funding and resources. Thus, as can be seen in the case of Carl in Box 6.1, students on these awards report far fewer financial difficulties in covering a living allowance and funding to support their research and develop their research networks. An added benefit is the ability for the student to obtain industry experience and to build connections for subsequent career development.

One disadvantage of the APAI is that occasionally an industry partner will pull out of the project. Where an industry partner does pull out and the project is terminated, the university may fund the affected APAI student as an APA student from its APA scheme funds. Further information can be gathered from the ARC web site: www.arc.gov.au/grant_programs/linkage_projects.htm.

Box 6.1
CARL

Carl is in his early fifties and is doing a full time PhD in management. He was working for a company who wanted some research done on organizational change and decided to fund a PhD through the Linkage-Projects scheme. The industry-funded scholarship was advertised in both the university and the company. Carl applied for, and received, the scholarship, and then as an additional bonus his company supplemented the scholarship to his previous salary amount. An advantage of having an industry-funded scholarship is that Carl has had all his resource needs funded without difficulty. Both the university and the industry partner contribute up to $5,000 a year each towards resource costs. This money has been used for transcription, research assistance, a computer and software, as well as travel and accommodation costs for fieldwork.

Source: The Doctoral Education Experience Project

Scholarships for international students

There are also various scholarship possibilities for international students, both from host countries and from their own country. In many cases the scholarships cover tuition fees, medical insurance and other set charges, but not a living allowance. It is worth checking carefully for the restrictions and conditions of such scholarships (see, for example, the case of Binh in Box 6.2).

One of the most comprehensive written guides on studying in different countries is by UNESCO (1999), which publishes information on courses and scholarships for most countries in the world. Details of the publication and lists of useful web sites are contained in Boxes 6.9–11 at the end of this chapter. Information on US graduate schools, rankings, research activity and scholarships can be found at www.usnews.com/usnews/edu/eduhome.htm. For similar information on Europe, see www.eurochoice.org.uk/. These sites provide a range of information on US study opportunities. The rankings and specialities of different colleges are provided, with an explanation of how they were obtained. The European site offers information and decision guides in surveying the range of universities offering research programmes in greater Europe.

Box 6.2
BINH

Binh is a student in his late twenties who has come to study in Australia from Thailand. The Thai government has provided him with a scholarship to complete a master's, followed by a PhD, which he is currently undertaking in engineering. The scholarship covers his tuition fees and a just adequate living allowance, and allows up to five years for the PhD. The Australian university that he has selected provides no extra money: for instance, he is not eligible for departmental grants to attend conferences that the Australian students are eligible for. He also does not get an opportunity to tutor within the department, because the places are filled with Australian students first. The project Binh is working on is in co-operation with a Japanese university, and the Japanese university paid for him to stay in Japan for three months to do experiments and learn to use their equipment. In his first year in Australia, Binh attended workshops provided by the university to acquire skill in writing academic English. He recommends that other international students look for such courses, as he believes they have helped him with his publications.

Source: The Doctoral Education Experience Project

Institutional scholarships

For students missing out on government-sponsored scholarships, there are also opportunities through institutional scholarships. In the main, each university has its own postgraduate research scholarships, and may attach different conditions to its scholarships. Some are open to all postgraduate research students, whilst others are targeted to specific disciplines and topic areas. Further information and links to the individual universities can be found at either the JASON web site or the DEST scholarships web site. In general, however, institutional scholarships are not transferable to other universities. The stipend is usually on a par with, or slightly higher than, the APA award.

Increasingly, individual university scholarships are connected with institutional research strengths and concentrations. Areas of research concentration are defined as areas in which a university has particular strength, has concentrated its research resources and has attracted external funding (DEST 2002).

Part-time teaching and research assistance

Another avenue of financial support is through employment in the university, preferably in an area as closely connected with your research topic as possible. There are essentially two main avenues, either in part-time teaching or as a part-time research assistant. Such opportunities can be particularly attractive to students.

There is a fairly long tradition in Western universities of postgraduate research students, especially those studying full-time, teaching in their department on a part-time basis during term time. This gives the double advantage of earning extra income while teaching in the discipline you are researching in and hence gaining career expertise and skills (see also later in this chapter). Most universities have rules on how much teaching can be undertaken by those enrolled as full-time students in order not to detract from the research process. However, the reality is, even if only teaching a small number of hours per week, many students find that they need to put considerable time into course preparation, consultation with students and marking – often more than they expected. Similarly with accepting research assistance work, you may be able to gain additional valuable research skills, but the time commitment could be substantial.

Hence it is important to weigh up just how much time can be devoted to earning additional income and increasing career skills without seriously detracting from your actual thesis research. In terms of remuneration, working as a research assistant will pay a lower hourly rate than teaching. There is some evidence, however, that research assistance work has less effect on a timely thesis completion than teaching (Leonard 2001).

Institutional resources to support research costs

The funding that universities receive from the government, from endowments and from fees for research students means that institutions have financial resources to distribute to support postgraduate research. Just how this funding is allocated varies across the institutions, since the funding also covers university costs such as supervisor time and research infrastructure, for example equipment, technical support and library resources.

In general, postgraduate research students should look for two types of institutional funding. The first is university-wide funding, which is likely to be available to students of all disciplines. The second is funding available through their faculty or department and available only to students enrolled in that area. Students are not always clear what financial entitlements or opportunities are available to them. They often hear about funding opportunities by word of mouth, but may find it hard to track down precise information. If this is the case, check the university web site under 'postgraduate research students' or the research office, or speak to a faculty postgraduate co-ordinator and to your supervisor.

Nearly all such funding is now competitive, meaning that you will need to apply for it, justifying how you plan to spend the money and how your request relates to your thesis topic. If you are awarded the money, a report on how you have used it and its contribution to your research will usually be required. Do not underestimate the time that such applications and reports take. However, the process does make you focus on your topic and help develop skills in application processes. Universities will also vary on what such additional funding can be used for. The most common use is to support conference attendance where the student is presenting a paper on their research. However, students may be able to make a case for spending some time with an eminent researcher in their field, learning a specialized research technique central to the research and not otherwise available, defraying data collection costs and possibly limited research assistance – for example, in the case of transcription in case study research.

For students with a scholarship, there is often also a thesis allowance to cover the costs of producing a thesis, such as binding and copying. Students should also check to see whether their university has specific initiatives that provide funding to students for particular purposes. Recently several universities have offered 'completion scholarships' and 'publication scholarships', which provide financial incentives to students to complete early, or to publish their research. These sorts of scholarships will vary enormously between universities, but the important lesson is that by making an effort to find out what is available at your university, you may find that you have access to unexpected sources of funding.

Another important avenue for additional resources is increasingly a student's supervisor. This tends to be more in fields where external research grants are essential for the research topic. However, in such situations, students can benefit greatly from the resource opportunities available to them through their supervisor's research grants. The case of Vincent in Box 6.3 is not an isolated example, but still not a common one for many students. However, it does illustrate what is possible. Finally, it is worth checking with external research and professional bodies to see what support is available to research students. For a discussion of financing issues for student intending to study in the US, see www.cgsnet.org/ResourcesForStudents/financing.htm. This site explores the financial options many research students face in the US, such as reduced-interest loans, fellowships and assistant teaching positions.

Box 6.3
VINCENT

Vincent is in his early twenties, doing a PhD in physics at a large research university in Australia. He chose to undertake his PhD with this particular physics group because he knew that the main researcher was very highly funded. Vincent has received a 'top-up' salary grant for his scholarship and has many travel opportunities. Although only mid-way through his PhD candidature, he has been overseas, particularly to the United States, on many occasions to present his work at major conferences. This has been enjoyable, and, more important, he also recognizes that it has provided him with career development skills, such as becoming confident at presentations, that will help him in his goal to become an academic. He has also been able to make contact with researchers in the same field from other parts of the world and has learnt a lot from associating with them. Vincent states that his experience is not unique and that many of the students in his research group have these opportunities.

Source: The Doctoral Education Experience Project

RESOURCE CONSIDERATIONS: PHYSICAL

Ideally, universities should have policies specifying minimum resource provision for postgraduate research students. Included in such resource provision are desk and office space, some storage space, access to photocopying, stationery, technical support, computers, standard software and e-mail facilities. This information may be posted on the university web site, detailed in university student handbooks or available from the faculty postgraduate co-ordinator. However, the actual provision of resources can vary significantly across fields of study, even within the same institution. Therefore students contemplating enrolling in a research degree should carefully consider the provisions made by different departments and universities.

The availability of computing and office space impacts considerably on the doctoral experience. At the very minimum, students should expect a desk in a communal room set aside for postgraduate research students, as well as access to a computer room for postgraduates. Often universities provide postgraduate research students, especially doctoral students, with their own computer, and sometimes with their own office, which is preferable for most students.

It is a high priority for both full-time and part-time students to have access to a dedicated personal space for several reasons. Aside from providing the requisite physical conditions for working, it also provides a sense of belonging and somewhere students can feel is their 'home' within the university. Security of personal material varies with the number of people who have access to the room, but if it is a small number of students and the office is secure, students are able to store their research material there so that they have it at their fingertips when they need it.

Another advantage of working in a dedicated research student area is the opportunity for mingling with other people in the department. Contact with members of staff and other students helps to alleviate feelings of isolation, as well as providing an opportunity to be part of the academic culture of the department. Students can find it very useful to have people around to ask questions, and bounce ideas off. In the long process of a thesis, it can be easy to lose a sense of perspective. Molehills can become mountains and regular contact with supervisor/s, peers and other departmental staff can help balance these sorts of 'problems' quickly.

Full-time students are more likely than part-time students to have access to this type of facility. In the sciences, particularly, it is usually taken for granted, but it is equally important in other fields. Judith's story in Box 6.4 highlights the perseverance that may be needed to gain the resource space needed for your research.

Part-time students are often professionals, and are not around campus as much during the day. They commonly work at home, where they may already have established an office with a computer. While this can sometimes be more convenient for part-time students, they should also consider their role within the department. The case of Annabelle in Box 6.5 highlights the feelings of marginalization that part-time research students can feel. If it is possible, they should try to gain access to a work space within their department so that at least from time to time they can come in and have contact with their peers.

As the case of Annabelle illustrates, universities and departments vary in the extent to which they are attuned to the needs of their part-time students. Some departments work at making students feel part of the department, and studying in this sort of environment is likely to make the thesis experience less stressful, and possibly more rewarding.

Box 6.4
JUDITH

Judith is a mature age student who has almost finished a PhD in accounting. She is a very talented student and found that the difficulties she experienced during her PhD candidature were related not to her academic ability or problems with her supervisor, but to the availability of a suitable office space. At the start of her candidature, the department assigned Judith an office in a building that was at the far end of the campus, in a very isolated position. Not only did this make her feel disconnected from everybody else, it was also a major security hazard. When the space was required for another purpose, she went through a series of temporary offices while a permanent one was being found. It was very difficult because she didn't have anywhere she could call her own and she never knew quite when she would be asked to move again. At various points, the university attempted to place her in a room of thirty students from different disciplines, and in a room next to an extremely loud machine, neither of which Judith found acceptable because she is the sort of person who requires quiet to work. In the end her supervisor managed to secure Judith a permanent office, but she felt quite demoralized by the whole process.

Source: The Doctoral Education Experience Project

Box 6.5
ANNABELLE

Annabelle is in her mid-thirties and is doing a PhD in ancient history part-time. She is employed in a different capacity in a completely different faculty on campus but needs to have a space where she can work on her PhD research undistracted by her employment. She is particularly sensitive to the fact that every time she needs to go to the ancient history department, whether for a seminar or for an appointment with her supervisor, there is no place for her to go and wait. She describes feelings of lurking in the corridor, feeling like 'a bump on a log', waiting for her supervisor to finish a meeting prior to her own appointment and then scuffling away. There is no place in the department to sit and have coffee or a chat with other research students or even to pull out a book and read when she is there. After three years of study there she feels unwelcome and like an outsider – as if she has no right to be there.

Source: The Doctoral Education Experience Project

RESOURCE CONSIDERATIONS: COURSES, SKILLS AND LEARNING SUPPORT

All postgraduate research students come to their research degree equipped with many skills – often taken for granted, as they have quietly accumulated over the years of learning. The research process requires many skills, not all of which are directly related to the content of the research topic. It is not always possible to anticipate what skills will be needed and what support may be required. This section discusses the range of procedural and technical knowledge that is likely to be needed and highlights where the resource support for these may be located.

Understanding thesis requirements and processes

On undertaking a research postgraduate degree some students will have entered via an honours route and hence are likely to have undertaken a research project and a previous thesis. However, others enter through coursework master's and other professional experience routes without undertaking a thesis or larger research project independently. Either way, it is important to understand clearly the institutional thesis requirements and also the disciplinary expectations of research in your field.

Increasingly universities are offering commencing postgraduate research students induction programmes, often complemented by on-line support material. Such programmes typically include a general orientation to the university and department; sessions on institutional thesis requirements and student entitlements; information on pitfalls to avoid and on managing the supervisory relationship, and information on the availability of learning support within the institution.

You should also seek out university and faculty handbooks, which cover much of the information that students need during the period of their research. Such handbooks typically cover the institutional thesis requirements; formal reporting periods during candidature; student entitlements; existing institutional codes of behaviour and learning; helpful tips on research; avenues for dispute resolution and institutional provision of learning support.

Various parts of the university's web site can also be very useful. In particular, students should become familiar with the web sites of their university's graduate school (if they have one), the postgraduate student association, the research office, the career development office and the library, although this list is by no means exhaustive. Don't just stick to the web site for the university in which you are enrolled, since other universities' web sites may have useful information that is not covered by your own. Other useful web sites include the Education Portal, found at www.education.gov.au, and the Education Network Australia site (EdNA), found at www.edna.edu.au/highered.html. EdNA has a search engine

Box 6.6
DEPARTMENTAL POSTGRADUATE CO-ORDINATOR

'We get all the new students at a meeting to help orient them. We discuss what's involved in the administrative sense, for example. We talk about the annual report that they have to write every September, the sort of research training courses and then what sort of resources are available within the departments – that sort of general induction aspect. Then as part of the research training course one, we also talk about things such as the format of the thesis, the relationship with the supervisors and then we again emphasize who you would contact if you were having problems, and there is a departmental PhD committee that includes myself and a couple of other academics and we say, "You can approach any of us." Also we go through the annual report issues . . . and I think in some cases there is a perception that if they are having a problem they shouldn't mention it in the annual report. We emphasize that they need to, so that we can monitor the situation and if they find it difficult to say it, they can certainly again approach the departmental PhD committee members to discuss these issues.'

Source: The Doctoral Education Experience Project

which will locate information on government sites and other relevant educational sites across Australia. American web sites also have lots of tips on how to survive your candidature. One particularly succinct and helpful one is the Graduate School Survival Guide, Stanford University, available at www-smi.stanford.edu/people/pratt/smi/advice.html, which includes advice on a range of issues relevant to research students.

Courses on research and research skills

Many universities provide short courses on research skills. Such courses can last two hours or run for several days. They cover a diverse range of topics, for example: research ethics, using qualitative analysis packages, quantitative statistics, designing questionnaires, 'how to' guides on writing a thesis or a literature review, making presentations at conferences, writing journal articles, computer skills, library and database searches, and bibliographic management software.

Courses and workshops that focus on skill development are often offered by university bodies such as a central student learning unit, library, university graduate school or postgraduate student association. Universities increasingly complement these offerings with web site offerings and on-line resource materials which you may be able to access on line, even without doing the courses.

83

Not all students, of course, will need such courses. Generic courses are often of most benefit early in the research degree, particularly to those who may not have had general research method training in their undergraduate study. In instances where highly specialized research skills or techniques are needed, these are usually acquired on a specific course or through a period of intensive learning with an expert, either within the university or outside.

Finally, nearly all universities offer workshops and seminars on intellectual property. Understanding intellectual property rules and rights and the university's policies on ownership of intellectual property is an increasingly important area for research students to understand, particularly if they are involved in industry-supported projects or industry collaborations. In undertaking a thesis, you are involved in independent research inquiry designed to generate new knowledge, skills or practices. Universities are increasingly conscious of the financial aspects and implications of generating knowledge and techniques that may produce patents or other commercialization opportunities. As a researcher, this involves you (not just your supervisor/s) and you should make sure that you are aware of, and understand, intellectual property issues that may be raised by your research. Intellectual property issues are likely to be particularly important if you are in a science field or in another area where results may be commercialized, for example, if you are developing new financial management models.

Library resources

The university library is an extremely important resource and will nearly always have additional services for postgraduate students, compared with those provided to undergraduates. These include services such as inter-library loans and Document Request, the ability to request books and articles from other universities, and possibly the ability to borrow from other university libraries. Such services are usually free for research students, and can provide you with access to much wider literature sources, particularly important if you are studying at a smaller university. The library will also have services for locating past theses. It can be very helpful to read theses in the same area as yours so that you can get an idea of what kind of standard is expected from you and the different ways that research material can be organized.

A good university library will help enormously in skill development, through courses and workshops that they run and/or by providing face-to-face support for specific problems or issues. Library courses may cover various stages of thesis production, including advanced courses in using databases and locating information, maintaining and organizing the information, and courses on using bibliographic software to manage references and formatting theses. The latter courses will cover topics such as the use of templates, 'outline view', tables and figures, and illustrating theses.

84

Dissertation abstracts

Copies of the abstracts of other students' theses are widely available through digital databases. Different universities will subscribe to different databases, and information about how dissertation abstracts can be obtained at each university can be found through the relevant university's library web page. An example of a very good database is ProQuest Digital Dissertations, which includes abstracts of all dissertations published since the first US dissertation in 1861 up to very recently accepted dissertations. Some databases require a subscription from the university, while others require a fee per abstract, and there are also some free databases. Two examples of free databases are the Networked Digital Library of Theses and Dissertations (NDLTD), found at www.theses.org, and UNESCO Electronic Theses and Dissertations, found at www.unesco.org/webworld/etd.

Bibliographic software

In order to manage the numerous citations and references acquired during the course of your research, it is highly advisable to use a bibliographic software package. These are specialized software packages with bibliographic management capabilities more specific than regular databases such as Microsoft Access and Corel Quattro Pro. Among the most widely known is EndNote, distributed by ISI ResearchSoft. ISI also produce a number of other programs, such as ProCite and Reference Manager. Other alternatives include Biblioscape and Biblioexpress, Citation, Bibliographix, Papyrus, Resource Mate and Esprit, although there are many more. AutoBiblio and Bookends Plus are specifically available for Apple Macintosh computers, and the ISI programs also have Mac versions. It is worth checking with your library and also your department to see if there are institutional site licences for any packages, which would mean that the program and all upgrades will be available to you at no charge. It will also mean that there is likely to be good institutional support available to you in learning to use the program and troubleshooting.

Different bibliographic packages will have different features, with some packages designed for highly particular uses. However, in general the main uses of this sort of software are for storing references, importing references from external sources, and compiling bibliographies and reference lists in any style required. The references are stored in a database style, where users can search by field, such as author, title or key words. Increasingly, bibliographic software packages are compatible with the Internet, with features such as posting reference lists on to the Web and downloading reference lists from the Web into the database. For example, references can be downloaded directly into EndNote from on-line databases. It is well worth devoting time at the start of your research to learning to use such software. It will pay dividends countless times throughout your research.

85

As the number of packages available increases, selecting the appropriate one may be quite difficult. There are several web sites available that have compiled links to the relevant bibliographic software companies as well as providing reviews of the main programs on the market and advice on how to choose a package that suits your individual needs. Two examples of these web sites are Biblio-Tech Review, found at www.biblio-tech.com, and UKOLUG, found at www.ukolug. org.uk/ and follow the links to the bibliography.

Career development

Students come to postgraduate research from a variety of backgrounds. Some continue directly from undergraduate study, while others have spent time in the work force, often with considerable professional experience. Career benefits from a research degree also vary. In the past students undertaking a PhD usually did so because they wished to pursue an academic career, but this is no longer the case. For example, in 1998 only 33 per cent of Australian PhD graduates went on to an academic career and there was a doubling of PhD graduates in the industry and commerce sectors (GCCA 1999). Similar trends can be found in the UK and the US. Strategically, students should consider the various career development possibilities that a research degree can offer and work to capitalize on the opportunities.

One important career development opportunity is writing for publication, as discussed in Chapter 16, 'From thesis to publication'. It can be valuable experience to get an idea of the processes involved in having a piece of work published in a journal, especially if you are planning a career as an academic. Presenting at conferences is another way to further your career during the course of your candidature. Both publication and presentation can help students become known in their field and expose them and their research to others in the area. The writing and presentation process also helps you develop your thesis writing, often bringing disparate parts of your research together. An additional advantage is that what you have written can often be adapted into a chapter or part of the thesis. Support in writing and conference presentations is available from your supervisor and from the various institutional learning support locations discussed above.

Further career opportunities lie in teaching. Such opportunities may be more prevalent in the sciences and professional fields than in the humanities. Not all students who undertake tutoring necessarily desire an academic career, but developing teaching skills can be useful for all types of leadership roles. Because tutors are paid, this can also be a good way to supplement your income. The universities and their departments vary in the way that tutorial work is allocated and, if you want tutoring work, it is best to start by talking to your supervisor. You should also speak to tutors currently employed at your university if you are interested, to find out their experiences of tutoring. Tutoring can enhance your communication and presentation skills. It also provides a way out of becoming completely absorbed in your own research, as well as broadening your knowledge of the field. However, beware, since it is not uncommon for students to undertake too much teaching, interfering with progress on their thesis. Students should be particularly careful about tutoring during the later stages of their candidature, when many people find that they need undisturbed large blocks of time to complete their write-up.

Publications and research networking are generally considered more important for an academic career than teaching experience. Alternative career development opportunities can include activities such as developing web pages, maintaining equipment and working as a research assistant.

RESOURCE CONSIDERATIONS: PERSONAL ORGANIZATION AND MANAGEMENT

A key to success in undertaking a research thesis is to work regularly and consistently on your project. While the odd day off will not do much harm, and indeed may be a good thing, keeping the flow going through regular time spent on the thesis is vital. This becomes even more crucial for those studying part-time. A break of continuity in contact with your research, supervisor and department can easily lead to feelings of isolation and marginalization. It does not take long for a downward spiral to eventuate, which can take a lot of personal energy and commitment to break.

Even if you think that you are efficient at managing time, it may be helpful to take a time management workshop, to make lists of tasks and to prioritize these. If you find that you can let yourself get distracted easily, then identify the distractions and find ways to overcome or remove them. Leonard (2001: 116–22) has particularly good tips for women with family responsibilities and domestic commitments. Above all, no matter what your personal situation is, make sure that you are doing something on your thesis every day, but also be sure to build in regular time to relax and switch off.

From the very start of your research it is worth establishing good filing and organization systems. The research process generates much material and data which if not appropriately organized and filed becomes increasingly difficult to locate. Bibliographic software, discussed above, is just one means of storing and organizing your data.

It is important for students to set out a timeline that includes reasonable goals and deadlines for the completion of the various research stages. Your supervisor should be able to help with this, as should other support people in your university – the departmental postgraduate co-ordinator or the dean of postgraduate research students. Many universities are developing more stringent annual reporting mechanisms for research students, which may include an expected timeline for completing thesis tasks. Volunteering to present a paper at a seminar within the department can be a good way to set a goal with a deadline. Not only does this give something finite to work towards, it is also a means of getting feedback from other students and faculty members on your progress.

Writing is another important skill. Many students and experienced supervisors stress the importance of writing from day one. Writing involves thinking, and is an important means of organizing your thoughts and ideas. Cumulatively it builds your thesis. For example, when reading articles, write some notes about the main points of each paper so that it can serve as a memory jog later. Writing a summary of groups of papers on a particular topic can help keep the flow going. As you undertake different parts of the research, write up what you are doing and the rationale for your decision making. On days when you have 'writer's block', work on something descriptive or factual rather than the more difficult conceptual parts. It helps to do an outline of your thesis from the beginning, putting in the various chapters that you expect to have, and jotting down headings and sub-headings within these. As your work progresses, this outline will be continually modified and developed, but will help your thesis to maintain a coherent structure.

As your thesis gradually develops, you will find that time invested in acquiring advanced word-processing skills pays off. It is a good idea to determine from an early stage how you would like the format of your thesis to look and to design a template to work in which conforms to any formatting requirements of your university. Microsoft Word provides a variety of templates, including thesis and

Box 6.7
ELIZA

Eliza is in her late twenties and is doing a PhD full-time in political science. She is also working part-time two days a week. Eliza speaks very highly of the advantages of writing continuously from the start of candidature. This initially started with a paper that she put together for a seminar. Her supervisor also encourages her to write papers that cover the different aspects of her research on a regular basis. Eliza has found that the biggest advantage of writing is that it helps her to understand the focus and direction of her thesis. It also provides something concrete that she can take to her supervisor for feedback. Although she may have more than she needs when the time comes to tie it all together, she recognizes that she will not be in the same position as many other students who find they have an awful lot of writing to do in the last six months of their candidature.

Source: The Doctoral Education Experience Project

report templates. It is worth investing time early to understanding templates, since they save enormous time at the end in terms of editorial work. For example, consistency of headings, a table of contents, lists of figures and tables are all easily managed and changed within a template. It is also encouraging to see your own work looking professional and in its final format, and can act as a motivator on those 'down' days.

OTHER SUPPORT

Finally, it is important to realize that during the course of your research there may be times when you have more personal support needs. The importance of carefully balancing research, social and family life has already been mentioned. Universities also have health and counselling services which can be very helpful with those unexpected problems that arise in the course of life, particularly coupled with the pressures of postgraduate research. Most universities also offer a range of other services that may be useful to students. For example, they often provide child care on campus and may offer discounted fees for postgraduate students. There are also grievance or dispute resolution officers and in many instances university deans for research students to help you should you have the misfortune of experiencing supervision or other difficulties during your research degree. Many universities also have an international office dedicated to the specific needs of international students. A list of such services is usually provided in the postgraduate student handbook and on the web site.

Finally do not forget the support possible from your peers. If a peer support group does not exist in you department, there may be opportunities within your university to set up a support group, as in Faith's case (Box 6.8). If members

Box 6.8
FAITH

Faith organized a support group, together with about six other people who were conducting research in related areas. She found this constructive because it provided a forum where members could discuss problems, share ideas and encourage each other through challenging times. They regularly organized speakers to talk to them about different aspects of postgraduate study and research. Members were at varying stages of their candidature and were both part and full-time, which provided several different perspectives. Knowing that others had also gone through the same issues as she was going through, and had completed, gave Faith the inspiration to persevere and not to be disheartened.

Source: Listserve QSR Forum, April 2003 posting

89

cannot meet in person, an e-mail group may be possible. Several universities have listserv computer systems that can support an on-line support group, so if you are interested you should approach someone in the university's information technology section.

CONCLUSION

When embarking on a thesis, it is always important to remember that it is a long-term commitment which requires independent work and direction. In such situations it is essential to understand the scope of the undertaking as well as the resource needs that you will have at various stages of the process. These needs include sufficient time and long-term financial support, appropriate physical resources and conditions, as well as an array of both broad and specific research skills. Often, these wider skills and support needs are overlooked, as students focus on the more obvious issues of supervisor choice and relationship and topic development. However, as a research student it is important to be aware of the broader context of your research and thesis and the range of resources that may be needed. When contemplating a thesis it is worth investing time to identify additional needs that you may have and to inform yourself of the support, beyond your immediate supervisor, available in the department and university at which you want to undertake your thesis.

REFERENCES

DEST, Department of Education, Science and Training (2002) *Higher Education: Report for the 2002–2004 Triennium.* Canberra ACT: DEST.

GCCA, Graduate Careers Council of Australia (1999) Postgraduate Destinations Survey, 1998. Parkville VC: GCCA.

Leonard, D. (2001) *A Woman's Guide to Doctoral Studies,* Buckingham: Open University Press.

Neumann, Ruth (2003) *The Doctoral Education Experience: Diversity and Complexity.* Canberra ACT: Evaluations and Investigations Programme, Research, Analysis and Evaluation Group, Department of Education, Science and Training.

UNESCO (1999). *Study Abroad 2000–2001,* Paris: UNESCO.

Box 6.9
WEB SITES: FUNDING OPPORTUNITIES

- *Joint Academic Scholarship Online Network (JASON).* Australian postgraduate scholarships database
www.jason.unimelb.edu.au

- *Council for International Exchange of Scholars.* Fulbright scholarships programme
www.cies.org

- *Department of Education, Science and Training (DEST).* Sources of funding for study and/or research in Australia
www.dest.edu/au/highered/scholarships.htm

- *National Health and Medical Research Council (NHMRC).* Information on funding and scholarships within Australia, particularly in the medical and science fields
www.health.gov.au/nhmrc/funding/scholarships.htm

- *Education.gov.au.* Information on a variety of Australian educational sites, including scholarships, funding, procedures, resources, policy, etc.
www.education.gov.au

- *AusAID scholarships.* AusAID web site on Australian and international scholarships
www.ausaid.gov.au/scholar/default.cfm

- *Research Councils UK.* Homepage links to various research councils within different disciplines, and information on scholarships, funding and information
www.research-councils.ac.uk/

- *British Council.* Sources of funding for international students
www.britishcouncil.org/education/funding/index.thm

- *British Chevening Scholarships.* Information on a scholarship programme for international students to study in the UK
www.chevening.com/

Box 6.10
WEB SITES: HELPFUL EDUCATIONAL INFORMATION

- *Council of Australian Postgraduate Associations.* CAPA homepage details role of CAPA and related publications and resources
  www.capa.edu.au

- *British Council Australia.* Information for students interested in studying in the UK
  www.britishcouncil.org.au

- *Association for Support of Graduate Students.* British web site with resources and advice for postgraduate students
  www.asgs.org

- *Education Network Australia – Higher Education.* Comprehensive Australian higher education resource site
  www.edna.edu.au/highered.html

- *UK Council for Graduate Education.* Links to relevant postgraduate literature
  www.ukcge.ac.uk/post_graduate_information.html

- *Higher Education Funding Council for England.* Information on HEFCE on funding schemes, policy, publications, research, etc.
  www.hefce.ac.uk

- *National Postgraduate Committee.* UK Postgraduate Committee web site, with resources, policy information, scholarships and funding
  www.npc.org.uk

- *US News and World Report.* Information on US graduate schools, research activity and funding options
  www.usnews.com/usnews/edu/eduhome.htm

- *Department for Education and Employment.* Provides information on European study options
  www.eurochoice.org.uk/

- *Association of UK Higher Education European Officers (HEURO).* Information on higher education in Europe
  www.heuro.org

- Association of Commonwealth Universities. Detailed information on graduate study opportunities in Commonwealth universities
  www.acu.ac.uk

- Council for Graduate Schools. Information on graduate education in the US and Canada
  www.cgsnet.org

Box 6.11
WEB SITES: RESEARCH SKILLS AND SOFTWARE

- *Biblio Tech Review*. Reviews of bibliographic software and other key resources
  www.biblio-tech.com

- *The UK Online User Group*. Information on bibliographic software
  www.ukolug.org.uk/links/biblio.htm

- Endnote. Bibliographic software program web site
  www.endnote.com

- *ProCite*. Bibliographic software program web site
  www.procite.com

- *Networked Digital Library of Theses and Dissertations (NDLTD)*.
  Electronic theses and dissertations
  www.theses.org

- *UNESCO Guide to Electronic Theses and Dissertations*. Electronic theses and dissertations
  www.unesco.org/webworld/etd

- *UTS: STAR*. One university's web site, with all types of useful information for postgraduate students
  www.star.uts.edu.au

- *Graduate Student Advice – Stanford*. A survival guide on the thesis process, writing and supervision
  www-smi.Stanford.edu/people/pratt/smi/advice.html

Part II

Operational issues and the medium stage

Chapter 7

The motivational journey

PAUL NESBIT

> Great works are performed, not by strength, but by perseverance. Yonder palace was raised by single stones, yet you see its height and spaciousness. He that shall walk with vigor three hours a day will pass in seven years a space equal to the circumference of the globe.
>
> (Samuel Johnson)

MOTIVATION

It will be no surprise to read that a thesis is a goal that you will have to persist with for a long period, and one that will take substantial energy and effort to achieve. In many ways a thesis can be likened to a long journey across terrain where you have never been before. You have a clear destination but you have little knowledge about the best path to get there. You are told to expect obstacles and problems on the way but you don't know exactly what those problems and obstacles will be until you encounter them. It is a difficult journey that many more people start than finish. While each thesis journey is different, all share the need for students to manage their thinking, emotions and behaviour, in order to produce the necessary persistence and intensity of effort. In other words the thesis is as much a motivational journey as a journey of research and discovery. This chapter discusses what you can do to help develop and maintain your motivation as you travel the thesis journey.

Motivation has been the subject of a substantial amount of research which has provided considerable insight into the nature of motivation and what one can do to help maintain the drive and energy necessary for successfully achieving difficult goals. This chapter is not an academic treatise on the literature of motivation, but is instead presented as a series of motivational strategies, to help you think about and deal with some of the motivational issues you may encounter while undertaking your thesis journey. However, it is important to note that there are no motivational strategies that will simply allow you to set a goal and reach it without effort on your part. There is nothing I can write that will substitute for your own effort. As the sixteenth-century astronomer and mathematician Galileo said, 'You cannot teach a man anything; you can only help him find it within himself.' In other words, the ideas discussed in this chapter can help you to engage your own capacity for self-motivation.

When I talk to prospective students about doing a research degree, I am reminded of a story about a party where one of the guests attending was a concert pianist. After some coaxing from the host and various guests he agreed to play a few songs on the grand piano. The music was magical and everyone was enchanted. Later a person went up to the pianist to tell him how much he had enjoyed it. 'You know,' he said as he shook the pianist's hand, 'I would give my life to play like that.' 'I have,' replied the pianist. There are many people who would like to play the piano, but few are prepared to give the time and effort in practice to reach a proficient level, let alone the high skills of the concert pianist. In the same way, many students I talk to would like to get a research degree, but few are willing to put in the time and effort that are needed to make their dream a reality. Part of the value of completing a thesis is that it is hard to achieve. Things that are easy to get are not highly valued. You might prefer the path to the goal of a thesis to be easy, but having travelled a difficult path, you will find more pleasure in arriving at the destination.

The fact that you have set off on the thesis journey, or intend to do so in the near future, is evidence that a thesis is a goal that you aspire to, and one that you believe is worthy of your effort. The more you value completing the thesis, the more useful will be the motivational strategies discussed in this chapter. It is easier to stay focused and ignore or deal with competing demands when you know how valuable it is for you to reach a goal. The more you commit to the thesis, the easier it is to decide to spend more time on it, and to spend less time on other goals that you value less. In addition, if for some reason other events in life do distract you for a time, a valued goal will keep returning to centre stage in your life.

MOTIVATIONAL STRATEGIES

This chapter discusses a number of strategies to help you develop and maintain motivation. The essence of these motivational strategies is that they help you organize your environment to increase the likelihood of you carrying out desired behaviours and limiting undesired behaviours.

Think of the thesis as a lifestyle change, not as a degree

An important starting point is to think differently about research studies. Rather than seeing them as another degree, think of your studies as a lifestyle choice! By lifestyle choice I mean that you need to integrate behaviours that will help you to build your goal into your current lifestyle. This is harder for part-time students who have to integrate doctoral studies into a life already packed with work and social commitments. But there is no way round the fact that unless you make choices to engage in action to advance your thesis you will not be successful. Thinking about your thesis as requiring a new lifestyle does two things that boost motivation. First, it helps you recognize the level of effort and the intensity of effort needed, and second it helps you to reflect realistically on how you spend your time now, and on ways that you can integrate the tasks associated with the thesis into your existing lifestyle.

The importance of this strategy is vividly illustrated in a story that I first read in Stephen Covey's best-selling book *First Things First* (1999). The story is about an instructor in a class on time management who takes out a large glass jar and proceeds to put a number of large rocks into the jar. He then asks the students if the jar is full. Some say yes, but most are wondering what he is going on about. He then pulls out a bucket of gravel and pours the gravel into the jar and shakes the jar so the gravel goes into the cracks and spaces left by the big rocks. He asks again if the jar is full. Some say yes, but a few suggest that there is still space left between the gravel. The lecturer pulls out another bucket, but this time filled with sand. He pours sand into the jar so that it begins to fill up many of the cracks and spaces left by the larger gravel and rocks. Again he asks if the jar is full and this time more students say no. The lecturer pulls out a pitcher of water and proceeds to pour it into the jar, filling it to the top. He then asks the students what is the point of the exercise. One student volunteers an answer. 'I guess you are saying that if you really try hard you can do more and more in life and fill life up.' 'No,' says the instructor, 'that's not it at all.' He waits a few moments. 'The point is,' he says at last, ' that if you didn't put the large rocks in first then you would not have been able to put them in at all.'

Life is like the glass jar in that we can put only so much into it. The big rocks are the things that we would like to achieve, the goals we set for ourselves. The sand, gravel and water are like many of the demands on our time that are easily able to fill up our days. Much of life is filled by routines and habits so that if we wish to add new goals, like studying for a thesis, we need to give considerable thought to how we organize our daily life. Whether we like it or not, the glass jar (our time) will get filled up – by others, by the demands of life. By setting goals, and by making choices to carry out behaviour to meet those goals, we begin to make our own destiny, rather than allowing the hustle and bustle of life to take total control over our lives and fill up the glass jar of our life. As the American motivation author Alfred A. Montapert said, 'Your life will be no better than the plans you make and the action you take. You are the architect and builder of your own life, fortune, destiny.' You need to make deliberate choices about using some of your time to engage in the activities of the thesis. Each day, all the hours will

99

be filled up. You never go to bed with a few spare hours saved up that you can devote to your thesis tomorrow!

There is usually nothing in the tasks associated with working on a thesis that will insist on immediate attention. If you don't work on your thesis when you have set yourself time to do it, then nothing bad will happen to you. In contrast, in our undergraduate degree, if we did not hand in an assignment on the due date then we would lose marks. If we didn't study for an exam we would get a lower mark than we could have received. These pressures built up as we came closer to the date the assignment was due, or to the date of the exam. Eventually the pressures reached such intensity that we would choose not to go to a party, or to sleep less, or to avoid other activities so we could study for the exam or complete the assignment. But the tasks of the thesis are different in that they do not generally build up in intensity, so we can continue to ignore them, for days, weeks or even months! But gradually you come to the realization that you have made very little progress on your thesis and suddenly you begin to feel less able to make progress.

The point is that unless you integrate the activities of the thesis into your daily lifestyle you risk not reaching your goal of successfully completing your thesis. We have to put the big rocks in consciously and deliberately! I am trying not to depress you about your chances of doing a thesis but to draw out the reality that you must think about how you will shape your current lifestyle to accommodate the demands of the doctorate.

To successfully complete a thesis we have to engage in new behaviours and avoid or limit other behaviours. That is, our lifestyle will need to change by embracing new behaviours, the tasks associated with the doctorate. Given the reality of finite time each day, we must also limit the attention and effort devoted to other tasks not associated with the thesis. That is, we must actively shape our social and physical environment to support and enhance our effort to meet our goals.

Goals are the basis of action. Break down long-term goals into short-term goals and write them down

Both academic researchers and popular writers on motivation stress the importance of intention in human achievement. An important first step to integrate new behaviour into your lifestyle is to be clear what that new behaviour looks like. You do this by articulating the behaviour you need to be carrying out, in the form of goals. As J. C. Penney, the American entrepreneur, said, 'Give me a stock clerk with a goal and I'll show you a man who will make history. Give me a man with no goals and I'll give you a stock clerk.' Goals are the foundation of success and achievement. Without consciously set goals, life would be aimless and the pressures and demands of your environment would simply carry you along.

Goals are the 'big rocks' of life. However, while the thesis is itself an important long-term goal, it is far too complex and distant a goal to adequately establish the short-term activities that you need to focus on at any particular time. There are distinct areas to most theses – reading and reviewing the extant research literature, collecting data, analysing data, writing up the thesis – but these activities are themselves long-term goals. The way to deal with long-term goals is to break them down into smaller short-term goals that will guide your behaviour. As the old joke goes, 'How do you eat an elephant?' Answer: 'One bite at a time.' To be able to reach long-term goals like a thesis, you need to break the thesis into clear and achievable short-term goals that you can focus on and use to help energize your efforts and so lead eventually to the long-term goal.

Goals have been the subject of a substantial amount of serious academic research, which has shown the positive effect of goals on personal achievement. Research suggests that goals will be more effective if they are framed in a way that specifies what needs to be done, and by when. By giving specific details of what is to be achieved and by when, you are in a better position to judge how much effort is needed. Goals should also be sufficiently challenging, so that they should stimulate the need for effort and the mobilization of ability. Research also suggests that goals should be realistic. You gain nothing by developing lists of goals that are 'pie in the sky' aspirations. Goals should be grounded in the reality of your current abilities, skills, knowledge and capacities. For example, if the time demands of family and work are particularly great, then your goals should accommodate that reality and should reflect the actual time available. Being realistic in goal setting is thus an important aspect of driving our motivations. The final lesson from research on goals is that they should be written down. By writing down goals, you keep the value associated with them centre-stage in your attention. This makes it easier to avoid distractions and maintain your focus and effort.

However, simply developing a set of goals and sub-goals and writing them down is not the same thing as carrying out the action to reach those goals. Goals and plans of action do not compel behaviour in the sense that once goals and plans are decided the necessary behaviour always follows. Goals and plans of action are important because they prepare the way forward. The more we value their achievement, and the more we have thought about how to fit the necessary time into our lifestyle, the more likely we are to carry out the behaviour needed to reach them.

Keep a research journal

Research has shown that keeping track of your progress towards reaching goals is a powerful aid to motivation. Keeping a research journal to write down your goals, sub-goals and tasks and to keep track of your progress is a good habit to get into. The journal doesn't have to be kept as a tidy, comprehensive and

101

systematic account of all your goals and activities. The purpose is to keep the information in a central location that you can easily review if necessary. In addition to recording your goals and the activities you undertake, you can also keep your ideas and thoughts about your research in one place. Ideas are easy to lose if they are not written down.

By keeping track of progress you do two things that contribute to your motivation. The first benefit is that tracking progress generates additional energy for forward motion. Progress activates thoughts like 'I've travelled this far, so I should continue,' which help maintain progress. If we do stop, the information in the journal also suggests where we might be able to restart. We don't have to spend considerable time and effort in getting back on top of material.

The second benefit of keeping track of progress is that you quickly become alert to any discrepancy between the goals you set and your actions. When you become aware of these discrepancies you are more likely to recognize the need to adjust your behaviour and to think about different approaches and strategies. For example, you may need to reflect on the characteristics of the goal. Is it too challenging or even unrealistic? Is it too broad to guide action? Thinking about the possible reasons behind the failure to reach goals allows you to think of solutions to the problems.

The specifics of the research journal are very personal and should fit into your preferred style of working. Some academics I know keep a journal of tasks and research on their computers. I personally like to use an exercise book where I record long-term and more immediate goals. Each time I work on research I put the date at the top of the page and then write a brief discussion of my work intentions and progress. As well as research I also note future plans and ideas. By keeping a central place for my ideas and notes, I know where to look for past information and I get a sense of progress.

Always keep moving in your thesis, because even small steps are progress

My supervisor's favourite piece of advice about motivation during my doctorate was that 'movement is everything'. By this he meant that one achieves goals by action and one should be constantly acting in ways that will help to reach goals. By action one gets closer to one's goal and the closer one is to the end the less likely it is that one will stop. Activity also helps to create order and focus for later action. As you begin a thesis you begin to know what needs to be done next, to know what works and what doesn't work.

It may seem obvious, but the importance of making progress a habitual way of working cannot be overstated. It is tempting to try and make progress in huge steps but this strategy is unlikely to be sustainable. If you want to spend all day on your thesis, by all means do so, but rather than do nothing the next day, spend a little time to make a little more progress. The point of this strategy is that habits form by constant repetition of action. Of course there will be days when little can be done, and there will be times when you are not sure what should be done, as well as some days when you will simply want to stop work on your thesis. The problem with giving way to the temptation to inaction for a few days is that it can go from a temporary rest to a longer-term stoppage. The longer you don't work on your doctorate, the harder it is to restart.

One of the problems with a complex goal like a thesis is that it is not always clear what you should be doing. What is the highest priority of the myriad of activities that you could be doing? At moments like this, it's sometimes said that 'if you don't know where to start, then it doesn't matter where you start'. By getting into a project, by just starting it, one creates a sense of momentum that leads to further action and progress.

However, there is an important caveat on this view of action. As Alfred A. Montepert advises 'Do not confuse motion and progress. A rocking horse keeps moving but does not make any progress.' We should be sure that our actions are related to goals. This is good counsel to counter the view that one should just do anything. You may have heard of the guidance to writers to 'just start writing, it doesn't matter what you write – just write'. The advantage of this advice is that it develops the habit of sitting down and writing. The disadvantage is that if you are writing rubbish, or material that doesn't move you towards your goal, eventually you begin to lose the motivation to continue writing. We do things because we are rewarded. The major reward while writing a thesis is ultimately a sense of making progress.

Thus, while action is everything in making progress, there is also the need for planning and for making our actions count. As Abraham Lincoln once said about the importance of planning, 'If I had eight hours to chop down a tree, I'd spend six sharpening my axe.' To the extent that you can plan and organize sensible interconnecting parts, you should do so. Remember, plans don't have to be perfect before you start on them. Momentum tends to create order and focus that aid the development of future plans of action.

One way that you might try to develop the habit of continual progress is always to stop work knowing where you will start the next time. It's easier to start again if you know where to start. It's also easier to start again if you leave something interesting to do for the start of the next session of work. Authors know that the best way to get readers to continue a book is to end each chapter with the promise of answering something interesting and mysterious in the next chapter.

Avoid negative thinking and keep away from negative people

Our thinking has a substantial impact on our behaviour. As much as you can, you should not let yourself dwell on the negative thoughts that will arise from time to time during your thesis. Things do not always go the way you would like, and this can lead to periods of negative thinking. The problem is when the occasional doubts become sustained self-doubt and pessimism.

The idea of positive thinking is often taken to extremes in popular literature on motivation. The notion of positive affirmations such as 'Every day I am getting better' and 'You can do anything that you can dream of' has for some people given positive thinking a flaky New Age image. However, the notion of keeping a positive outlook and keeping problems and obstacles in perspective is an important element in staying motivated. Even personal exhortations can raise your motivational energy. You often see athletes engage in self-talk just prior to competing. You can be sure that they are not convincing themselves that they will fail on this attempt! Positive self-talk and positive thinking can both play an important role in temporarily enhancing your motivation to do a critical task.

Stanford psychologist Albert Bandura considers self-belief in one's ability as a central capacity in the pursuit and achievement of goals. He refers to this self-belief as 'self-efficacy', and regards the self-efficacy belief system as the foundation of human motivation. Indeed, self-efficacy has become one of the most well researched and well regarded concepts in the field of motivation and self-regulation. A substantial amount of empirical research has shown that people who have high self-efficacy tend to set themselves more challenging goals, and will be more persistent and energetic in reaching those goals, even in the face of obstacles.

There are a number of ways of increasing one's sense of self-efficacy. The most effective method of creating a strong sense of efficacy for a particular task is through mastery experiences, that is, by successfully dealing with similar tasks. While many research students may not have the degree of experience of research required to have developed strong self-efficacy for research, they typically have successful experience with many of the basic skills needed. For example, they may have experience in researching and analysing literature, in writing and expressing ideas, and in developing and articulating coherent and persuasive arguments, etc. You may in fact have already carried out some research. Thus you have efficacy for many of the tasks needed to research and produce a thesis. Your research efficacy will develop in time, as you gain experience through setting challenging but realistic sub-goals and reaching them.

The second way of creating and strengthening self-efficacy is through observing people similar to oneself succeeding by sustained effort. Thus an important strategy is to mix with others also doing their thesis, especially those who are successfully dealing with the tasks and demands associated with their research. Spending time getting to know others is useful because it helps you in setting a standard to guide your own intentions, as well as giving you insight into the skills and approaches that others have successfully used to deal with similar problems. Research students share a common experience and can give each other the necessary support when things are not going so well. Thus seeing others successfully progress and eventually complete long-term goals like a thesis can reinforce your own motivation. Others can also help your motivation through their encouragement of your efforts. People who are concerned about your progress, especially those whose opinion you value, can persuade you, when doubts enter your thinking, that you possess the ability to reach your goals. Thus supervisors, colleagues and family members can all play a role in stimulating and supporting your motivation.

Of course, boosts to self-efficacy from verbal persuasion will soon decline if you do not also reinforce efficacy through realistic and appropriate actions. It is important to follow up the effects of encouragement from others with goal-directed behaviours. Making progress will then inspire further motivation effort.

Contact with negative people can also eat away at self-efficacy and reduce efforts to reach solutions. The idea of associating with successful students and limiting contact with negative thinkers may sound a bit calculating. However, research has shown substantial support for the view that the immediate social environment, including people, influences our thinking and behaviour. Being around other students who are successfully dealing with the demands of a research thesis, and being around people who support us in our endeavours, is a lot more pleasant and motivating than having the misery of failure echo in one's ears!

Take responsibility for helping your supervisor to increase your motivation and self-efficacy

In Chapter 3 you read about how to manage your supervisor. Here I want to discuss your relationship with your supervisor from the perspective of motivation. Clearly the supervisor can play an important role in developing your self-efficacy and contributing to your motivation. As well as helping to guide your research efforts, your supervisor's expectations act as an external source of pressure to carry out the tasks of the thesis. In other words, your supervisor's expectations pressure you to perceive the tasks of your thesis as 'big rocks' that you have to deal with and fit into your lifestyle.

Unfortunately, the extent that a supervisor has this effect will vary considerably. Some students get very good support from their supervisor, while others rarely see them or seem to get little benefit from the relationship. Irrespective of the skills and abilities of your supervisor, you should and can take significant responsibility for ensuring that your supervisor does contribute positively to your motivation. The student/supervisor relationship is too important to let it go to waste. That your supervisor may not contribute much is not the point. You must take charge to see that you benefit from the relationship.

Many research students make the mistake of seeing their supervisor as someone checking up on them, as someone in authority and with greater knowledge casting a wary eye over their progress. Thus, if the supervisor does not take an active interest in the student's progress, some students seem almost relieved that their supervisor is not too vigilant about their work and progress. Gradually meetings with the supervisor occur less and less often, until contact is infrequent at best. The result is that an important source of motivational stimulation and knowledge is lost.

It may seem harsh to focus on you, the student, rather than the supervisor, to maintain and control the student/supervisor relationship, but leaving it solely to the supervisor's interest and motivation is to risk limiting a potentially significant source of motivational support. Supervisors respond to their social environment and, like you, have many demands on their time and attention. By taking the initiative to maximize the benefits of the relationship, you will help shape the environment of the supervisor, who is then likely to increase his or her supervisory efforts.

For most students, contact with the supervisor will usually be by meeting face to face and it is at these meetings that you have most capacity to influence the relationship. All meetings should have an agenda of items to discuss. If your supervisor does not have a clear agenda you should provide one, and you should be clear about what you would like to get out of the meeting. You don't have to make a show of these items but you simply ensure that each of the items you need to discuss is dealt with. If you want your supervisor to comment on something you should send it to him or her prior to the meeting. Don't expect your supervisor to read early drafts with spelling mistakes, containing only broad ideas. Even the most diligent supervisor will become frustrated if asked to read poorly developed work. Think of your supervisor's time as a limited resource and think about how you can use it best. If you have problems, then come to the meeting with some ideas about how to deal with them, rather than relying on your supervisor to be the source of all wisdom. Remember, your supervisor is not there as a substitute for your own thinking!

Meetings with your supervisor should be regular, especially in the early period of your thesis, until momentum and progress have been established. But again remember that time is a limited resource for your supervisor, so use it wisely. The purpose of your meeting should be to report on what you have done, what you have found out, to identify and discuss the next steps in the process, and to agree on what will be done by the next meeting and when that meeting will be. If your supervisor does not set you tasks or timelines, then you need to ensure that these are established. It can be as simple as both agreeing on what is expected of you and by when. If possible you should also end meetings with a commitment from your supervisor about their contribution to your thesis, such as when he or she can read and comment on any writing you will submit.

If you don't live in the same city as your supervisor there is obviously less opportunity for personal meetings. However, even in these situations there is the same need for you to take responsibility to use your supervisor to help your motivation. In these cases communication by e-mail, telephone and on-line meetings can be a substitute for physical meetings. Just as in the physical meeting, you need to make these 'virtual' contacts as useful as possible. You can use e-mails to list agenda items, to identify sub-goals and tasks, to establish timelines for activities and commitments, and to discuss problems and offer solutions.

Organize your work environment

The organization of your work environment can also have a significant impact on your motivation. Some people have very tidy work environments while others appear very disorganized and untidy. Generally speaking, the more time and effort you need to spend on organizing your environment before you can make progress on your thesis, the more likely it is that disorganization will reduce your likelihood of starting work. The reason is that you may realistically feel that it will take too much time to set yourself up to work effectively in the time you have available. Nevertheless, many of the most productive academics I know have untidy desks and offices. Thus it is not being untidy that is the problem, but rather whether you can start easily on tasks that will give you a sense of progress.

The thesis is a long-term project, and during it you will collect a great deal of information, research articles and other documents pertaining to your thesis. The amount of written material collected over time will be substantial. There will also be many document and data files related to your thesis on your computer. You should make an effort to think through how you will organize these items. When information is handy and easily reached, you will be able to concentrate your effort on your thesis. If information is difficult to locate, you will erode some of your energy and focus. There are also many items you will need to use or refer to while working on your thesis. For example, pens, paper to write on, paper for the printer, computer disks, other stationery items, reference material such as a dictionary, writing style guide, statistics textbook, etc. If, when you need these items, you have to go on a grand search to find them, you not only waste time and effort, but also risk an even greater danger. On your search you may find something more interesting to engage in (watching television, chatting to a friend) or more pressing to do, and so find yourself distracted from your research. In summary, the thesis is already a difficult enough process, so you should limit obstacles to progress by planning and organizing your work environment.

While discussing the organization of information, I also offer this common, but commonly ignored, piece of advice: always back up your computer files regularly and keep the backup data of your thesis in a separate place to your computer. Computer hard drives do crash and computers do get stolen. Losing a substantial amount of data and files is not only immensely stressful but can also destroy your motivation.

'I've lost the plot.' How to get back on track?

Despite one's best efforts, sometimes the fire of enthusiasm for one's thesis goes out. A long period of unavoidable inactivity can lead to a crisis of progress where one can't seem to find the energy to get back into research. The solution to this problem is to use a two-step strategy. First, simply wait until one's motivation and mood improves. This is not as asinine as it seems. We all go up and down in mood in our life. There are moments of high optimistic energy and moments of depressed energy and lack of interest. It is virtually impossible to reactivate the thesis while one is feeling deeply depressed or negative about it or when one is totally engaged in some other important aspect of life. Rather than beat up on yourself and add more guilt to your woes, it is better to let go for a while. If you value the research thesis highly enough, then the desire to do it will resurface. (If you do not come back to the thesis, then you can set yourself another goal in life . . . like learning to play the piano!)

You can also help increase the desire to get back into your thesis by reconnecting with what it is that you value about completing the thesis. There are many ways of doing this. Popular motivational writers often refer to 'visioning' successful completion of a desired goal. In your case, you would imagine, in as much detail as you can, what it would be like at your graduation. Imagine who would be there, imagine what people would be saying to you, imagine accepting your degree, etc. You can also help re-energize desire by talking to others, such as your supervisor or friends, by reading a motivational book, watching a film on your topic area, or by reading a biography about a person you admire, etc. I know of one (ultimately successful) student who during his darkest moments while undertaking a PhD would visit the stock exchange to re-energize the desire to learn about management.

Assuming that the desire returns, the second step is to approach starting the thesis from the aspect that you find the most enjoyable. Think about past activities associated with the thesis. What aspect did you like the most? Searching databases for interesting articles? Going to the library and reading the latest journals? Thinking about and writing theoretical models? Whatever tasks associated with your thesis that you enjoyed the most should be your starting point. The logic is as powerful as it is obvious; we are more likely to do something if we find it intrinsically interesting and enjoyable. By starting on that aspect we find enjoyable we are more likely to continue working and so create momentum for action which in turn leads to experiencing the satisfaction of having done something that creates more commitment to the thesis. Eventually, you can begin to plan and think more seriously about the tasks necessary to start making rapid progress.

The point is to re-ignite a spark of interest that will generate the motivation necessary for progress on the thesis. Once you start back, you need to build up

Box 7.1
MOTIVATIONAL STRATEGIES

- Recognize that your thesis is a lifestyle choice that requires you to reorganize your life to do the thesis.
- Set realistic, specific, yet challenging goals and sub-goals.
- Keep a research journal to monitor your goals and activities and to track your progress.
- Always keep moving on your thesis, because even small steps contribute to progress.
- Organize your work environment to help you work on your thesis.
- Keep a positive attitude and mix with others making progress on their theses.
- Take control to maximize the benefits of your relationship with your supervisor.

'wood for the fire' as quickly as possible so that the fire takes off again. You build up the fire of motivation by using the strategies we have discussed. Box 7.1 lists these strategies again.

CONCLUSION

One thing is certain about the research thesis journey. The intensity of your motivation will vary across the period of your thesis. At times you will feel energized and excited by the process and at other times you will feel uninterested and depressed. Rather than expecting yourself to be highly engaged all the time, you should be realistic about the process. However, you should guard against relying on working on the tasks of your thesis only when the mood comes over you. You should make a conscious and deliberate effort to reflect on the process of reaching the long-term goal of successfully completing your thesis. As part of this reflection you should think creatively about strategies to maximize your energy and effort to carry out the tasks of the thesis. Using the strategies mentioned above will not guarantee progress and successful completion of your thesis. However, by taking note of these strategies, by thinking about them and by putting into action those that suit your work habits, you will enhance your motivation and increase your likelihood of completing your thesis journey. The American author Henry Miller summed it up well when he said, 'in this age, which believes that there is a short cut to everything, the greatest lesson to be learned is that the most difficult way is, in the long run, the easiest'.

Chapter 8

Learning to learn

Lessons from ancient Chinese proverbs

YIMING TANG

学力根深方蒂固, 功名水到自渠成 – 范成大 (1126–93) 南宋诗人

Where water flows, a channel forms; where a solid foundation is laid, a tower rises.

(FAN Chengda, 1126–93; poet, South Song dynasty)

Nearly every research student, but especially those who undertake the dual challenge of studying in another country, will become frustrated with an apparent lack of progress at some time during their thesis. In this chapter we draw on the wisdom of ancient Chinese proverbs to guide candidates in developing a proper perspective for pursuing their thesis. While the lessons offered in this chapter originate from the Chinese culture, they have universal application for students involved in the challenging experience of completing a thesis, particularly in an environment and culture that is unfamiliar.

LEARNING TO LEARN

Once there was a young man named Qiu Zhi who lived in a village at the foot of a mountain. Qiu Zhi loved the martial arts and dreamed of one day becoming a *Gong Fu* master. The best way to achieve that goal, he was told, was to learn from the monks of a Buddhist temple in the mountains. So one day he packed a bag and left for the temple. The distance from the village to the temple was not very far, but it was not an easy climb. It was already afternoon by the time Qiu Zhi knocked on the door of the temple. A young monk responded.

'How can I help you?' asked the monk.

'I want to join your temple and learn the martial arts,' answered Qiu Zhi.

'For that, you will need the permission of the master,' said the young monk.

'OK. Can I speak to him, then?' asked Qiu Zhi.

'The master only meets visitors in the morning. Please come back tomorrow,' said the monk.

So the next morning Qiu Zhi got up earlier than the day before, and again set out for the temple. This time the journey took him less time, as the way was more familiar. By the time he reached the temple, it was still morning, though the sun was already high. Again he knocked at the temple's door, and the same monk responded.

'Oh, the master is doing his meditation. I'm afraid you must come back again.'

Qiu Zhi was disappointed, but he understood that he needed the permission of the master, and he was determined. The next morning he rose much earlier than the previous day and reached the temple just as the sun appeared on the horizon. Again he knocked loudly on the temple's door, and again the same monk responded.

'I am sorry but the master is with his students, and they have just started their morning practice together. I am afraid that you will have to come back another day if you wish to meet him,' said the monk.

Again Qiu Zhi was disappointed. 'This is my third visit, but I still cannot meet the master. Perhaps the master does not want another student,' he said to the monk.

'Since this is your third visit, let me try to speak to the master and see what I can do,' the monk replied.

Soon the monk came back with a bowl of hot rice porridge, and said to Qiu Zhi, 'I am very sorry but the master cannot be disturbed as he is leading his students in their morning martial arts practice. But since you have travelled so far and so early, you must be hungry. Please have this rice porridge as breakfast. And while you eat, let me tell you a story.'

Together they sat down on the stone steps at the temple's front door, and the monk began this story:

A young man worth educating (Ru zi ke jiao, 孺子可教)

One day Zhang Liang met an old man while crossing a bridge. When the old man saw Zhang Liang, he removed his own shoe and threw it down from the bridge. 'That's curious,' Zhang Liang thought. But his curiosity soon turned to agitation when the old man asked him to go and fetch the shoe. Nevertheless, out of respect for the man's age, he did so. When Zhang Liang returned with the shoe, the old man asked him to put it on for him. Again, out of respect, Zhang Liang knelt down and complied. Satisfied, the old man praised Zhang Liang as *a young man worth educating*. He asked Zhang Liang to meet him back at the bridge five days later, and promised to bring something for him.

Five days later, Zhang Liang returned at daybreak. The old man, already waiting there, reproached him for being late and asked him to come back again after another five days. And so a second time, five days later, Zhang Liang came to the bridge at rooster's first crow, only to find that once again the old man was already waiting there. Angrily the old man insisted that he must come back again in five days' time. The third time Zhang Liang came to the bridge before midnight and waited a long while before the old man arrived. This time the old man was pleased and he gave Zhang Liang a rare book about the art of war. Zhang Liang studied it day and night and ultimately became a famous military strategist.

(Based on Situ Yan 1986: I, 281–2)

Having heard the monk's story, Qiu Zhi suddenly realized that his seriousness as a martial arts student was being tested.

'Ah,' he said, 'I will sleep outside the temple tonight so I will not be late again to meet the master tomorrow morning.'

Having learned of Qiu Zhi's determination, the master monk ordered that he should be permitted to spend the night inside the temple. The next morning Qiu Zhi was brought to the master.

'What is your name?' the master asked, 'And why have you come here?'

'My name is Qiu Zhi. I want to join the temple to learn martial arts from you, and one day to become a *Gong Fu* master!'

'You have high ambition, Qiu Zhi!' the master replied. 'Before we go any further, though, let me tell you a story.' And so he began.

Exercises at rooster's crow (Wen ji qi wu, 闻鸡起舞)

Liu Kun and Zu Di both had great aspirations to serve their country even when they were very young. Room mates, they often debated far into the night about how they might do so. Late one night, and still debating even in bed, they suddenly heard a rooster crow.

'The sound of the rooster crow stirs people to action. Let's get up and practise swords,' Zu Di said.

'Yes, let's go!' Liu Kun agreed.

So the two jumped out of bed and began practising their swordsmanship together, accompanied by the rooster's crow. From that day on, they continued this practice for many years. Later, both became great generals who led their armies to victory and recovered lost territories of their country.

(Based on Situ Yan 1986: I, 254–5)

When he had finished this story, the master turned to Qiu Zhi. 'Learning the martial arts is very hard work. It requires great determination and endurance. Are you willing to follow the examples of Liu Kun and Zu Di?'

'Yes, I am!' replied Qiu Zhi.

'Good!' said the master. 'From tomorrow on, your first task is to fetch enough water to fill the water vats in the front yard. You must get up at the rooster's first crow. Take two empty buckets to the other side of the rushing stream behind the temple, and fill them with water. Then, stepping on the stones in the stream bed, you must carry them back. If you spill any water you must return to where you started, and refill the buckets. When you are able to fill the vats before noon each day, come and see me. Then I will start teaching you the martial arts.'

Qiu Zhi thought to himself, 'It must be another test, but I have been fetching water back in my village for years, so it should not be difficult.'

He got up very early the next day. Taking the buckets to the other side of the stream, he filled them with water and started to carry them back, stepping carefully on the stones in the stream bed. But it turned out to be much more difficult than he had anticipated. First, it was not easy to spot the stones under the rushing water. Second, the stones were very slippery. Qiu Zhi could find his way only by slowly and carefully feeling for a footing on the slippery stones. Often he would slip and spill some of the water. When that happened he had to return, refill the buckets and start again. It all took great time and effort. Even so, by the end of the day the vats were still not yet full.

But the master came to encourage Qiu Zhi. 'It is only your first attempt,' he said. 'You are not expected to manage it in one day. You will get better in time.'

Encouraged by the master's words, Qiu Zhi put his head down and continued fetching water each and every day. Over the next six months, he learned more about the stones, their number, location, size and how slippery they were, etc. Soon he was able to remember where the big and less slippery ones were located under the water, and he was able to handle the less stable ones with greater skill. As he progressed, he managed to spill less water each trip. And so, gradually, he was able to fill the water vats a little earlier each day. But still he was unable to fill them all by noon. Discouraged by his slow progress, he went to the master and said, 'Maybe I am not cut out for this. Besides, what has fetching water to do with martial arts? Maybe I should just go home.'

Instead of responding directly to Qiu Zhi's frustration, the master smiled and said, 'Let me tell you another story.' And so he began:

Giving up half-way (Ban tu er fei, 半途而废)

Le Yangzi, a scholar, left home to study. One year later, he returned.

'Finished your studies already?' asked his wife, who was sitting at her loom weaving cloth.

'No. I've come back to see you because I missed you.' said Le Yangzi.

His wife took out a pair of scissors and said: 'The cocoons are unreeled and spun into yarn. The loom then weaves the yarns one by one into cloth. It takes months to finish a bolt of silk cloth. If I cut it with a pair of scissors, all I have done will be wasted. It is just the same with your studies. Knowledge must be accumulated day after day and month after month. If you give up half-way, isn't it like cutting the yarn with scissors?'

Le Yangzi was deeply moved by his wife's words. He left again and did not return until he had finished his studies several years later.

(Based on Situ Yan 1988: II, 64–5)

When the master had finished this story, he turned to Qiu Zhi and said, 'You have only just started your long journey to learn the martial arts. You don't want to give up this easily – only half-way – do you? Besides, fetching water has everything to do with learning the martial arts. As you fetch more water each day you build up the muscles in your arms. You gain steadiness in your steps. Without these, you cannot master any form of martial arts. Therefore, this is a necessary stage that every serious student of martial arts must endure.'

Enlightened by the master's words, Qiu Zhi continued to fetch water for another six months until he was able to carry the full buckets across the rushing stream quickly and steadily without spilling any water, and to fill the water vats in good time.

'At last,' he thought, 'my learning will begin in earnest.' Eagerly, he went to the master and said, 'I am ready to learn martial arts with you now!'

'Good!' said the master. 'Come with me, then.'

The master led Qiu Zhi through a zigzag alley, and through a heavy wooden door. Then, for the first time since his arrival at the temple, Qiu Zhi was allowed into the temple's back yard. He saw the master's students practising, some with fists, others with various kinds of weapons, including sword, spear, whip, bow and arrow, etc. Seeing all these activities in front of his eyes, Qiu Zhi was very excited.

'Which style would you like to learn, then?' came the master's question.

'I want to do the sword dance on top of the standing posts. I also want to learn the fists dance and the spear as well.'

The master smiled, and he said to Qiu Zhi: 'You want to do many things. Let me tell you another story, then.' And so he began:

Concentrating one's attention (Zhuan Xin Zhi Zhi, 专心致志)

Qiu was a famous chess player of ancient times. No one in the whole country could beat him on the chessboard. Two students came to learn from him. One always kept his mind focused on the game, and on learning from the master. The other also sat there, listening and looking at the chessboard. But his mind was often on the wild geese flying by, wondering how to shoot them with his bow and arrow. The first student learned to play very quickly, while the other made little progress. Was one student cleverer than the other? No. It is only that one concentrated his attention while the other did not.

(Based on Situ Yan 1986: I, 199)

When the master had finished this story, Qiu Zhi replied, 'I understand. I must focus all my attention on one form of martial arts if I am to master it. And so I have decided to learn the sword dance on posts.'

Indeed, this is truly an ambitious young man! thought the master. 'That's a very good choice, as it is one of the most difficult forms of martial arts to master. I am very pleased to see your ambition. Come with me, then.' The master led Qiu Zhi back to the front yard, where he put several half-bricks on the ground, leading from the front door to the water vats. 'From tomorrow morning, when you carry the water buckets back from the stream, you must make sure to step only on these bricks to reach the water vats. When you manage to do that without spilling any water, let me know.'

Qiu Zhi felt his heart sink. He thought to himself, 'What I really want to learn is the sword dance on the posts, but all I have been asked to do so far is fetch water. There are only so many hours in each day. If I keep fetching water, when will I have time to practise martial arts?' And so Qiu Zhi resolved to learn at night while everyone was asleep. One night he got out of bed, and very quietly sneaked out into the training yard. The posts were about two metres above the ground and a metre apart. Qiu Zhi managed to mount one of the posts, though, needless to say, he was not very graceful. Before long his foot slipped. He fell off the post, bumping his head and knocking himself unconscious. He landed hard on the ground, dislocating an arm in the process. When Qiu Zhi finally awoke, he found himself in bed with severe pain in his arm and in his head. Sitting by the bedside, the master smiled.

'Drink this medicine.' He said. 'It is bitter but it will take the pain away.'

As he took the cup Qiu Zhi said, 'Master, I am truly sorry about the trouble I have caused. I only wanted to learn to handle the posts sooner.'

The master smiled. 'Let me tell you another story, then.' And so he began:

More haste, less speed (Yu Su Bu Da, 欲速不达)

Before taking up his position as a country magistrate, Zi Xia came to Confucius for advise on how to govern. Knowing that Zi Xia tended to focus his attention on the immediate interests and that he was impetuous, Confucius exhorted him: 'Attention to minor and immediate interests prevents one from accomplishing great things. Whatever you do, do it step by step instead of pursuing mere speed. The more haste, the less speed.'

(Based on Situ Yan 1986: I, 203–4)

115

When he had finished this story, the master said to Qiu Zhi, 'This has happened in your case. Wanting to progress faster is very good, but moving too fast when you are not ready for it will only take you backwards. It may not have been apparent to you, but stepping over those bricks as you carried the water buckets was like doing the sword dance on posts. But doing it on the ground is a necessary first step before attempting the posts.'

'Now I understand!' said Qiu Zhi. 'But how long will it take me to recover from my fall?'

'If you take your medicine daily, it should not take long for you to recover fully,' said the master. 'Fortunately, your arm is only dislocated and not broken. Otherwise, not only would it take much longer to heal, but I fear that it would always be much weaker than before. Now, while that arm heals, I will teach you to use your other arm to handle the sword.'

In a couple of months Qiu Zhi had fully recovered. And again he was able to carry the filled buckets, stepping on to the bricks, though it was still not an easy thing to do. The bricks were placed loosely on the ground. As Qiu Zhi stepped on to them, carrying the buckets full of water, the bricks would slip and slide. Nevertheless, Qiu Zhi was determined. He practised daily. And in time he began to make steady progress, gradually spilling less water. From time to time the master would come to see how Qiu Zhi was progressing. And just when Qiu Zhi seemed to have managed the previous arrangement well, the master would change it. He would move the bricks further apart, and add a couple more bricks at the end. Qiu Zhi noticed these changes, of course. But now he was more philosophical, thinking it must be necessary to better prepare him for the real tasks ahead.

Then one day the master came to Qiu Zhi and said, 'You seemed to have progressed very well. Now I want you to also move sideways and backwards as well.'

This added much greater difficulty, of course, but Qiu Zhi continued to do what the master told him to do each day; and he continued to make steady progress. Finally one day the master, pleased with what he saw, said to Qiu Zhi, 'I think you have managed these bricks very well. From tomorrow I want you to practise on top of the standing posts.'

Now Qiu Zhi was very excited. At last he was ready to practise on the posts. But of course, it was not an easy task. And initially, with the memory of the first fall still fresh in his mind, Qiu Zhi was somewhat apprehensive, afraid that he would fall again and, perhaps, hurt himself even more seriously.

But the master encouraged him, saying, 'Don't be afraid to fall. You will not be the first. Everyone who has mastered this form of martial arts has fallen from the posts many times. When you fall, however, you must keep your eyes open to see where you are falling in order to avoid bumping into things. And you must reflect on what you did wrong just before you fell in order to prevent the same thing from happening again.'

So, as he continued practising on the posts day after day, Qiu Zhi kept reminding himself of what the master had said. As he continued practising another year went by. In that time he made great progress and was able to move from post to post with increasing confidence. But still he would fall off occasionally.

Then one day Qiu Zhi came to the master and said, 'I have worked very hard, and I have learned to move from post to post. But I still fall off the post several times a day. It is now three years since I came to the temple. During that time I have seen several other students who have already mastered their chosen armory very well. I feel discouraged by my slow progress, and now I doubt that I have what it takes to ever succeed at this. Perhaps I should have chosen another form of martial arts?'

The master looked directly into Qiu Zhi eyes and smiled. 'Let me tell you another story,' he said. And so he began:

Great vessels taking longer to complete (Da qi wan cheng, 大器晚成)

Ma Yuan lost his parents at early age, so his elder brother, Ma Kuang, raised him. Ma Kuang wanted his brother to become a scholar. But there was a neighbouring boy named Zhu Bo, who could recite the Book of Odes and the Book of History at age twelve. Discouraged, Ma Yuan feared that he was not as smart as Zhu Bo. So he asked his brother to let him become a shepherd instead.

Ma Kuang advised his brother: 'For Zhu Bo it is a case of "small vessels taking a short time to complete", owing to their limited capacity. For you it is a case of "great vessels taking longer to build", because of their great capacity. Be resolute and work hard, and you will definitely have a bright future.'

From then on, Ma Yuan no longer abandoned himself to despair but studied diligently. Eventually he became a governor and a general.

(Based on Situ Yan 1988: II, 25–6)

Having finished this story, the master said to Qiu Zhi, 'What you have been practising over the last three years is one of the most difficult forms of martial arts. It is much more difficult than those practised by other students. Naturally, it takes much longer to learn. That is why so few ever attempt it. You should be very proud of what you have accomplished so far. If you persevere, you will one day master it.'

Encouraged again by the master's words, Qiu Zhi continued to practise. As he did, his progress continued. Before long, he was moving from post to post at will and with greater confidence and ease.

Pleased with his student, the master said to Qiu Zhi, 'You have made very good progress so far, and I hope you have not forgotten your goal to become a *Gong Fu* master eventually.'

117

'Of course not!' said Qiu Zhi, 'But how can I achieve that?'

'There is a national championship each year. If you win the title in this category, you will be recognized as *Gong Fu* Master in the Sword on Posts technique. But to gain that title, it is not enough only to perform the task. You must also meet certain standards, as determined by a panel of judges.'

'What are these standards?' asked Qiu Zhi.

'Well, each player must complete two programmes within the time limit. For the compulsory programme, you must complete a series of standard poses. For each mistake you make, you will lose points. If you exceed the time limit, you will also lose points. Some judges are adamant about these standard poses. Should you make any deviation, however, slight, they will be very strict. For the personal programme, you must complete a series of poses of your own choice. In addition to completing these poses correctly in the time allowed, you will be judged on their level of difficulty and on your creativity. Some judges may even ask you to justify your choices. You must be fully prepared for it. Fortunately, in what you have done so far, you have always followed these strict standards. That is another reason why it has taken more than three years for you to reach this point. That is why, with further practice, I think you will be ready in good time for the national championship.'

Encouraged by the master's words, and excited at the prospect of earning the coveted title, Qiu Zhi continued to work very hard, practising each and every day. Finally, when the time came to attend the championships, he endured one round of competition after another. And, in the end, Qiu Zhi won the championship and the title. It was a very proud day, both for Qiu Zhi and for the master.

WIN YOUR SUPERVISOR'S HEART

In many ways, doing research work is like Qiu Zhi's journey to become a *Gong Fu* master. First you will need a supervisor. Like the master in the temple, your supervisor is also a very busy person. Therefore you must *make yourself worth educating* in the eyes of your supervisor.

Most research candidates show great enthusiasm for their studies by always providing detailed and carefully written documents for review, by preparing well for meetings and by completing on time the tasks assigned by their supervisors. These are the candidates most welcomed by supervisors. In return, these candidates receive their supervisors' best and most timely support.

Unfortunately, though, there are also those few who submit for review draft documents that are poorly written, and with many loose ends. There are those who come to see their supervisor with little or no preparation, sometimes having made little progress since the last meeting. Whatever circumstances give rise to such incidents, they nevertheless leave their supervisor with the impression that these students are not fully committed to the rigorous process of doctoral studies. Consequently, given other demands on their time, supervisors will be less motivated to work closely with these students. Eventually, unless there is significant improvement, such students will lose the heart of their supervisor. Without a supervisor, one cannot complete one's studies. In the story above Qiu Zhi understood this. So too should research students.

FOCUS ONE'S ATTENTION

Many people who have earned a doctoral or master's degree from a reputable academic institution have told me that the most critical decision for them was probably at the very earliest stage of their programme, when they were trying to pin down and settle on a topic. This is critical because the outcome of this decision becomes the focus of all your attention, and provides direction for the effort to follow. From the beginning, Qiu Zhi focused his attention on mastering the art of the sword dance on posts. It was a most challenging goal. In pursuing his dream, Qiu Zhi came to early acceptance that he could master only one thing at a time. This helped him to *focus his attention* from the beginning on pursuing his dream. This has significant implications, too, for doctoral and master's candidates.

Obviously, candidates must choose a topic with which they are so fascinated that they are willing to spend at least several years of time and effort on it. While most people probably realize this even before starting their programme, some candidates continue to wrestle with their choice of topic even after they have completed the coursework component of their programme. Indeed, just the other day I received an e-mail from a candidate who, after working on it for two years, was considering abandoning the topic of his thesis and switching to an entirely different subject area. While this candidate may have good reason(s) for switching direction in the middle of a programme, it is nevertheless a most costly exercise, both for the candidate and for the supervisor. One should never take the decision lightly.

ADVANCE STEP BY STEP

Naturally, every candidate would like to finish his/her degree in the shortest time possible. However, they cannot hope that a reputable academic institution will award a doctoral degree, the highest academic achievement one can earn, or a master's degree, without their having met certain rigorous standards. All candidates must therefore be prepared to follow a step-by-step process, ensuring as each step is completed, and before taking the next, that it conforms to rigorous academic standards.

119

You will recall that our martial arts hero, Qiu Zhi, was very clear about the goal he pursued. Nevertheless, it took several stages and several years for him to achieve it. He began by carefully feeling his way over the slippery stones under the water, buckets of water perilously balanced on his shoulders. For months he practised, slowly and carefully crossing the stream, over and over again, until gradually the way became familiar to him. But then, despite his apparent progress, he had to spend many more months stepping on the bricks. Indeed, it was several years before, finally, he was about to mount the posts. Similarly, there are several key stages a candidate must successfully negotiate in order to complete their thesis. These include a critical literature review and theoretical framework, research hypotheses and measurements, data collection, data analysis and thesis documentation.

Not unlike Qiu Zhi, groping with his feet through the water, a candidate must become very familiar with the pathway to their intended field of study. The way to do that is by conducting a critical literature review. The candidate must first search out and access key pieces of relevant research literature, and then carefully study them, making sure to achieve a thorough understanding of their field of study.

To properly conduct a critical literature review, a candidate must:

- Thoroughly cover the field of previous studies on the chosen topic, so as not to miss any important pieces of the research literature. Moreover, candidates must assess the *original* literature. To merely rely on reading reviews by other people, one runs the risk of using results that may have been misinterpreted.
- Understand the issues studied in the field to date, the key outcomes and the related methodologies applied in these studies.
- Critique the findings and the research methods of these studies.
- Identify the knowledge gaps of the previous studies and future research direction(s), which, hopefully, will form the research question(s) for your thesis.

All this takes considerable time and effort, of course. But without a thorough review of the relevant research literature a candidate cannot build a solid theoretical framework to guide their thesis. Recall that if Qiu Zhi happened to spill any of the water, the master required him to return all the way back to where he started, fill the buckets again, and start over. Similarly, if a candidate were to discover at a later stage that, owing to lack of thoroughness, s/he had missed a key piece of original research on the chosen topic, it might force a revisit and/or even a major revision of the theoretical framework. This can significantly delay progress with subsequent tasks. A candidate, on the other hand, who invests the time and effort to conduct a thorough critical literature review can proceed with confidence to build the theoretical framework of his/her thesis. The next stage, then, is the development of research hypotheses and the measures for testing those hypotheses.

Once the research hypotheses and measures have been formulated, a candidate may be eager to surge ahead to data collection. But, as happened to the martial arts student, undue haste may result in a major setback if the candidate is not truly ready. In his quest Qiu Zhi progressed from traversing slippery stones under water to an apparently more solid footing over bricks in the yard. But, despite their solid appearance, even those bricks were sometimes unstable. Similarly, no matter how good they may look on paper, a candidate must validate and pre-test his/her identified measures before proceeding to data collection. In addition, a candidate must also make sure to properly handle key methodological issues, including research sample selection, contact method(s) and response rate, etc., for their data collection.

Sadly, I recall one candidate who, having identified his measures, rushed into data collection before properly validating and pre-testing them. Since invalid measures were used to collect them, a significant portion of the data could not be used. The candidate had no choice but to revise his instrument and to collect the data again, resulting in lengthy delay. Furthermore, owing to the refusal and/or changed circumstances of some respondents, it was not possible for the candidate to obtain all the data needed. Clearly, the lesson to be drawn here is, as the master put it, 'The more haste, the less speed.'

The master required specific tasks and much hard work from Qiu Zhi before he was deemed ready to attempt what he had set out to accomplish. Though it was not always evident to him, each of those tasks served a purpose. Each stage laid the foundation of the next, each in turn contributing to the greater likelihood of ultimate success. In order to succeed, each stage must be successfully negotiated, one at a time, and in a logical order. And so it is with research theses.

Having established a firm foundation, the candidate can now proceed, confident that they will not fall off the posts – or, if they do, it will at least be without suffering any major injury. Once valid research data have been collected, the candidate is ready, at long last, to begin to analyse the data and to document the results. Challenging as the remaining work may be, they can be assured that, if they have come so far, they have already overcome most of the major hurdles in completing a thesis, and are well on their way to successful completion of their degree.

CONFORMING WITH THE STANDARDS (FORM AND SUBSTANCE)

Qiu Zhi understood that, in the end, it did not matter where he came from and how much effort he had made. He would ultimately be judged not only on the difficulty of his poses, and on their successful completion, but also on his presentation and form. The same principle applies to research degrees. In addition to adhering to rigorous academic standards, candidates must ultimately be able to communicate their study clearly and effectively, in a well written document that conforms to generally accepted standards for academic writing. This, of course, assumes a very high standard of proficiency in written English, which is often a challenge even to those for whom English is their first language. Obviously it presents an even greater challenge to candidates whose first language is *not* English. Nevertheless, a degree is awarded not on the basis of what a candidate starts with, but on the basis of where they finish.

For overseas students, there is often a lack of face-to-face interaction between a supervisor and a candidate. More often than not, communication is by e-mail, possibly with draft documents attached. In any case, each and every time a candidate communicates with the supervisor is an opportunity to obtain feedback, not only on their research progress, but on their writing skills as well. It also provides an opportunity to work on developing those writing skills. Your supervisor wants you to succeed. Any criticism of your work is not intended for you to lose face, but to teach you to conform to the rigorous standards expected, and to prepare you to face tougher questions from the examiners. A candidate who submits to a supervisor a document that contains many language deficiencies will undoubtedly receive an unfavourable review. If it happens consistently, a supervisor may have increasing difficulty taking that candidate seriously. They may even form the impression that they are *not worth educating*. Any work you submit to your supervisor, therefore, must represent your 'best effort' in terms of writing style. Sometimes, particularly for your thesis document, it may be necessary to use an editorial service.

PERSEVERANCE

Meeting the exacting standards of a doctoral degree will inevitably require repeated revisions and the revisiting of specific research issues, often many times. It is a process that can be frustrating and discouraging. At times you may be tempted, as Qiu Zhi sometimes was, to simply give it all up. When that happens, you must remember Qiu Zhi. Remember that he did not give up. Remind yourself too, as Qiu Zhi demonstrated, that you must persevere if you want to fulfil your dream.

CONCLUSION

Completing a thesis is never an easy task. It requires a step-by-step approach, focus, diligence, attention to detail and perseverance. Candidates should also remind themselves that *great vessels take longer to fill*. And that is why the degree carries such prestige and honour.

122

REFERENCES

Situ Yan (1986) *Best Chinese Idioms* I, trans. Zhao Shuhan and Tang Bowen, Hong Kong: Hai Feng.

Situ Yan (1988) *Best Chinese Idioms* II, trans. Tang Bowen, Hong Kong: Hai Feng.

Chapter 9

Fundamentals of a literature review

PETER STEANE

> You can never truly call yourself educated unless you study not only the best arguments of your own side, but the best arguments of your opponents.
>
> (J.S. Mill)

This chapter discusses the literature review, a critical part of the thesis. The literature review is also the foundation of the research project, on which the rationale for investigating the problem and for the chosen methodology is based. The chapter begins by discussing the role of the literature review within the thesis. Skills helpful in studying theory are provided. The metaphor of a tapestry is used as an illustration of the researcher's skill in weaving together ideas, argument and schools of thought in composing a literature review. Examples are offered from different disciplines to explain these skills, from the broadest view of a general theory, down to the more detailed analysis of an individual theory represented in a particular piece of writing. Finally, the literature review is discussed as an ongoing and evolving task that you must constantly revisit and update in the course of writing your thesis.

THE ROLE OF A LITERATURE REVIEW IN A THESIS

A thesis is a significant piece of work, and one of its most important parts is the review of the literature or theory pertinent to the research area. In the literature review you must do two things. First, you must demonstrate an understanding of both the previous research and general writings that are relevant to your research area. Second, you must demonstrate to the examiners your ability to critically integrate and evaluate this literature, rather than provide a simple summary of previous research. This second point is important, and can often be overlooked by research students. It is one thing to summarize your reading of different writers; it is quite another to be able to categorize studies by certain assumptions or approaches, identify their key contribution to a field, criticize others because of flawed methodologies and highlight gaps in the relevant research area. By the end of the literature review chapter, an examiner should be able to reasonably conclude that the researcher has competently evaluated all the theoretical positions relevant to the topic of the thesis.

The word 'thesis' is derived from the Greek *tithenai*, which generally means a position advanced for argument. This idea of a 'position' hints at all the component parts of a thesis: proposition, justification, evidence and findings. The proposition is the central research statement, question or hypothesis that you wish to defend or prove. There must be a justification about why this proposition is worthy of study. In the justification, you are expected to demonstrate how your research will contribute to knowledge, or to professional practice or to society, depending on the specific requirements of your thesis. Evidence is provided by the data or logic that support the proposition. This evidence can be derived from empirical research, from statistics or from the tracing of historical events. Whatever evidence you use, there should be some coherent logic to its presentation, rather than a simple listing of the summary points from previous research. The findings are the concluding points you make to support or refute a hypothesis, or to answer a research question.

These different parts form the basis of the classical thesis, consisting of five chapters:

- introduction
- literature review
- method and data collection
- analysis of data
- findings with contribution.

Not all theses follow this model, but almost every thesis will contain a chapter that analyses the literature and, on the basis of that analysis, proposes a model and/or research question. While all the parts of a thesis are important, it is this critical review of the theory, practice and previous research that builds the foundation for the research question, and for the thesis, regardless of its overall structure. All the parts of the thesis are strengthened by the comprehensiveness and rigour of your review of relevant theories. Understanding the literature sharpens the focus of your argument, and will help to clarify your proposition or research question. Reading previous studies helps to define the arena of your study, and can suggest the hypotheses that you need to test, methodologies appropriate for your study, and perhaps even a sample size. The literature review chapter in the thesis, then, justifies the proposed research by identifying trends or gaps in the literature, and, by a review of relevant studies, demonstrates that you understand the relevant literature and shows how your study will contribute to that body of knowledge.

CATEGORIES OF RESEARCH

There are a number of ways of classifying research. Understanding the different types of research is important in understanding and developing a critical review of the literature, as each type of research tends to generate particular types of analysis (e.g. exploratory or evaluative) or method (e.g. survey or case study). According to Hart (1998), research can be:

- *basic research*, contributing to theory by testing hypotheses;
- *applied research*, analysing theoretical insights and testing their application;
- *summative research*, assessing the generalizability of previous research;
- *formative evaluation*, assessing by case method;
- *action research*, joining with respondents in researching themselves;
- *ethno-methodology*, a close scrutiny of everyday causal practices;
- *exploratory*, to investigate a poorly understood area;
- *descriptive research*, to understand and describe social phenomena;
- *explanatory research*, to explain the causal connections between phenomena.

This list of types of research can be expanded to include the diverse forms that research can take, such as before-and-after studies, longitudinal and retrospective studies. In the literature review you need to identify the particular contribution of different studies as part of the overall evaluation of knowledge in the field. For example, you may find that no action research has been done in the area you wish to investigate, and so the field lacks the particular contribution of this type of research. Or you may be able to argue in your review that a combination of research approaches is worthy of investigation and may better explain some behaviour or phenomenon. Or again, that a longitudinal approach is needed to fill some gap left from previous empirical research.

STUDYING THE LITERATURE

Defining what constitutes the relevant 'literature' in any research field is always a difficult thing. If you reflect too long, you may never start writing. Once you have a general research question or problem, the best advice is to start by seeking out key articles, and by summarizing what you have read and the patterns and questions that emerge. This helps to formulate your ideas into a coherent structure, and is a foundation stone for the more developed writing you will submit to a supervisor for advice. These key articles will then suggest other relevant articles, which will suggest others, and so on.

This task of identifying the relevant literature can be likened to a journey of discovery, like tracking a river to its source. If you are exploring a river, there will be tributaries and creeks that invite exploration, but these are side trips and

diversions from the main task and from the general direction – some of them fruitful and some of them not. If you explore every small creek and stream that flows into a river, you will have a much greater understanding of the whole river, but you also run the risk of becoming so distracted by the small streams that you will never reach the source. So you need to decide what are the important branches of the river that need to be explored, and to decide what branches are less important and can be ignored. Similarly, as you progress in the task of the literature review, you are likely to become more and more focused and less inclined to be distracted by diversions. You will be able to recognize the signs of what promises to be a useful article, a help in understanding the theory and in building a better review. You will also become better at recognizing the articles that are likely to be less useful or even a waste of time, because they do not contribute new information.

RECOGNIZING KEY SOURCES

In order to make sure that your reading and your literature review cover all the relevant literature, you need to have a system to seek out and identify key sources. Some methods of doing this include:

- In focusing your field of inquiry, base your reading around a specific research question. The research question may change or develop as you read more, but the more specific your research question, the more specific you can be in your reading.
- Think about both the history and context of study in this area. This will help define *what* the field and focus of your research will be.
- Your university library is likely to give you on-line access to many excellent databases providing abstracts and/or full-text versions of peer-reviewed journal articles, and these should be your prime source of references for a thesis. So you should identify the key databases in your area, enter specific search terms and look for relevant peer-reviewed articles. While you might include references to practitioner or unrefereed material to show trends in practice, there is a lot of junk in the cyberspace of knowledge, and your literature review should primarily reflect peer-reviewed sources.
- While electronic databases are invaluable for research students, if there are key journals in your area that aren't available in abstract or full-text form from an electronic database, you will need to ensure that you have searched for and obtained relevant articles from these journals.
- Don't overlook encyclopaedias, compendiums, general books and textbooks, in order to get a general appreciation of the writing in the field.

127

- Talk to both practitioners and academics about your interest. This can help to clarify the research topic as well as provide referrals to good references.
- Try to identify the names of scholars or theories that are referred to by multiple sources. These are likely to be the key theorists and clusters of theoretical knowledge in the field.
- Ask yourself what studies emerge as seminal, and what are the methodological assumptions underpinning such studies that you may need to include in your research.
- Consider the benefit of differentiating between practitioner and scholarly or peer-reviewed writing. It may vary across disciplines, but usually there will be some value in demonstrating your familiarity with both peer-reviewed scholarly writing (which receives prominence in an academic thesis) as well as with the debates among professionals or themes evident in non-reviewed writing in practitioner journals.
- Always remember that others have gone before you. Almost all journal articles will include a brief literature review that can provide small-scale models that you can build on. These articles can also suggest potentially important references that you may have overlooked.

In some science-based theses, particularly in medicine, documenting the procedure that you used to search for relevant areas is a critical part of demonstrating that you have included all relevant sources. This is known as a 'systematic review' where the researcher documents the databases searched, and search terms used, to ensure and demonstrate that all relevant sources have been evaluated. (For an in-depth discussion of the systematic review process see Mulrow and Cook, 1998.) While this procedure is less common in non-scientific theses, the systematic review process is likely to become more common in other research areas, so it is a good idea to document the procedure that you use for identifying relevant sources for your literature review.

FROM SUMMARY TO SYNTHESIS

Supervisors have many good tips for research students in starting the literature review. Common among this advice is the exhortation to start reading and start writing. The reason for this is that momentum appears to be a key factor in the successful completion of a thesis. However, there are two phases of writing when developing the literature review. Phase one is the writing that summarizes and clarifies your ideas. Each time you read an article, it's usually a good idea to write some sort of summary, even a very brief one. Otherwise you will rapidly forget what you have read, and the time spent reading will be wasted. Phase two writing starts only when you have a sufficient overview of the theory, and is the basis of the literature review that you will submit for comment to your supervisor. It's

important not to confuse the two stages; students who start writing the literature review before they have a sufficient overview often lack a broad understanding of the field. Their literature review can then become a sequence of summaries of different articles, rather than an integrated synthesis of the areas that are relevant to their particular thesis.

Studying the literature starts with analysing and summarizing lots of individual pieces of work (journal articles, chapters, books), and after you have done a lot of these, you can start to recognize overlaps, and then finally start to integrate your reading and reflection. One helpful concept is Rudestam and Newton's (1992) idea of a *short*, *medium* and *long* shot evaluation of literature. The short-shot evaluation is a critical analysis of one article or chapter or book. It involves you recording or assessing an article according to certain categories. After recording the author, title and journal details, you could evaluative the article as follows:

- *What is the central thesis (argument) of the article?* In this question you are trying to determine clearly what the problem is, and whether it has been clearly defined.
- *What is the theoretical framework?* In this question you are attempting to see linkages between variables; whether they are explicit and reasonable, and whether the problem or hypothesis is stated in a way that is really testable.
- *What is the research design?* This question helps to focus you on the appropriateness of the methodology in the article, as well as provide insight into issues of validity and reliability.
- *What are the findings?* Decide whether the findings are within the scope of the aim and related to the central thesis.
- *How proficient is the analysis?* In this question you are attempting to assess the appropriateness and adequacy of the analytical section or discussion, given the data and research question.
- *How does it contribute to the body of knowledge?* This question invites some assessment of the implications of the study to the field of knowledge.

You may wish to modify this sequence to suit your own particular study style. For example, some students record this analysis using bibliographic software such as Endnote. However you adapt and record it, a major benefit from the analysis is to ensure you apply some critical rigour to your reading and some order to your note taking. You may not make a detailed analysis of every article you read, but it's important to make a basic summary, so you remember what you have written.

The medium-shot analysis involves recognizing the overlap between studies. When you start to make comparisons or links between authors and studies, you are moving from the short-shot approach into medium-shot analysis. This is

important because it assists in building proficiency in explaining patterns and gaps in your field of study.

The long-shot analysis is an overview of studies in a field. It is the conceptual ability to stand back and recognize that some writers take one line of argument while others take another line of argument, or to identify that one school of thought is divergent from other schools. The long-shot analysis is closest to a true *review* of the literature as a body of knowledge. It is a more expansive overview, and can only be achieved after the heavy work load of having to read hundreds of articles and book chapters and record many short-shot reviews. It is at the level of the long shot that you are in a credible position in the eyes of an examiner to truly weigh up the contribution of particular ideas or positions or approaches in the field of knowledge you are going to research.

The strategies listed above will help you to recognize the authoritative sources and patterns in the literature that build the credibility of your review in the eyes of a supervisor or examiner. As you collect and read more articles, you should be making at least brief summaries for yourself of each article, so you gradually develop your understanding of the literature. However, while your search for relevant sources and literature should be very broad, don't make the mistake of thinking that everything you read will, or should, go into the literature review. The literature review should include *relevant* literature, not *all* literature. If lots of work has been done before, you will also need to decide what is *most* relevant, because there will be too much relevant literature to include all of it. While it is important that your literature review is comprehensive, examiners are likely to become irritated by a long literature review that includes discussion of articles or issues that aren't clearly relevant to the research topic. This is why the distinction between phase one (summary) and phase two (integration) writing is so important. Your phase one summaries will help you to structure the literature review, and to decide what to include and what to leave out. So once you believe that you have identified the relevant literature, and made brief summaries, you are ready to start phase two writing – structuring and writing your literature review.

STRUCTURING THE LITERATURE REVIEW

Once you have developed a sufficient overview of the literature, you are in a position to begin to structure your literature review chapter. Most literature reviews will start by a justification of why the research area is an important one, and this section will require its own referencing, usually from influential sources, to justify that the area is worth researching. Or you may start by presenting a problem, and by showing how the research will help to address the problem.

Once you have justified the research area, your literature review needs to present the relevant background literature, not as a sequence of summaries but

as an integrated overview of previous work. You need to decide how you will draw together the threads of previous literature to present a structured, consistent summary of what is relevant to your own research.

One possible metaphor for this process of drawing together, or synthesizing, the literature is that of a tapestry. Just as a tapestry can show a picture from a particular long-range perspective, a closer scrutiny reveals knots, threads and colours not apparent from a long-distance perspective. So it is with reviewing literature. Close analysis of one or many studies or authors is one thing. However, a critical overview should provide more than just a series of authors on a topic, but should instead illustrate a pattern in the range of schools-of-thinking and theoretical debates between scholars. It may reveal culturally or gender-biased studies and conclusions, which you can use to illustrate divergence and disagreement as well as convergence and agreement.

Your review should not only suggest you know *what* has been written, but also *why* the author(s) wrote it, *when* it was researched, and *how* such studies were undertaken. To return to the image of a tapestry, you should weave together and integrate the threads or arguments that are contained in previous writings on the topic. While one scholar presents a thesis or argument, another may offer a different view, an anti-thesis. Perhaps there are different scholars you could categorize into one theoretical point of view distinct from another theoretical view. Figure 9.1 illustrates how a well developed literature review can be a dialectical process, where contesting theories are compared and contrasted, examined for strengths and limitations, and finally integrated to come to a conclusion or synthesis of different theories. This is the key to an effective literature review: the author identifies key studies, compares and contrasts them, and ultimately comes to an opinion as to what theories are supported, or what theories are worth further investigation, and so justifies the planned research.

A good example of this dialectical process is the debate among anthropology scholars concerning the origin of man. One group of scientists hold to a thesis called the 'multi-regional hypothesis', that *Homo erectus*, the ancestor of modern man, originated in Africa about 1.5 million to 2 million years ago and migrated to Asia and Europe, then gradually evolved into *Homo sapiens*, modern man, wherever these migrations took them. Another group of researchers argue an antithesis that could be referred to as the 'out of Africa hypothesis', that *Homo erectus* originated in Africa about 1.5 million to 2 million years ago, and from there evolved into *Homo sapiens* as Africans, and then migrated to Asia and Europe about 200,000 years ago, replacing more archaic humans in the process. There is research supporting both views. Some scholars take one or the other view, and some take a more compromise view, which could be described as a synthesis between the two theories. In this case, a synthesis is similar to a compromise, which may not always be possible. It depends on the field of your research and the maturity of theory in the discipline. Your literature review should not only summarize one

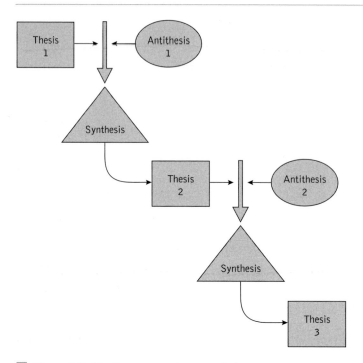

Figure 9.1 *The literature review as a dialectic process*

thesis or another, but should show a body of knowledge as an ongoing dialectic, perhaps with different assumptions, contexts and methods. This is sometimes referred to as 'mapping the literature', and usually there are multiple maps, or multiple ways of summarizing the literature. As a consequence, it is important to focus your overview around your particular question or problem. If this is not done, you could find yourself drowning in a quagmire of theories and superficial evaluations. You hope to be able first to demonstrate your familiarity with the debates and, second, to show the context of your study in what has already been researched and written before you.

An additional way of categorizing theories and synthesizing the literature in the debate may be to differentiate between literature which is research-based and that which is practitioner-oriented. A good example is the literature in the field of electronic commerce, popularly referred to as e-commerce. Technology is changing so rapidly that the often long delay in getting a refereed journal article published means that the content of the article may be out of date before publication. So many cutting-edge contributions to e-commerce appear in refereed conference proceedings and in practitioner literature. While the scholarly journals are important to cite in the literature review, a comprehensive review will illustrate the complexity and diversity of the field by demonstrating the patterns of how theory is evolving.

SYNTHESIZING THE LITERATURE

Early drafts of literature reviews nearly always reveal a common failing, a tendency to simply summarize what you have read. A string of key quotes is not a review – it is just a series of quotes. Similarly, a string of small summaries such as 'Smith says . . .' and 'Brown argues . . .' is not a literature review – it merely demonstrates summary skills. Quotes are often useful, but they are not sufficient. Similarly, knowing what one theorist says is essential, but it is not sufficient. A literature review should build upon these quotes and reveal themes and schools of thought that are either convergent or divergent.

Consider an example of a literature review on strategic management:

The positioning approach to strategy has provided the dominant framework for strategy from the 1950s, with contributions made by Andrews (1987), Ansoff (1987) and Learned *et al.* (1965). Although the basic framework for this positioning approach appears to have been formulated in the early 1950s, it has been elaborated on and developed by a number of writers. Arguably, amongst these the most important contributor has been Porter (1980, 1985, 1987, 1993), with his development of the concept of the five forces model used for industry analysis, the value chain as an instrument for assessing internal organizational strengths and weaknesses, and the generic strategies as a tool to assist in strategy evaluation. Theorists such as Ansoff (1968), Porter (1980) and Selznick (1957) have discussed the importance of internal analysis and developed the *competence grid* and the *value chain* as aids to this analysis. But the major focus has tended to be on the external environment, with the common assumption underlying the approach that the environment largely determines the organization's freedom to manoeuvre. Therefore the structure of the environment is seen to be of overwhelming importance, and a strategy for delivering competitive advantage will be one that positions the organization within that environment. The problem for the strategist then becomes one of finding a position that is defensible against the threats from existing and potential competitors and also from the bargaining power of suppliers and buyers . . .

The first thing to note is that key scholars are referenced and woven into this analysis of the theory and development of the positioning school of strategy. The writer is demonstrating familiarity with the theory. The second point to note is that the quality of analysis is far removed from simply summarizing what one or another scholar has said. Instead, convergence, divergence and assumptions are discussed, and the implications for those who practise strategy in the field are drawn out. The example illustrates how a dialectical approach to theory (which includes debates) is developed in a literature review, rather than a series of summaries.

Schemas and figures are excellent ways to reinforce what you are trying to demonstrate in your evaluation of the literature. These can include the inclusion of a model that a particular theorist uses in your short-shot analysis, but can also include broader conceptual frameworks that visually link what you have explained in text. Figure 9.2, from Petty and Guthrie (2000), illustrates the various concepts associated with intellectual capital, assuming that the central concerns of intellectual capital are strategic or measurement issues. This view of intellectual capital as an important strategic resource is more of a long shot, assisted through different means such as knowledge development or leverage (medium-shot), with each being linked with more specific (short-shot) studies.

ORGANIZING AND WRITING THE LITERATURE REVIEW

While developing the literature review, it is important to keep good bibliographic notes and to be organized in filing. First, this means ensuring that you have full bibliographic details when you first download or copy journal articles. Second, it means filing articles where you can find them again. You are likely to use your sources more than once – first, as you seek to clarify and focus your research, and later, when some of these sources assume greater significance once the research topic has been refined and you return and re-read them. There is no ideal method of filing articles. Some researchers file articles alphabetically, some by subject area, some by the order that the article was obtained. The important thing is that you develop a system where you can retrieve any sources when you need them.

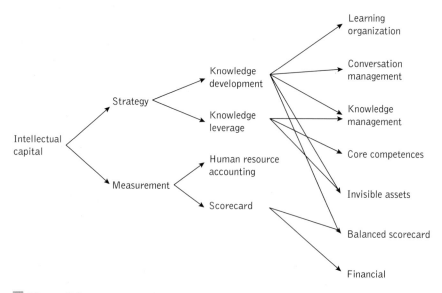

Figure 9.2 Dimensions of intellectual capital

Some research students ask the question 'When do I know I have read enough?' This is a legitimate question and it is worth a couple of comments by way of advice. When references continue to reveal divergent views and new information continues to emerge, it can indicate that you need to continue reading. Alternatively, if you have read large amounts, and still continue to find new information, it may suggest that your topic is not sufficiently focused. Topics that are too general can generate multiple interconnections and theories, rather than building towards some coherent understanding. You can gauge that you have read enough when there are diminishing returns from reading. This means that if nothing really new is emerging from what you read, then you have probably identified the bulk of the relevant literature.

Approaching your field of inquiry with criticism and rigour is important, but is a skill that is easier for some people, and for some cultures, than for others. Some cultures are less familiar, or less comfortable, with the critical genre typically seen in Western universities. For example, some Asian cultures and research students from those cultures may take a more deferential and respectful approach to an author (particularly if they possess the title of 'Professor'). This can present the challenge of a mind-shift for Asian research students studying in the Western tradition of rigorous and critical evaluation. This does not mean Asian scholars or students are not rigorous or critical in their evaluation. But cultures are different, and criticism is expressed differently in different cultures. In contrast, some Western students, more experienced in criticism, sometimes approach the literature review as if it were an exercise in identifying the faults in every study. This can result in the student being seen as arrogant and unrealistic. The challenge of studying and undertaking research in a culture different from your own is discussed in Chapter 2. However, a critical approach to the literature means that postgraduate students must develop the attitude of a dispassionate investigator in their evaluation of the knowledge in the field. One needs to be prepared to identify weaknesses in the literature. But as with all things, there are times to bring some balance into your investigation. One does not have to be critical *all* the time.

In striking a balance between criticism and deference, there are prudent and judicious ways to use the English language to both recognize the contribution of a scholar but also to critique the assumptions or methodologies of such a contribution, and hence invite reservations about the perfection of the piece of writing. For example, the following text is adapted from a journal paper published by the author about the current debate over, and criticism of, a leadership instrument (the MLQ5X) used in a research project.

One of the healthy signs of research is that debate appears in the disciplinary literature. Scholars in leadership have devoted attention to the benefits and concerns of the MLQ5X (Bass and Avolio 1993; Carless 1998; den Hartog,

Muijen and Koopman 1997; Tracey and Hinkin 1998). Critics suggest the proposed dimensionality of the MLQ is not sustained, that is, problems reside in the area of internal validity. . . . Such debate suggests that concerns, and consequent problems in valid measures, can arise from the description of trans-formational attributes in managerial language. As Tracey and Hinkin's (1998) study indicates, Bass and Avolio's construct possesses predictive validity, even though concerns about dimensionality remain. However, Avolio (1998: 63) argues for maintaining a broad range of leadership styles in research studies in order to capture subtle behavior in organizations, and that more samples, particularly of a cross-cultural nature, would help build robustness. This study contributes to this ongoing debate . . .

This example reinforces how important it is to recognize any criticism of a theoretical framework or instrument you might wish to use, and illustrates how the views of such scholars can be included. It is not wise to ignore views contrary to those of your argument, nor to arbitrarily dismiss them. Your task is to try and present a balanced view of the theoretical discussion in your field of know-ledge or practice, using judicious and prudent language.

The careful use of language and the importance of continually re-editing is covered in greater detail in Chapter 12, 'Writing the thesis'. Perhaps even more than any other section of the thesis, writing the literature review is an iterative process rather than a linear process. This means it evolves and changes, and is rarely completed without numerous drafts, corrections and editions. Most of the time you will take the initiative in editing for improvement. But sometimes it may be forced upon you, for example when the research findings are surprising or unexpected, and compel you to undertake a substantive restructure of the liter-ature review.

CONCLUSION

In summary, the literature review is a crucial part of the thesis, demonstrating that you have mastered a relevant area of knowledge, and as a result possess a critically informed mind, and have identified a gap in theory or practice worthy of study, and can justifiably proceed to question, hypothesize and investigate. Developing an understanding of the literature in the research field, and demon-strating that understanding in the literature review, will always take substantial amounts of time. However, the time will be rewarded, because this understanding of the literature is the foundation of the research question, the analysis, and the discussion of the results of the thesis.

REFERENCES

Hart, C. (1998) *Doing a Literature Review*, London: Sage.

Mulrow, C. and Cook, D. (1998) *Systematic Reviews: Synthesis of Best Evidence for Health Care Decisions*, Philadelphia: American College of Physicians.

Petty, R. and Guthrie, J. (2000) 'Intellectual capital literature review: measurement, reporting and management', *Journal of Intellectual Capital*, 1 (2): 155–76.

Rudestam, K.E. and Newton, R.R. (1992) *Surviving your Dissertation*, Newbury Park CA: Sage.

Chapter 10

Quantitative research and analysis

SUZAN BURTON

Errors using inadequate data are much less than those using no data at all.
(Charles Babbage)

The component of a research thesis that scares students most is nearly always the statistical analysis. This fear is not completely unfounded, because statistical analysis is a complex area where you can be, in the opinion of experts (including your examiners), completely and utterly wrong. It is also an area where your supervisor/s, with the best will in the world, sometimes can't give you much help, because they may lack confidence in statistical analysis. If you make mistakes in your data collection and analysis, they can be difficult or impossible to correct at a later stage, which can result in serious problems if those mistakes are detected by examiners, rather than by you. This chapter aims to demystify the quantitative research process and give you some guidelines for performing quality quantitative analysis. It can't make you an expert in statistics, or guarantee that the quantitative component of your thesis is well done, but following the recommended steps can decrease the likelihood that you will make disastrous mistakes.

So you think you'll get someone else to do your analysis? Many students think that they can avoid much of the pain of quantitative analysis by getting someone to do their analysis for them. This is a dangerous strategy. While it can be quite acceptable (and, as this chapter will discuss, desirable) to seek expert help in areas of your thesis where you lack expertise, expecting that someone else can perform your analysis for you is almost always a bad idea. For a start, it is usually expensive, because it's never easy to do analysis for someone else's research questions. Whoever you get to help you will almost never understand your research questions and your objectives as well as you. Without taking a lot of time, they won't understand your data collection methods, your measures and/or your coding. As a result, in order for them to perform an adequate analysis, they will need to spend substantial time and effort, which usually translates into high costs for you. Most important, because they don't usually understand the objectives, the background or relevant previous research, it will be difficult for them to provide a thorough analysis that is interpretable in terms of previous research.

The unfortunate reality for almost all students ('unfortunate' if you are nervous of statistics, but the problem is so common we will take some nervousness for granted) is that you will need to do most of the statistical analysis and interpretation yourself. If this sounds depressing, there is also good news: by asking the right questions at the right time, and by thorough planning and preparation at each stage of your data collection, you are likely to end up with a better analysis and a better (which equals more interpretable) set of results.

PLANNING YOUR ANALYSIS

The basis of effective quantitative analysis is good planning, starting before you even collect any data. Your data collection is the one step of your thesis that you have to get right the first time. You can redo every other section of your thesis, but if you don't get your data collection right, it's time-consuming and usually expensive to redo it, and will almost certainly lead to substantial delay in the completion of your thesis.

Planning your data collection effectively means starting with a good grasp of the relevant literature, so you can identify:

- the gaps in the literature
- variables of interest
- appropriate measures
- the hypotheses of interest
- data collection techniques
- the likely methodology to analyse the data.

Once you have identified these six areas, you should sit down with your supervisor, or with someone who has quantitative skills in the appropriate area, and discuss whether your proposed measures and data collection strategies are appropriate. Each step is critical, however, in performing a good analysis, so let's go through each one in turn.

Gaps in the literature

Your literature review chapter should have identified gaps in the literature, and demonstrated (1) that your topic is worth researching and (2) how your thesis will extend previous work. The best way to justify a gap in the literature that is worth researching is to quote an important author in the field.

For example, Weiner (2000) has identified the relative absence of attribution theory in consumer psychology research, and argued that this is an important

139

avenue for understanding consumers' reactions to product or service failure. (Attribution theory is broadly concerned with a person's explanation for the cause of a particular event.) Weiner is an authoritative figure in the field of attribution research, so his call for further research is a very good starting point for a justification of research into consumer attributions for problems with a product they have purchased.

Variables of interest

Your literature review should identify what measures have been identified as important by previous authors. For example, Weiner (2000) discussed the importance of understanding the stability of attributions (i.e. whether someone thinks that a problem was a one-off or is likely to continue). A person's judgement is also likely to be influenced by whether they have experienced the product before, so you would probably want to obtain a measure of the person's previous experience with the product.

So there are at least two variables that you need to investigate: stability of attributions and experience with the product. A review of other research on attributions will identify other relevant variables. For example, it would make sense to also collect measures of consumer responses such as customer satisfaction and/or intention to repurchase the product.

Appropriate measures

Once you have identified the variables that you are interested in researching, you need to decide on the best way to measure them. Large amounts have been written on the need to justify the reliability and validity of measures, but the major issue can be broadly summarized as the need to justify that your measures are an appropriate way to measure whatever it is you are interested in. If possible, the best way to justify the use of a scale is to use one that has been used in a high-quality publication. For example, Oliver (1997: 284–5), another authoritative author, recommends the use of a particular scale to measure stability of attributions (Box 10.1).

The advantage of using a scale developed and recommended by an authority in the field, such as Oliver, or used in a prestigious publication, is that your supervisor/s and examiners are unlikely to criticize your use of the scale (as long as you have used the scale appropriately). Sometimes, however, there may be fundamental issues involved in deciding how you measure a variable. For example, will you measure experience with the product as a categorical measure, or on an ordinal or linear scale (Box 10.2)? Each of these scales will give you a measure of a subject's experience with the product, and will allow (and possibly exclude) different methods of analysis. If you choose the categorical scale, you won't be

Box 10.1
SCALE TO MEASURE STABILITY OF ATTRIBUTION

The following items reflect feelings you might have about *why* the purchase outcome turned out as it did. Circle the number that best reflects *your* feelings about this.

Outcome will always happen this way	1	2	3	4	5	Not sure that the outcome will happen this way again
Expect the outcome to be the same over time	1	2	3	4	5	Expect the outcome to vary over time
Reason for the outcome will never change	1	2	3	4	5	Reason for the outcome will always be different

able to make any assumptions about whether a person's attributions or other responses become more fixed as the person becomes more experienced, beyond their first experience of the product. If you use the ordinal scale, you won't easily be able to analyse your data with regression techniques, but you will if you use the interval scale. To decide which scale is most appropriate you need to think about what information it gives you, and what analysis techniques it is consistent with. Again, looking at the measures that have been used in previous research in your field can help you to develop and justify your measures.

Scale discriminant validity

The decision described above is really a matter of establishing whether a scale has sufficient 'discriminant validity', or in other words whether it will be able to detect small changes in a response (for example, changes in experience). If your scale is very restricted (like the categorical scale for experience) you won't be able to investigate differences between individuals who have lots of experience and others who have very little experience. A scale like this with too little discrimination can make people look similar when they aren't. For example, if you are investigating customer satisfaction, you will usually find that most customers of most businesses are satisfied (because otherwise they would stop being customers). The five-point dissatisfaction/satisfaction scale in Box 10.3 won't separate these customers very well, because you will find that almost

Box 10.2
DIFFERENT SCALES TO MEASURE EXPERIENCE WITH THE PRODUCT

Categorical scale

Have you ever used this product? (*Tick one*) ☐ Yes ☐ No

Ordinal scale

How many times have you used this product? (*Tick one*)

☐ Never ☐ 1–5 times ☐ 6 or more times

Interval scale

Approximately how many times have you used this product?

Approximately _____ times

Box 10.3
DIFFERENT SCALES TO MEASURE CUSTOMER SATISFACTION

How satisfied are you with your experience with _____ ?

Five-point scale

1	2	3	4	5
Extremely dissatisfied		Neither satisfied nor dissatisfied		Extremely satisfied

Seven-point scale

1	2	3	4	5	6	7
Extremely dissatisfied			Neither satisfied nor dissatisfied			Extremely satisfied

everyone will mark themselves 4 or 5. In contrast, the seven-point scale will allow you to discriminate between the *very* satisfied customers who rate themselves 7 out of 7, and those who may be just a *bit* satisfied, who might rate themselves 5 out of 7.

In summary, you should choose a scale which (1) can be justified and (2) differentiates sufficiently between groups of customers. Sometimes you won't know whether your scale will differentiate sufficiently without pilot testing, but in general a scale with more categories will discriminate better than one with fewer categories. It's usually better to err on the side of putting in more categories than fewer, because if a scale is too broad you can usually combine categories later. However, if the scale has too few categories, you won't be able to do anything to fix it after you have collected the data.

Hypotheses of interest

Quantitative research will usually be framed in terms of specific testable hypotheses. Specifying these hypotheses before you collect your data helps to ensure that you have a measure for each of your variables, and provides a check that your hypotheses can be tested with your anticipated analysis technique. For example:

Hypothesis 1. Consumers' attributions of the cause of problems with a product will be more stable for those who are more experienced with the product.

The stated hypothesis requires that you have measures of (1) the stability of the attribution and (2) the experience of the customer. If you have a categorical measure of experience you will be restricted to a comparison of the mean or median stability of attributions between experienced and inexperienced individuals (for example, a *t* test to compare the means of the two groups, or a non-parametric test to compare the medians). If you have an interval measure of experience, you will be able to investigate whether stability of attributions changes in a linear or non-linear fashion. Which of these methods is more important to test depends on your theoretical argument, developed from previous research and argued in your literature review.

If this discussion doesn't mean a lot to you, don't panic. You should take away three key messages: first that you can't choose the right scale without some understanding of the statistical methods that you will use and, second, that a statistician alone can't tell you which is the right scale unless you can explain the main issues in the literature very clearly. However, even if your knowledge of statistics is poor, working with an expert can help you to choose the right scale. Finally, and in summary, don't rush in to choose a scale without thinking carefully about both the literature *and* the statistical issues, because otherwise you are likely to choose the wrong scale, which can seriously limit your analysis and interpretation.

143

Data collection techniques

Data can be collected using a variety of methods, such as surveys (e.g. satisfaction scores), direct measurement (e.g. score on a test) and historical records (e.g. share prices over time). The most appropriate method will depend on your research area, but your data collection technique will raise critical questions. For example, if you are doing a postal or e-mail survey, you need to think about:

- *How many surveys should be sent out?* The more complex the planned analysis, the more responses you will need.
- *What is the likely response rate?* An anticipated lower response rate means that you need to send out more surveys.
- *Is there some incentive for people to respond?* If there is no incentive for people to respond to your survey, your response rate will almost certainly be much lower, so you will need to send out more surveys.
- *What is the variability in the population?* If there is limited variability in the population in your variables of interest, you will need to send out more surveys to ensure you capture some variability in your sample.
- *What is the estimated effect size?* If you are estimating the effect of a variable that has limited impact, you will need to collect more data to be able to detect any effect.
- *What is the power of my measurement instrument?* If your measurement instrument isn't sensitive to small changes in your variable of interest (for example, if you use a five-point scale rather than a seven-point scale), you will need more responses to detect any differences between groups of subjects.

Likely methodology to analyse the data

Certain research questions will typically be tested using particular methodologies. For example, the relationship between customer satisfaction, perceived performance and intended behaviour will often be investigated using structural equation modelling. Customers' probability of choosing one product over another might be tested using some form of choice modelling technique. It's beyond the scope of this chapter to go into detail about when each methodology might be appropriate. However, every technique will have particular requirements about the number of responses required, the measurements, format of the data, and so on. You should check with an expert, or if you are confident in your own statistical ability, do extensive research yourself, to ensure that your data will be suitable for your proposed analysis technique, *before* you collect the data. By doing this checking before you commit to a particular form of data collection you are likely to minimize your risk of severe problems later.

Unless you are very confident in quantitative analysis, when you have decided on your measures, your hypotheses and your data collection technique, it's a good idea to make a written summary and discuss it with your supervisor, and/or with someone who has particular expertise in your analysis technique. For example, Box 10.4 shows an example of an analysis summary. With a summary like Box 10.4 you can go to your supervisor and check whether they are happy with your theoretical contribution, and then to a statistics expert, to check whether your proposed measures and analysis are suitable to test your hypotheses. Your supervisor may suggest that you need to investigate the effect of other variables, and your statistics expert may argue that you should use a different measure or methodology. Having this discussion *before* you collect your data is likely to ensure that your analysis is easier to complete, and more rigorous.

We can't stress too strongly that time spent planning like this before you collect your data is time well spent. Lack of planning can mean that you collect your data, and then realize that you have neglected to measure a key variable. Or you may collect data, and then discover that you need a more sensitive scale (for example, a seven-point rather than a five-point scale) to increase the discrimination of the scale, and/or to compare your results with other researchers.

SURVEY DESIGN

One of the most common methods of data collection in the social sciences is a survey, so survey design is a critical issue for many students. There are many good books covering survey design, and if you intend to collect data by a survey, you should consult one of these books, some of which are listed at the end of this chapter. Unfortunately, perhaps because we all see many surveys, some students think they can develop a survey without any experience and without a lot of effort. This will usually result in a poorly planned and executed survey, with the result that many of your target respondents won't bother to fill it in, and you won't collect enough data to analyse. The most critical factor in assuring a good response rate to a survey is whether it is easy to fill in, and succeeds in inducing respondents to complete and return it. A well designed survey can achieve a response rate over 50 per cent, while a poorly designed survey can result in a response rate as low as 5 per cent. A response rate as low as 20 per cent or less means that the people who answered the survey are very different from the majority of the population, and research based on such a small sample (even if you have a large number of responses) is likely to be considered unacceptable by any examiner or journal reviewer. This means that if your response rate is very low, you may need to start again, which is expensive and time-consuming. However, good planning can avoid this sort of disaster.

Survey design is a specialized area, and it is beyond the scope of this chapter to fully cover how to construct a survey. However, there are some key principles which are worth summarizing. In developing your survey, you are trying to achieve two things: first, to ensure you have suitable measures for all your variables. Making a summary like Box 10.4 should help you to do this. Second, you are trying to ensure that a large number of your target subjects will take the time to complete the survey and return it. But most people have many demands on their time, and completing a survey, especially if it is from a total stranger, is often low on people's priority list. So how can you design a survey that people are prepared to fill in?

Most people will decide whether they complete a survey based loosely on the effort involved (how much time it is likely to take, and how difficult it is) and by the value to them, or to others, of filling it in. So if you can decrease the perceived effort involved, or increase the perceived value of completion, you are likely to increase your response rate. Some ways to achieve this include:

Decreasing the effort

- Other things being equal, longer surveys will get a lower response rate. This doesn't mean that you can't achieve a high response rate with a long survey, but it is more difficult. Keep the survey as short as possible. Don't add in questions that you are unlikely to analyse, because they make the survey longer and add little or no value. Whether you add an extra question also depends on the overall length of the survey. If you add one extra question, and the survey goes from four to five pages, the extra question will make the survey appear much longer. If one extra question can be contained within the four pages, the question is unlikely to add significantly to the actual or perceived length.
- Make it easy to fill in. A long survey can still achieve a very good response rate if it is easy to fill in. A short survey which asks difficult questions, or which appears to be difficult, by asking hard questions at the beginning, is likely to receive a low response rate.
- Use tick boxes (which are fast and easy to fill in) as much as possible. Avoid open-ended questions. If you must have open-ended questions, put them at the end of the questionnaire. Reconsider any question which will take more than a few seconds to read and complete.
- Review the instructions for every question carefully to make sure they are clear and easy to read.
- Check the formatting of the survey carefully to ensure that it is easy to read and looks professional. If you don't appear to have put effort into your survey, people are less likely to put effort into filling it in.
- If you are using a postal survey, always provide a reply-paid or stamped envelope (of course!).

Box 10.4
SAMPLE SUMMARY OF QUANTITATIVE ANALYSIS

Research question

Is satisfaction related to customer expectations and experience in a linear or non-linear function?

Hypotheses

1 Satisfaction will be positively associated with pre-experience expectations.
2 Satisfaction will be positively associated in a non-linear fashion with pre-experience expectations.
3 Satisfaction will vary as a function of experience and expectations.

Measures

● Satisfaction, measured on a seven-point scale, from Smith *et al.* (1999).
● Expectations, measured on a seven-point scale, from Oliver and Burke (1999).
● Experience, measured as length of time used, based on Burton *et al.* (2003).

Data collection

Survey data from random sample of 400 customers. Estimated response rate 25 per cent, leading to a projected sample size of 100 subjects.

Planned statistical tests

– Linear regression to test the association between satisfaction and expectations.
– Regression, including polynomial forms, to test for non-linear associations between satisfaction and expectations.
– Multiple regression, including polynomial forms, to test for different functional associations between experience, expectations and satisfaction.

- Most important, you should trial your survey very carefully to ensure everything makes sense, and it is easy to complete. Fill it in yourself, pretending to be a typical subject. Ask your friends and family to fill it in, and see if they have problems with any of the instructions or questions. If they do, revise the section to make it easier to complete. Finally, watch typical subjects filling it in. If they have problems with any of the questions, it is likely that other subjects won't bother to finish the survey. At each stage of trialling you should be constantly revising the survey, making it clearer and easier to complete, till you get to the stage where trialling with potential subjects no longer identifies problems. It is this final and critical stage of trialling that will ensure that you have an easy-to-complete survey, which people are more likely to fill in and return.

Increasing the value

Your covering letter should give people a good reason to fill in the survey. This may be some sort of reward, but doesn't have to be. You might offer to send subjects a copy of the results, or you might be able to justify that your research is useful for society. If you make it clear that you are a student, and the survey is part of university research, more people are likely to complete it than if they get the idea that it is commercial research. If the cover letter appears on university letterhead, and/or if it is signed by an academic who sounds important, (a professor or a doctor), people are more likely to fill it in.

Address subjects' concerns

You should think carefully about possible reasons why people might not return a survey, such as concerns about privacy, or about what will be done with the information. You can then address these concerns in the covering letter, for example by assuring them that information about them won't be made available to other people or to commercial organizations. If you provide a contact phone number where people can call you, and/or your supervisor, if they have concerns, people are more likely to regard the research as coming from an individual, who they might want to help, rather than from an anonymous institution, who they are less interested in. (It is the author's experience that only a very small number of people will bother to phone you, but the presence of a phone number on the covering letter is probably useful in addressing concerns.)

ENTERING YOUR DATA

When you have collected your data, the next step is entering them into some type of spreadsheet or analysis package. Even if you intend to use a statistics package such as SPSS or Minitab, it is usually a good idea to first enter the data into a common spreadsheet like Excel. If you have the luxury of getting someone else to enter the data, they are likely to be more familiar with Excel, and the package offers some additional features such as searching, formatting and (unless you are an expert with statistical packages) easier manipulation of data. Excel also allows you to format columns in advance, so only appropriate responses can be added. This can minimize data entry errors.[1]

Even if someone is entering the data for you, you will still need to design a coding sheet (the spreadsheet design for entering the data). Good guidelines for design of the coding sheet are suggested in Box 10.5.

CLEANING YOUR DATA

Once your data have been entered, you need to check them for errors, or 'clean' the data. There are different ways of cleaning data. Sometimes the data are entered twice, by two people, and differences are checked. This is a very rigorous test, but expensive and time-consuming, so it is rarely used. A simpler, more common procedure for cleaning data is to do a series of checks to ensure that all data are within the appropriate range and that there are no other obvious signs of errors.

- Go to the last column of data in your spreadsheet. Move one column to the right, to what should be an empty column. Page down to the last row, checking that the column is empty for all rows. (Entries in this column probably mean the data entry person has missed a column and entered data for a subject one column to the right.) If there are any entries in this column, recheck all data for that subject to find and correct the mistake.
- Check that all data are within appropriate limits (for example, that all values in a seven-point scale are between 1 and 7). Other entries probably mean the data entry person has forgotten to change columns, and all subsequent columns for that subject are likely to be wrong. In a statistics package, this can be done by a 'frequency' or 'tally' command. In Excel you can check values in a column using the 'Filter' function.[2]
- Once you have cleaned your data, lock the file so no one can overwrite it by mistake.[3] Make a second copy of the file, and store it in a safe place. When you are ready to work on the file, you can save it under a different file name, and remove the read-only restriction.

UNDERSTANDING YOUR DATA

When you are ready to begin analysing your data, it's always a good idea to start by printing out histograms of every variable, showing the range of the data. This

Box 10.5
DESIGNING A CODING SHEET

- Rows represent respondents, numbered in order of data collection, and columns represent items in your survey or data collection procedure.

- Keep the column names short, so more columns are visible on the screen at any time.

- Variable names should be able to be recognized and distinguished in the first eight letters (the average width of a spreadsheet column).

- Each column should represent one measure. Don't use multiple columns for multiple answers to a question, because this is likely to result in data entry mistakes.

- Use the 'Freeze panes' function on Excel so column names are still visible as you enter more data.* Otherwise a data entry person can easily lose their place and enter data in the wrong column.

- Build in simple checks to minimize data entry errors. For example, if you are entering survey data, colour the column corresponding to the last item on each page a different colour (using the 'Fill' colour function in Excel). This serves as a check for the data entry person that they are entering the data in the right column.

- Always enter some responses yourself, to check that the coding sheet is easy and fast to use. If your data entry is difficult or complicated, whoever does the data entry will take much longer (which is more expensive if you are paying) and will make more mistakes. You can always rearrange your spreadsheet or recode your data later to make it easier to analyse.

- Anticipate problems. How do you code a response with two boxes marked, when subjects have been asked to choose one? How do you code a scale marked half-way between two categories? If someone else is entering the data for you, don't rely on their judgement. Give them a pad of Post-its, get them to mark any responses they aren't sure of, and discuss with you later how to code problematic responses.

* If your variable names are in row 1, click on cell A2. On the toolbar menu, select 'Window', then 'Freeze panes'. As you page down to enter more data or to select another row, row 1, with the column names, will still remain visible. Similarly, freezing panes in cell B2 also leaves subject details (in column A) visible.

provides an extra check that no data are outside the appropriate range, and helps you to begin to understand your data, by looking at the ranges. What proportion in the sample were males? What were the range and distribution of ages? Describing your sample in terms of descriptive statistics is often the first part of reporting your results, and can also alert you to anomalies or problems in the data. For example, if you were hoping to analyse differences in attributions across age groups using a random sample of the population, and analysis of your sample shows that you have few or no subjects over sixty years old, you know that you won't be able to extend your analysis to that age group. If this age group is important to you, you may need to collect additional data, using a targeted sampling approach.

Missing data. An important component of initial data screening is reviewing your data to see if you have missing data (for example, where respondents did not answer a survey question). Missing data present problems for some methods of analysis (such as structural equation modelling) that can't include subjects which have even one variable missing. This may not present a major problem if you have a very large sample, but it can mean that your available sample size becomes much smaller, and as a consequence, less powerful. There are many ways to cope with the problem of missing data, such as replacing the missing value with the group mean or median response, deleting the variable from the analysis, or simply ignoring respondents with missing values. Different authorities argue for different solutions, so there is no clear answer, but part of your discussion of the data should include an explanation of the frequency of missing values, and how they were dealt with.

ANALYSING YOUR DATA

A common mistake made by students is thinking that they will do their data analysis once. While this sounds logical, in practice it almost never happens. Most data analysts find that they examine the data, realize they need to recode some variables, and reanalyse the data. Suppose, for example, that you are investigating use of Internet shopping, and you have asked respondents to report their experience of shopping on-line by reporting the number of times that they have bought physical products on-line. Experience is thus coded as an interval variable. On investigating your data, you may, however, find that about half your sample have never shopped on-line (experience $= 0$), but those who have shopped on-line have nearly all done it more than twenty times, and there is a substantial group who have shopped on-line more than 100 times. You have a very non-normal distribution of shopping.

A logical response to this problem is to recode your experience data into a categorical variable, using either two categories (those who have shopped and those who haven't) or three categories (non-shoppers, 'shoppers' and 'super-

151

shoppers'). Your decision as to how to distinguish 'shoppers' and 'super-shoppers' will need to be justified in some way, such as by natural groupings in the data. You can then reanalyse your data using the new groupings of experience. (*Hint*. If you decide to recode your data in a way like this, always enter the new coding in a new column of your worksheet, not by overwriting your original data. You should always preserve your original data, because at some stage you may want to use your original coding.) This method of recoding data is also referred to as 'collapsing categories' and is particularly useful if you only have a small number of respondents in some categories. In that case, combining categories will permit more accurate and more powerful analysis.

This process of recoding and reanalysing data will often continue for some time, as analysis suggests unanticipated patterns in the data that should be investigated. A new method of coding data will sometimes require a new method of analysis, with the result that you will have to abandon what you have already done. This means that in the early stages of data analysis, it's not usually worth spending much time writing up your results. Keep a record of analyses that you think you will use in your thesis, but don't start to formally write up your results until you are fairly sure of the final form of your analysis.

One warning: this method of analysis, while commonly used, is unpopular with some researchers. The basis of hypothesis testing is often said to be what is called 'hypothetico-deductive research' where the researcher derives hypotheses from the literature, tests those hypotheses and reports the results. Changing or adapting your hypotheses or data analysis procedures after collecting your data is sometimes criticized as '*ad hoc*' or 'empirical'. The best (honest) defence against this sort of accusation is to carefully justify what you have done, perhaps with a detailed explanation in an appendix, where an essentially technical argument won't interfere with the flow of the thesis.

REPORTING RESULTS

Deciding how to write up your results often presents a challenge for research students. What's the best way to summarize results? How much detail should you put in your thesis? Should you include discussion of the results in the results chapter, or put discussion in a separate discussion chapter? As always, there are no hard-and-fast rules, but a very good general rule is to remember that your whole thesis should attempt to present your research in a coherent and readable fashion. Dumping large amounts of output from a statistical program into the thesis is only likely to irritate examiners, and make them look at a thesis more critically. Don't fall into the trap of believing that it will look as if you have done more if you include large amounts of material. It is more likely that it will look as if you don't understand your analysis, and so don't know how to prioritize. You can always put supportive material in an appendix, but your results chapter,

Box 10.6
DATA ANALYSIS MADE EASIER

Since different researchers will use such a variety of methods, it's impossible for this chapter to give specific advice on different analysis techniques. However, some useful general guidelines if you are using a technique that you aren't very comfortable with include:

- Use the Web for general advice and background on the technique. Sitting at your computer, you can download a variety of information and explanation on almost any statistical technique. This is a good way to get a general understanding of the technique. However, most of the material on the Web is unreviewed and may contain errors, so the Web is insufficient for justifying or referencing what you do.

- Find some general statistics books and/or specialist textbooks in your university's library. These will usually give you a very clear explanation of the technique, and can often be used to justify what you do.

- Find some published articles in your research field that use your intended research technique. These can give you a template for how to justify your use of the technique, and how to report your results.

- If you are still having problems with your analysis, look for sources of expert help. Even if your supervisor isn't an expert, they may be able to recommend someone who can help you. For many techniques there are also on-line discussion groups where researchers pose problems or discuss applications. Posting a question to these sorts of groups can be a good way to get expert advice for free.

as with other chapters, should provide a consistent flow of relevant information, presented in such a way that the reader doesn't have to struggle to understand what you are writing.

Follow an authoritative example. As with every procedure in quantitative analysis, if you follow the procedure used by an authoritative author or publication, you are less likely to be criticized. This means that when you are summarizing statistical results in a table, you can report the estimates and values that are given by someone else of standing, and omit variables that they don't include. Beware, however, of differences between journal articles and theses. Most of the examples you see will be in journals, where authors will be severely restricted in the amount of material that they can report. This means that published journal articles often omit lots of detail that should be reported in theses, such as full details of measures, discussion of data cleaning, testing of analysis assumptions, etc. You have space to present more material in a thesis, so looking at other theses that have used a similar quantitative method can provide another model of what to present, and how to summarize results.

Put what's less important in appendices. Readers are likely to become annoyed and distracted if you include large amounts of non-essential material. Students, however, often have a tendency to include large amounts of non-essential material in an attempt to show that they have been thorough. One way round this dilemma is to put all non-critical material in appendices, with an appropriate reference such as 'Evidence of testing of the assumptions of the analysis is shown in Appendix III'. The examiner is thus reassured that you have followed proper procedures, but isn't distracted by a long digression that serves only to argue that your analysis is valid. Most examiners won't read appendices in detail, but the material is there if they want to. As with the body of your thesis, you should never dump large amounts of statistical output in an appendix without appropriate introduction, formatting and explanation of the purpose of the material. If you do that, you may suggest to an examiner that you are sloppy in your work – the last thing you want to imply.

HOW TO AVOID LOOKING FOOLISH: WHAT NOT TO SAY WHEN REPORTING STATISTICAL RESULTS

Quantitative analysis is an area with strong conventions, where specific wording is important. It is also an area where students can easily write something which can make them look foolish to a quantitative expert. So some things to be careful with:

Avoid claiming that you have 'proved' something. The dominant convention in scientific and philosophic thinking is that, strictly speaking, you can't 'prove' something, though you can disprove things. The often quoted example is that, even if every swan you had ever seen was white, it would be impossible to 'prove' that all swans were white, because there might be an undiscovered one of another colour out there somewhere (as was found when black swans were discovered in Australia). Now we have found black swans, we have disproved that all swans are white, but we haven't proved that all swans are white or black, because there may still be undiscovered swans of another colour. You can say that 'the data are consistent with' or 'suggest' or 'support' that all swans are black or white, but you could never say that the observed data on swans outside Australia 'establish' or 'prove' that all swans are white.

Be careful of saying that one thing 'causes' another. Careless researchers often claim causation (that one thing causes another) when all that they have tested is an association between variables. For example, you might perform research on employee pay and company profitability, and find that companies where employees are paid more are more successful. Pay and company profitability may be positively associated, but it is not clear which causes the other (wealthy companies may pay employees more because they can afford to). You can say that pay and company performance are 'associated' or that 'the data are consistent with higher pay causing higher company profitability' or that 'companies which paid higher salaries were found to be more profitable', all of which report your results without claiming that one thing causes the other. If there is doubt about the likely direction of causality, your discussion might then discuss any evidence that might suggest that pay causes profitability, or vice versa, or perhaps some other explanation, such as a third variable (e.g. buoyant economic conditions) resulting in both higher pay and higher profitability.

To establish causation, you would generally need to have performed a controlled experiment, but a general rule is that causation should never be claimed unless (1) one thing precedes the other in time, (2) there is a reasonable theory to suggest that one factor causes the other and (3) that all reasonable alternative explanations have been excluded.

Never report the result of a statistical test as $p = 0.000$. Statistical tests are often reported with a given 'p value', for example, $p < 0.05$ or $p = 0.002$, with the p value taken from the statistical test. Sometimes a statistical test result will report that $p = 0.000$. Never report this, or you will make yourself look silly to a statistical reader. The correct interpretation of $p = 0.000$ is that $p < 0.001$, because p (that is, the probability of obtaining the observed result if the null hypothesis is true) cannot ever be exactly zero. (The statistical package sometimes reports $p = 0.000$, due to rounding of a very small value, but you will make yourself look silly if you report it in the same way.)

CONCLUSION

Quantitative analysis can be an intimidating process for many students, and it is often an area where a supervisor will have limited expertise in your particular method, so can't give you specific help. However, it is also an area where you can obtain an enormous amount of help from the Web, from textbooks and from published articles, providing advice on what to do, and templates for summarizing and reporting results. By following a careful planning process that starts before you collect your data, you can minimize the chance that you will make serious and time-consuming mistakes in your data analysis.

Box 10.7
CHECKLIST: DEALING WITH DATA

Before collecting the data, have I:

- checked that I have included all the relevant variables? ☐
- made sure I have an appropriate and justifiable scale for each measure? ☐
- checked that my measures are appropriate for my proposed analysis technique? ☐
- checked that my anticipated sample size is appropriate for my proposed analysis technique? ☐

If using a survey, have I:

- pilot-tested the survey on a range of people who are similar to the proposed sample? ☐
- checked to see that I have sufficient discriminative ability in my measures, based on my pilot testing? ☐
- checked to be sure that I have sufficient questions for all the information I need to collect? ☐
- checked that I am not including questions that are unnecessary? ☐

In writing up the data analysis, have I:

- explained and justified the measures used? ☐
- justified the use of the technique/s? ☐
- explained the incidence of, and my treatment of, missing data? ☐
- followed a recognized procedure to justify my analysis? ☐

In reporting the results of the data analysis, have I:

- reported appropriate statistics for each analysis? ☐
- reported a specific result for each hypothesis? ☐

NOTES

1 You can prevent incorrect data entries by highlighting a column by clicking on the letter at the top (e.g. 'A' for row A). On the tool bar menu, select 'Data', then 'Validation', then specify the values that can be entered. If someone makes a mistake and tries to enter an invalid response they will receive an error message.

2 To check data entries in a column only containing pre-specified values, first highlight a whole column by clicking on the letter value (e.g. 'A' for the first column). On the toolbar menu, select 'Data', then 'Filter', then 'Autofilter'. A small arrow will appear in the first row (e.g. cell A1). Clicking on the arrow will give you a list of all the values in the column. Any that are outside your appropriate range can then be checked and corrected.

3 If you are using Windows, to lock the file, first close the file, then locate it in whatever directory it is stored in. Right-click on the file, go to 'Properties' and tick the box marked 'Read-only'.

FURTHER READING

Any university library will have a large number of excellent books which cover different statistical techniques in detail. Many of these books, however, assume a high level of statistical ability, and can be intimidating to the average research student. The following list of references are books which students who are not experts in statistics are likely to find easier to read, and which can therefore be helpful in developing an overview of less common methodologies.

Further reading on developing surveys

De Vaus, D.A. (2002) *Surveys in Social Research* (5th edn), St Leonards: Allen & Unwin.

Alreck, P.L. and Settle, R.B. (1995) *The Survey Research Handbook*. Chicago: Irwin.

Further reading on multivariate techniques

Hair, J.F., Anderson, R.E., Tatham, R.L. and Black, W.C. (1998) *Multivariate Data Analysis* (5th edn). Upper Saddle River NJ: Prentice Hall.

Further reading on forecasting techniques

Armstrong, J.S. (2001) *Principles of forecasting*, Dordrecht: Kluwer.

REFERENCES

Burton, S., Sheather, S. and Roberts, J. (2003) 'Reality or perception? The effect of actual and perceived performance on satisfaction and behavioral intention', *Journal of Service Research*, 5 (4): 292–302.

Oliver, R.L. (1997) *Satisfaction: A Behavioral Perspective on the Consumer*. Boston MA: Irwin McGraw-Hill.

Oliver, R.L. and Burke, R.R. (1999) 'Expectation processes in satisfaction formation: a field study, *Journal of Service Research*, 1 (3): 196–214.

Smith, A.K., Bolton, R.N. and Wagner, J. (1999) 'A model of customer satisfaction with service encounters involving failure and recovery', *Journal of Marketing Research*, 36 (3), 356–72.

Weiner, B. (2000) 'Attributional thoughts about consumer behavior', *Journal of Consumer Research*, 27 (3): 382–7.

Chapter 11

Qualitative research

LEE PARKER

We do not see things as they are; we see things as we are.

(Talmud)

To most intending research students, particularly those in business schools, the prospect of undertaking a Qualitative Research (QR) study is unfortunately all too infrequently contemplated. There are several explanations for this. First, the dominant research paradigm in many business-related research journals is quantitative and positivist. Second, many academic supervisors are trained in quantitative methods but largely unfamiliar with qualitative methods. Third, there is a perception among many researchers and research students that QR is complex, ill defined, messy, time-consuming and difficult to circumscribe. Yet, despite these constraints, QR is becoming an increasingly important method of generating research theses and of contributing to the published research literature.

This chapter introduces QR as an attractive, relevant and potentially powerful research genre for project design, implementation and resulting thesis production. We shall review the essential characteristics of QR, consider the rationales advanced for employing such an approach, assess the research skills required of a qualitative researcher, and then outline the nature of, and basic methods employed in, a number of qualitative methodologies: namely historical methodology, ethnography, phenomenology, hermeneutics, field-based case study, grounded theory and action research. Finally we shall examine the relationship between qualitative and quantitative research.

BEHIND THE 'QUALITATIVE' LABEL

What does the label 'qualitative analysis' really mean? Shank (2002) has defined QR as the study of processes and behaviours in their natural settings, through which the researcher tries to make sense of phenomena and the meanings that people attribute to them. So the focus of qualitative analysis is the interpretation and understanding of phenomena in their social, institutional, political, economic,

159

technological, institutional and organizational contexts. The qualitative researcher employs a variety of methods in an attempt to interpret and understand the world, and, in so doing, offers multiple perspectives that incrementally add to our understanding of its operation and its implicit meanings (Denzin and Lincoln 2000).

In studying and describing multiple socially constructed realities of actors (the QR term for research subjects), the qualitative researcher often uses multiple methods to tease out the complexity, depth and richness of the natural settings being studied. These methods can include observation, conversation, interview and participative or archival research. One or more of these methods are often used to explore practices hitherto ignored or neglected, to interpret phenomena that have not been well understood, or to explain practices and behaviours in terms of their context, process and outcomes. So, with its focus on process and meaning, qualitative analysis deliberately encompasses complexity, uncertainty, context, rich/thick description and multiple analytical methods (Denzin and Lincoln 2000; Shank 2002).

Another distinctive feature of QR is the researcher's role as the primary research instrument, since the research is invariably conducted through the researcher's direct engagement in intense, prolonged and direct exposure to the field amidst 'live' situations that form the everyday activities and processes of people, organizations and institutions. This engagement serves the researcher's objective to capture the perceptions and understandings of the actors 'from the inside' so as to better understand how they make sense of and manage their daily activities (Miles and Huberman 1994). Finally, in comparison with the quantitative researcher's analytical reliance on statistics, the qualitative researcher's analysis is based on a careful and deep understanding and use of language, concept and argument.

WHY SELECT A QUALITATIVE RESEARCH STRATEGY?

QR facilitates unique opportunities for you as a researcher to have an encounter with people's actual experiences in naturally occurring events and situations. In most circumstances, this is achieved through the collection of data directly from the scene of action and through considering context in any investigation of phenomena. The primary goals of QR are insight, enlightenment and illumination. To achieve this, the researcher attempts to tease out the detail, richness and texture of organizational processes, events and relationships over sustained periods of time. So if you wish to move beyond the sometimes simplistic causal models of the quantitative study, and you are interested in developing deep-level, contextually informed, holistic understandings of how and why things happen as they do, then QR is for you (Miles and Huberman 1994; Shank 2002)!

So QR actively seeks to examine subject areas in their entirety and to grapple with the complexity, ambiguity and variability of life that is often ignored by researchers absorbed in attempting to develop and test generalizable models of behaviour. When you want to study routine everyday processes, an exceptional or unusual event, particular groups, situations or practices, then a QR approach is, therefore, a most appropriate choice. It allows recognition and appreciation of diversity, difference and uniqueness. QR also permits researchers to apply multiple theoretical perspectives as part of a strategy of accumulating understanding of the complex world in which we live, and allowing research and research findings to reflect many differing and changing social and organizational cultures, histories and contexts (Flick 2002).

In summary, if you, as a researcher, have a particular interest in contributing to understanding practices in your disciplinary field, in offering new perspectives on contentious issues in the field, in tendering constructive critique grounded on historical and field-based investigations, in inductive theory development, or in contributing to policy debate and formulation, then QR offers a viable research strategy. It is a research strategy that requires your direct, personal engagement with the field, its actors and the archives, and one that challenges you to grapple with 'real world' complexity, interaction and change.

BUILDING YOUR SKILL SET

Just as quantitative researchers must acquire and develop a range of research design, data collection and statistical analysis skills, so too must qualitative researchers develop a range of design collection and analysis skills. Some of these are method techniques specific to a particular selected methodology, but there are a number of generic skills common to many methodologies.

Participation

Most QR requires at least some degree of researcher involvement in the field site and with the actors being studied. This involvement may range from being a passive observer to being a very active participant in actors' and their organizations' activities. Participation can be a vital strategy that allows you access to otherwise obscured or hidden sources of evidence and interpretation. As a qualitative researcher you must therefore develop your abilities and processes for gaining access to such individuals and groups, developing mutually trusting relationships and effective communications, managing your actual and perceived role as researcher, organizational participant and, sometimes, facilitator.

Observation

While it might be assumed that everyone has observational skills, your qualitative observation skills must be more finely honed than usual, directed towards delving into any forms of data that may provide insights into your project's central research question. This involves observing actions, context, attitudes and inter-actions. These observations themselves are multi-dimensional, and may be visual, aural and emotional. This requires you to be sensitive to historical and cultural influences, to recognize whatever may be highly germane to the subject under investigation, to gather data from unexpected sources, take up unplanned oppor-tunities for observation, and be sufficiently flexible to switch methods and focus of observation, if necessary, in response to emerging data and issues.

Triangulation

In collecting data, you need to develop strategies and be alert to opportunities for triangulating data. Triangulation involves collecting data by multiple methods, or from multiple sources. It will enhance the credibility of data you collect, the associated analyses you conduct and the resulting assertions you make. To do this you need to collect information and/or perspectives on the same issue from different sources, different actors and at different points in time during your study or fieldwork period. Where these various sources give you a mutually consistent picture of a particular event, process, relationship or concept, the credibility and justification of your analysis and findings will be strengthened.

Communication

As a qualitative researcher engaging with actors in the field, you need to learn the subtleties, specific terminology and nuances of the actors' language in order to understand their communication with each other, their responses to your ques-tions and of course to make your own communications understood. It is important to recognize that your communication with actors is not confined to formal inter-view settings but, regardless of the method you use, will involve considerable informal conversation that can be an invaluable source of rich data. Finally you must train yourself to be a sensitive listener. This is no easy task, given most people's propensity to talk more than they listen. It is the actor's voice that is a vital focus for any QR, and by listening more, and speaking less, you will learn much more.

Interpretation

This is a primary skill that all qualitative researchers must develop, partly through study of the methods advocated in the literature of the selected methodology, and partly through their own experience in the field. You must discern the under-lying meaning of interviewees' responses and actors' interchanges in meetings and discussions. This involves first ascertaining what is relevant to, and significant for, your selected research question. It means that you need to unpack the messages implicit in any text (be it archival, interview or observation notes), reflect on the effect of your own background and predispositions on your findings, and continually review the effect of your engagement with the actors on the data collected. Most important, it means learning not to jump to premature interpretations of what you observe.

Analysis and narration

For the qualitative researcher, data analysis varies with the methodology selected: from formally structured and detailed method steps to informally, loosely specified steps. Some guidelines are given below for each specific methodology outlined. While space prohibits a detailed discussion of computer software packages, a brief comment on the use of these packages for qualitative data storage management and coding analysis may be useful. A variety of software programs is now available, including Ethnograph, Textbase Alpha, Qualpro, Atlas and NUD.IST. Substantial analysis can be done using only word-processing software, and you should be wary of unnecessarily adopting sophisticated package options. While these packages may assist in the speed and efficiency of data manipulation (depending on the amount of data you collect), they do not replace the intellectual skill you require for identifying themes, underlying agendas, codes, relationships, etc. This skill is the most important component of qualitative analysis, regardless of whether you use computer or manual methods. The computer software only offers an adjunct tool to your essentially important sociological, historical, anthropological and philosophical expertise. The risk you must avoid is that of becoming focused on the 'bells and whistles' of the software and distracted from the primary tasks of deep-level understanding of texts and contemplative reflection on what lies behind them. These computer packages are probably at their best for the organization and retrieval of data, while theorizing is best conducted using your trained intellect (Flick 2002; Hammersley and Atkinson 1995; Silverman 2000).

Unlike the quantitative researcher, whose discoveries are almost exclusively made during data analysis, the qualitative researcher makes significant discoveries at both the data analysis and the thesis write-up stages. Your writing will prompt further introspection, reflection, critique and conceptualization, so that analysis continues throughout the write-up stage. You must learn to discern patterns, trends and relationships, to think conceptually, to rise above the manifest appearance of the data collected in order to detect and discuss its deeper meaning and broader significance, and to develop concepts, frameworks and themes which can be compared with existing theories, concepts and assumptions. This task also often involves the construction of a narrative that presents persuasive themes and story lines, argues influences, connections and outcomes, and develops wider implications for the discipline in which the study is situated.

163

The above skill set represents a fundamental menu upon which all qualitative researchers almost invariably draw in pursuing their projects. It must be developed through your prior methodological study and preparation before entering the field, but also in the course of experiencing and reflecting upon your own involvement in, and execution of, the actual research process.

SELECTED QUALITATIVE METHODOLOGIES

What follows is a selection of qualitative methodologies from which you can draw for a QR study or for the qualitative component of a combined qualitative and quantitative research study. Of course, this selection does not constitute all the methodologies falling under the qualitative label. Nevertheless, it represents the methodologies typically used by researchers in the social science and management disciplines. As you can appreciate, within the space of this chapter it is not possible to offer detailed practical guides for implementing such a range of methodologies. The following section offers, for each methodology, a basic definition, its derivation and primary research aim or focus, and its basic characteristics. This is designed to help you decide which methodology may be most suited to the research question your study is trying to address. In addition, some basic introductory comments are made concerning the type of method steps that can be involved in implementing each methodology, and a number of introductory references are provided in the outline of each methodology.

Historical methodology

Historical research, particularly in the business, accounting and management fields, has made major contributions to our explanations of the past and our understandings of the present. Historical research can show how contemporary attitudes, practices and theories have emerged and can elucidate the influence of events, practices and policies upon organizations, groups and individuals. Rather than presenting a simplistic unitary perspective on policy and practice, it can facilitate multiple incremental interpretations of that past, thereby challenging received wisdom and offering new ways of addressing what has previously been considered settled. Multiple perspectives are made possible through a variety of methodological traditions, including Rankean historicism, the interdisciplinary *Annales* school, Marxian historical materialism, the Foucauldian disciplinary perspective and the postmodern school, with its sponsorship of minority group and oral histories. These different perspectives present opportunities for original archival research and for revisiting previous conclusions through new lenses that focus on issues and dimensions previously ignored. Such studies include the development of thought, biographical, institutional, social and critical histories (Carr 1961; Evans 2000; Parker 1997, 1999; Tosh 1991).

164

So historical research offers us the prospect of exposing the effects of events, practices and policies on people's lives and their behaviours. By analysing our past through multiple lenses and interpretations, actors and their contexts are brought into sharp focus and both past and present can be critically reappraised (Carnegie and Napier 1996; Hammond and Sikka 1996; Miller *et al.* 1991). Historians study what happened in a particular set of events, but also examine conditioning influences, consequences and events occurring long after (Lowenthal 1996). Revisionism is a natural feature of historical research whereby historians continually reconstitute the past through their accruing experiences, changing interests and accretions of knowledge (Heller 1982; Stanford 1998). So history is repeatedly rewritten as historians of different periods and persuasions re-examine old and sometimes new evidence, and transmit their accounts to new audiences living in a new 'present' (Hull 1979; Fleischman and Tyson 1997; Parker 1997).

In embarking upon historical research, you first need to decide whether your historical research focus is primarily biographical, institutional or a development of thought, and upon which historical school or theoretical perspective you elect to draw. You then need to determine what primary and secondary sources of evidence are most relevant to your research question and commence the usually time-consuming task of gathering this evidence. Remember that historical evidence is most likely to be documentary, but be alert for any possibilities of accessing oral sources (by your own interviewing or by taped interviews already contained in library and research collection archives). The data collected must first be assessed for its origins, time and place of production, its relevance to your research and for evidence of its authenticity and credibility. Analysis of the collected data can then be turned towards selecting and detailing the key events and their sequence. Then the analysis might search for and evaluate conditioning factors, interpreting processes of interaction between the environment, factors and people and, as a result, develop explanations of ensuing outcomes. Even in an ostensibly narrative account, interpretation and explanation are involved, and each factor's probability of significant influence on events must be judged. Even then, unlike the positivist researcher, you will find that further analysis and revelations will naturally take place in the course of your writing up the research.

Ethnography

Ethnography involves the researcher personally observing a group of people, their customs and behaviour patterns in their natural setting over a lengthy period of time. This research tradition focuses on describing and interpreting a group of actors and their cultural system. Its roots lie in cultural anthropology studies of primitive cultures by early twentieth-century anthropologists (Creswell 1998; Glesne 1999; Silverman 2000). The primary data collection approach is predominantly semi-structured or unstructured, carried out by participant observation and supplemented by interviews. The researcher becomes immersed in the daily lives and activities of the group, observing their behaviour, language and interactions, with a view to understanding the associated meanings they reflect. Such research projects invariably take the single-case format. Participant observation is a key data collection strategy, using one of the following approaches by the researcher:

- *Peripheral member.* The researcher interacts sufficiently with actors to be considered an insider but does not participate in activities central to group membership.
- *Active member.* The researcher undertakes a more central role in the group, participating in some of its core activities.
- *Complete member.* The researcher 'goes native' and immerses themselves entirely in the group's activities and experiences.

Selecting from these three categories of participant observation, the ethnographer can experience actors' context, perceptions, decision making and behaviour, and approach some understanding of their *Weltanschauung*, or world view (Adler and Adler 1994; Denzin 1978).

While outlines of ethnographic methodology typically focus largely on the narrative reporting of findings, ethnographic data collection is most often conducted by observation and semi-structured interviews. A key resource will be making detailed and meticulous observation field notes, while in the field and also immediately after each occasion of leaving the field. These notes should be as detailed as possible, clearly identifying the setting and context of observations or interviews, direct quotations, paraphrased descriptions of activities, events and interactions observed, and your own reflections. Audio-recorded interviews must be transcribed. Notes may also be taken summarizing documents inspected. Data analysis is more often undertaken through discursive, narrative and literary forms than through formal categorizing and coding of data, although the latter strategy can be used. Thus reflecting on and analysing your *experience* of the field sites is considered to be most important. Over time it is important that you progressively focus your analysis, clarifying and delimiting the focal research problem and project scope and determining what the story is *really* about. This can also involve a gradual shift from detailed descriptions of events and processes to developing key overarching themes and concepts that address the central research question and provide a more overriding theoretical explanation of the described accounts (Creswell 1998; Flick 2002; Hammersley and Atkinson 1995).

Phenomenology

Phenomenology involves penetrating and analysing the experiences of a group of actors about a phenomenon in which they are involved. The researcher aims to uncover what central meaning the actors derive from their experience of the phenomenon. This methodology has its roots in the philosophical thinking of Edmund Husserl, who argued that the relationship between objects and human perception of them is not passive, and that human consciousness actually constitutes objects of experience. Actors in his view are conscious of *something*, so that consciousness not only perceives the world, but also constructs it. From a sociological perspective, Schutz built on Husserl's ideas to investigate how people experience their ordinary everyday world. So like ethnography, phenomenology is concerned with how people make sense of their everyday activities and how they develop meanings from their social interactions. This approach is based on the fundamental philosophy that understanding is a product of human experience and that this experience is a product of human interaction, and not simply some construct developed by an external observer. The researcher studies the everyday world as produced and experienced by the actors. So the researcher employing the phenomenological methodology focuses on actors' descriptions and interpretations of their lived experiences in relation to a particular phenomenon that the researcher is investigating – how they experience it and how they perceive that experience (Creswell 1998; Glesne 1999; Gubrium and Holstein 2000).

The researcher should temporarily suspend or set aside his or her prior experiences, knowledge of and views on the subject, instead focusing upon encouraging the actors' interpretations of an event or experience in their *own* words. Data are primarily gathered through extended interviews with actors who give their personal account of their experience of the phenomenon being studied. The researcher focuses on actors' experience *and* actors' associated behaviour as a whole, and not simply its parts. In analysing interview transcripts, the researcher seeks to identify key statements that give an insight into the actors' experiences and perceptions of those experiences. The research does this through inductively ascertaining the meaning that these statements imply and categorizing into clusters the meaning derived from the interviews.

These meanings are then portrayed by textual outlines of what was experienced, and by structural outlines of how it was experienced by actors. In this way the researcher attempts to convey to the reader a sense of the essence of the experience, its underlying structure and what it was like to experience that phenomenon (Creswell 1998; Shank 2002).

Hermeneutics

Hermeneutics is essentially a methodology of interpreting text and is closely associated with phenomenology. It was first employed by scholars who strove to revisit and reinterpret the context, underlying messages and meanings implicit in the Christian Bible. The methodology was subsequently extended to the interpretation of any text, pioneered in particular by the phenomenologist Heidegger.

167

Hermeneutics treats writer, text and reader as constituents of a process of producing reality. It argues that the person reading a text about a subject, event or interaction is just as involved in constructing a view of reality as the author of the text. This view is not limited to the experience of reading written text, but applies equally to the verbal texts of conversation and interview. The actor experiences environments, events and activities, constructs texts to represent their experience, and the reader or listener then interprets and develops understandings and meanings from those texts. Thus the text transcends the meanings initially invested in it by its author(s) and develops wider meanings for other actors (such as listeners and readers) and in other social contexts. Acknowledgement of this hermeneutic potential permits researchers to offer accounts of events and circumstances that transcend the actors' initial self-understanding and present interpretations and meanings that synthesize the frames of reference of the actors and the researcher (Flick 2002; Kincheloe and McLaren 2000; Llewellyn 1993; Shank 2002; Schwandt 2000).

A hermeneutical approach allows the researcher to tease out antecedents (and) consequences of actions, even when these antecedents and consequences may not be clear to the actors themselves. Actors' self-understanding can thereby be evaluated. Consistent with its roots in biblical interpretation, hermeneutical methodology also requires the researcher to draw on the historical context as the setting for their interpretation (Llewellyn 1993). The hermeneutical researcher most often interprets and constructs new understandings via narrative exposition. The narrative constructs or reconstructs the past and anticipates the future by projecting various possible scenarios. The researcher constructs their narrative around a plot that may represent a romance (a quest towards a desired end result), comedy (evolutionary or revolutionary progress), tragedy (a decline from a previously successful state) or satire (where events overwhelm the actors). The narrative must offer a coherent account that includes all material relevant to the study's aim, and that presents events and themes in a logical progression, drawing on data which best represent the themes being explicated. The narrative exposition allows the researcher to recognize conditions of ambiguity and complexity, to set interpretation in its context, to 'see' events and circumstances in new ways, to offer new understandings and interpretations, and to project new future scenarios. By doing this, the narrative can be exploited as a tool for identifying conditions of possibility, and for configuring actors, events and themes in an explanatory sequence (Llewellyn 1999; Pentland 1999).

Field-based case study

Field research embodies the 'involved' researcher tradition whereby researchers personally insert themselves into the actors' world by going on-site and studying phenomena in their natural context over a period of time. Field researchers focus

168

on actual events, activities, processes, people and relationships, employing an evolving set of multiple methods as field observations proceed, and producing theses and publications that incorporate rich descriptions and analysis of contexts and practices (Adler and Adler 1994; Ferreira and Merchant 1992; Neumann 2003; Silverman 2000). Field-based case research is often classified as descriptive, exploratory or explanatory, and as single, collective, comparative or layered case studies (Stake 2000; Yin 1989). It can serve a variety of purposes, including presenting detailed accounts of organizational practices, penetrating the cultural perceptions and understandings of organizational actors, interpreting management practices in their socio-economic, institutional and organizational contexts, inductively generating theory from field data, and clarifying prior research contradictions and superficiality (Silverman 1985; Walker 1985; Werner and Schoepfle 1987). Rather than developing simplistic models that provide general predictions of aggregate behaviour, field-based case study produces theories that explain observations in specific contexts. Instead of statistical generalization, it aims at theoretical generalization, developing specific contextualized theories that explain actual observations made in the field (Dawson 1997; Scapens 1990).

A challenge for student researchers is often getting access to a suitable field research site. Personal introductions are often helpful to obtain leads to potential research sites. Consider your own contacts and those of your supervisor, colleagues, friends and relatives. In persuading any body to give you permission as a research site, you will need to justify the study to them. When you explain your study to a target organization or group, do it in their language, and show them what's in it for them, briefly explaining what you want to do, why, and what you need from them. You should also be well prepared to address confidentiality issues, in order to allay any concern that individuals or the group might have about their own privacy, or about other sensitive information. Potential field research methods range from semi-structured to quite highly structured processes, including observation of activities, processes and meetings, unstructured and semi-structured interviews, and documentary and archival research (Creswell 1998; Miles and Huberman 1994). The process usually involves a period of repeated site visits by the researcher, spread over a period of at least six months. Remember throughout the study to watch and listen, and to adopt the 'vacuum cleaner' approach, collecting all forms of potential evidence no matter how seemingly minor or peripheral. Target actors at all levels and functional groups for interview, and focus in particular on those who appear to be perceptive and articulate. You can design your interviews to be structured (closed-ended questions), semi-structured (open and closed-ended questions) or unstructured (open-ended questions) or a combination of these. Consider the reasons behind any question, the sequence, and transitions between questions, in order to make the interview situation relaxed, and thereby draw out maximum information from the interviewee. Maintain flexibility and, if relevant to your research topic, be prepared

169

to follow the interviewee down paths they wish to go. Judiciously use probe and follow-up questions such as 'What else?', 'Tell me more,' 'How did that happen?', 'Why?', 'Can you give an example of that?' and occasional silence, in order to elicit more detail and depth. Remember to listen 'between the lines' (Flick 2002; Shank 2002; Silverman 2000).

Data analysis of field-based research usually takes the form of either narrative analysis or the more formal coding, with intensive and interpretive memo writing and analysis of field data for understanding concepts, interrelationships and themes. You must continually search your data for hidden meanings, patterns and relationships, and gradually develop concepts and theory from your data. You are trying to build a holistic theoretical picture of process, context, influences and outcomes. You may use either a semi-structured approach to data analysis characteristic of the methodologies discussed above, or a more formal coding approach as outlined in the grounded theory methodology below. Your study write-up may take a narrative thematic form or a more formal concept and theoretical framework specification.

Grounded theory

Grounded theory is a methodology for the inductive generation and discovery of theory from collected and analysed field data. It attempts to produce an analytical representation and interpretation of a phenomenon in its contextual surroundings. North American sociologists Barney Glaser (1978) and Anselm Strauss (Glaser and Strauss 1965, 1967, 1968; Strauss 1987) originally developed this methodology. Instead of beginning with a deductively predetermined theory about a phenomenon and subsequently collecting field data to test that theory, the grounded theory researcher begins with a central question concerning a phenomenon or area of study and attempts to inductively generate relevant theoretical elements through data collection and concurrent iterative data analysis. This involves systematic analysis of the researcher's notes, interview transcripts and archival documents. The emerging theoretical framework then depicts the central phenomenon, its conditioning influences and its outcomes. The theory so produced should be meaningful for actors, researchers and readers (Parker and Roffey 1997). The paths of Glaser and Strauss separated when Strauss and Corbin (1990) devised a more structured process of developing theory. So divergent approaches to grounded theory have been advanced by Glaser (1978, 1992), modified by Strauss and Corbin (1990, 1998) and then further modified by Charmaz (2000).

Both the original Glaser and Glaser and Strauss approaches, and also the Strauss and Corbin approach, exhibit a 'post-positivist' tendency in their concern to lay down formal data analysis processes that aim towards validity and reliability in positivist terms. Activities and incidents are selected for observation and study, and interviewees are selected on a theoretical (non-random) sampling basis, so that selection is orientated towards those activities, incidents and interviewees most applicable to the phenomenon under study. Data are analysed by categorizing or coding field notes and interview transcripts and by writing interpretive memos concerning the characteristics of the 'open codes' assigned by the researcher. The resulting open codes are aggregated and sorted to produce macro-codes that represent a central phenomenon, its causal conditions, its consequential strategies and outcomes, and any intervening conditions or strategies. The relations between these so-called 'axial' codes are represented by a formal theoretical framework or by a theoretical story line that portrays a substantive-level theory (Creswell 1998; Parker and Roffey 1997).

Charmaz (2000) offers a postmodern constructivist approach to grounded theory in which researcher and actors are seen to be jointly interpreting and creating social realities. Her approach adopts a less objectivist orientation, rejecting the notion of a measurable, commonly agreed external reality, instead focusing on experiences and interpreted meanings of researchers and actors. The mythical 'independent' researcher is replaced by active engagement between researcher and actors in a dialectical process of joint meaning creation. Charmaz's data collection and analysis are less formally structured and more flexible than those of her forerunners. This social construction of a grounded theory takes the form of concepts and arguments for further exploration and debate, rather than presenting as objectively testable models. Inferences regarding causality are made conditionally and are left open to revisitation and revision.

Action research

Action research involves the researcher carrying out research in collaboration with organizational actors on specific projects in which they diagnose, design, implement and evaluate planned changes in iterative cycles, with the intention of improving actors' and organizations' processes, equity and self-determination (Greenwood and Levin 2000). It represents a general methodology of involved, co-operative research rather than a single unified methodology with a generally agreed set of method steps. Rather, it takes a variety of forms and descriptors (for example 'participatory action research', 'collaborative action research' or 'co-operative inquiry'). J.L. Moreno coined the term and co-researched with groups in Vienna in 1913. In 1929 the educational philosopher John Dewey promoted practice-based inquiry, and in 1945 John Collier employed the approach to research ethnic group relations. The social psychologist Kurt Lewin, working in the mid-1940s, has, however, generally been credited as the most influential founder of action research (Glesne 1999; Ottosson 2001; Reason and Bradbury 2001).

Action research can be applied to a spectrum of issues and settings, including systems improvement, change management, innovation, specific problem solving

171

or theory generation. It attempts to create a more direct link between theory and practical action, to improve the context, understanding and application of practice, and to involve practitioners in developing definitions of problems and in implementing change. Thus it is variously conceived as:

- a continuous process of research, planning, theorizing, learning and development;
- a process of analysis, fact finding, conceptualization, planning and execution, repeated multiple times;
- identifying practitioners' questions/problems in local practice contexts, building associated descriptions and theories and testing them through intervention experiments

(Coghlan 2001; Dickens and Watkins 1999; Heron and Reason 2001; Kemmis and McTaggart 2000; Shank 2002).

Lewin called for theory building to be combined with research into practical problems and envisaged action research as involving researcher and actor group decision making and commitment to improvement. This required engaging in an ever deepening investigation of the selected problem. In summary, Lewin's action research involved:

- experiments on real problems and change in social systems;
- iterative cycles of problem identification, planning, acting and evaluating;
- actors' re-education, by changing their patterns of thinking and action;
- challenging the *status quo* through group participation in research;
- contributing to basic knowledge in social science and to everyday social action.

Thus, for Lewin, action research comprised a spiral of repeated cycles of fact finding, planning, action and evaluation, each successive cycle bringing the action research group closer to its objective. In this process the researcher facilitates actor group deliberations, helps formulate planned change and may collaborate in implementing organizational change (Argyris 1997).

In practical terms, as an action researcher you need to initially negotiate not only access to an organization or setting but also the composition of a team with which to work and the subject area that will be of mutual interest to your project and the team. With that team you must negotiate the project goals, the team's purpose and the relative roles and authorities of yourself and the other team members. Then the team needs to identify the focal problem(s) to be addressed and gather background data (organizational, contextual and wider literature) on the nature of the problem, possible approaches and solutions, resources required, etc. Planning meetings will then involve organizing and analysing the data,

172

reflecting on team processes, reconsidering team objectives, presenting data to relevant other parties, developing optional solutions and selecting from among them. Action implementation then takes place, followed by further data gathering on implementation efficiency and effectiveness, related problems, and the resulting outcomes. This information is fed back into the team for further reflection, and revisions may be made to the strategies employed and their implementation processes for trialling in a further round of action. These steps may not always occur in an orderly sequence, but many times you may find it necessary for the group to revisit earlier steps or segments thereof, so that in fact your team may cycle backwards and forwards through action research steps. Thus the cycle continues through several iterations, while all the time, as a participant observer, you record the processes, deliberations, interactions, influences and outcomes occurring (Dickens and Watkins 1999).

POSITIONING QUALITATIVE RESEARCH

When you adopt a QR strategy, it is important to recognize what that strategy implies. First, it suggests direct engagement with, and investigation of, social processes and participants' experiences of them, rather than measurement from afar of causal relations between variables with a view to building a model that can predict outcomes. Instead, your primary agenda is the interpretation and understanding of phenomena and their induced meaning for actors. Second, your preoccupation will be to study the world in its natural state through close personal contact with the natural setting in order to observe, describe and interpret what happens, how it happens, and in what contexts. Your overriding research concern is the inductive investigation of the phenomenon under study, rather than testing a set of prior hypotheses. In QR, laws of behaviour are rejected on the grounds that actors' behaviour is continually reconstructed through their changing interpretations of their situations (Parker 2003).

In addition you must be prepared to become, to varying degrees, involved with your research site and actors, in order to access data and meanings that would otherwise remain hidden from your view. Indeed, qualitative researchers argue that the independence, neutrality and objectivity prized by quantitative positivist researchers is unattainable and that, just like QR, quantitative research is also infused with culture, stories, language, symbols, selective perception, cognition, social conventions and ideology (Alvesson and Skoldberg 2000; Flick 2002; Hammersley and Atkinson 1995).

QR is in no way inferior to or subservient to quantitative research. It may well assist the latter, but it also stands on its own merits and has its own purposes and contribution to make to our stock of knowledge. QR can offer a strong foundation for consequent quantitative survey research in presenting an inductive development of knowledge about practices and beliefs from field investigations of organizations' and actors' experiences and processes. Such findings may then be susceptible to modelling and statistical testing by quantitative methods. Alternatively QR can offer investigations that can help explain the reasons underlying statistically significant associations found in positivist studies.

CONCLUSION

This chapter has described the background to, and use of, a variety of QR methodologies. For you, the researcher, QR offers a major research opportunity in its own right: a unique window on to the enactment of social, business and professional practices and beliefs *in situ*. Your focus can be on the interpretation of observed phenomena, the critique of contemporary or historical policies and practices or the exploration and facilitation of organizational and institutional change. The qualitative lens allows us to use archival sources, oral sources and narratives of experience, and to focus upon specific situations, selected time periods and particular contexts. We can do this via alternative theoretical lenses and multiple methodologies, in contrast to the positivist's single rational, scientific, existentialist, objectivist perspective. In so doing we allow ourselves the opportunity to rediscover in multiple guises what we thought we already knew.

REFERENCES

Adler, P. and Adler, P. (1994) 'Observational techniques', in N. Denzin and Y. Lincoln (eds) *Handbook of Qualitative Research*, Thousand Oaks CA: Sage, pp. 377–92.

Alvesson M. and Skoldberg, K. (2000) *Reflexive Methodology: New Vistas for Qualitative Research*, London: Sage.

Argyris, C. (1997) Kurt Lewin Award Lecture 1997: 'Field Theory as a Basis for Scholarly Consulting' (Transforming Psychology: Interpretive and Participatory Research Methods), *Journal of Social Issues*, 53 (4): 1–11.

Carnegie, G.D. and Napier, C.J. (1996) 'Critical and interpretive histories: insights into accounting's present and future through its past', *Accounting, Auditing and Accountability Journal*, 9: 7–39.

Carr, E.H. (1961) *What is History?* London: Macmillan.

Charmaz, K. (2000) 'Grounded theory: objectivist and constructivist methods', in N. K. Denzin and Y. S. Lincoln (eds) *Handbook of Qualitative Research*, 2nd edn, Thousand Oaks CA: Sage, pp. 509–35.

Coghlan, D. (2001) 'Insider action research projects: implications for practising managers', *Management Learning*, 32 (1): 49–60.

Creswell, J.W. (1998) *Qualitative Inquiry and Research Design: Choosing Among Five Traditions*, Thousand Oaks CA: Sage.

Dawson, P. (1997) 'In at the deep end: conducting processual research on organisational change', *Scandinavian Journal of Management*, 13 (4): 389–405.

Denzin, N.K. (1978) *The Research Act: A Theoretical Introduction to Sociological Methods*, 2nd edn, New York: McGraw-Hill.

Denzin, N.K. and Lincoln, Y.S. (2000) 'The discipline and practice of qualitative research', in N. K. Denzin and Y. S. Lincoln (eds.) *Handbook of Qualitative Research*, 2nd edn, Thousand Oaks CA: Sage, pp. 1–28.

Dickens, L. and Watkins, K. (1999) 'Action research: rethinking Lewin', *Management Learning*, 30 (2): 127–40.

Evans, R.J. (2000) *In Defence of History*, London: Granta Books.

Ferreira, L.D. and Merchant, K.A. (1992) 'Field research in management accounting and control: a review and evaluation', *Accounting, Auditing and Accountability Journal*, 5 (4): 3–34.

Fleischman, R.K. and Tyson, T.N. (1997) 'Archival researchers: an endangered species?' *Accounting Historians' Journal*, 24: 91–109.

Flick, U. (2002) *An Introduction to Qualitative Research*, London: Sage.

Glaser, B. (1978) *Theoretical Sensitivity*, Mill Valley CA: Sociology Press.

Glaser, B. (1992) *Basics of Grounded Theory Analysis*, Mill Valley, CA: Sociology Press.

Glaser, B.G. and Strauss, A. (1965) *Awareness of Dying*, Chicago: Aldine.

Glaser, B.G. and Strauss, A. (1967) *The Discovery of Grounded Theory: Strategies for Qualitative Research*, New York: Aldine.

Glaser, B.G. and Strauss, A. (1968) *Time for Dying*, Chicago: Aldine.

Glesne, C. (1999) *Becoming Qualitative Researchers: An Introduction*, 2nd edn, New York: Longman.

Greenwood, D.J. and Levin, M. (2000) 'Reconstructing the relationships between universities and society through action research', in N. K. Denzin and Y. S. Lincoln (eds) *Handbook of Qualitative Research*, 2nd edn, Thousand Oaks CA: Sage, pp. 85–106.

Gubrium, J.F. and Holstein, J.A. (2000) 'Analyzing interpretive practice', in N. K. Denzin and Y. S. Lincoln (eds) *Handbook of Qualitative Research*, 2nd edn, Thousand Oaks CA: Sage, pp. 487–508.

Hammersley, M. and Atkinson, P. (1995) *Ethnography: Principles in Practice*, 2nd edn, London: Routledge.

Hammond, T. and Sikka, P. (1996) 'Radicalizing accounting history: the potential of oral history', *Accounting, Auditing and Accountability Journal*, 9: 79–97.

Heller, A. (1982) *A Theory of History*, London: Routledge.

Heron, J. and Reason, P. (2001) 'The practice of co-operative inquiry: research "with" rather than "on" people', in P. Reason and H. Bradbury (eds) *Handbook of Action Research: Participative Inquiry and Practice*, London: Sage, pp. 179–88.

Hull, D. L. (1979) 'In defense of presentism', *History and Theory*, 18: 1–15.

Husserl, E. (1970) *Logical Investigation*, New York: Humanities Press.

Kemmis, S. and McTaggart, R. (2000) 'Participatory action research', in N. K. Denzin and Y. S. Lincoln (eds) *Handbook of Qualitative Research*, 2nd edn, Thousand Oaks CA: Sage, pp. 567–605.

Kincheloe, J.L. and McLaren, P. (2000) 'Rethinking critical theory and qualitative research', in N. K. Denzin and Y. S. Lincoln (eds) *Handbook of Qualitative Research*, 2nd edn, Thousand Oaks CA: Sage, pp. 279–313.

Llewellyn, S. (1993) 'Working in hermeneutic circles in management and accounting research: some implications and applications', *Management Accounting Research*, 4: 231–49.

Llewellyn, S. (1999) 'Narratives in accounting and management research', *Accounting, Auditing and Accountability Journal*, 12: 220–36.

Lowenthal, D. (1996) *The Heritage Crusade and the Spoils of History*, London: Viking.

Miles, M.B. and Huberman, A.M. (1994) *An Expanded Sourcebook: Qualitative Data Analysis*, 2nd edn, Thousand Oaks CA: Sage.

Miller, P., Hopper, T. and Laughlin, R. (1991) 'The new accounting history: an introduction', *Accounting, Organizations and Society*, 16: 395–403.

Neumann, W.L. (2003) *Social Research Methods: Qualitative and Quantitative Approaches*, 5th edn, Boston MA: Pearson.

Ottosson, S. (2001) 'Participation action research: a key to improved knowledge of management', *Technovation*, 23 (2): 87–94.

Parker, L.D. (1997) 'Informing historical research in accounting and management: traditions, philosophies, and opportunities', *Accounting Historians' Journal*, 24: 111–49.

Parker, L.D. (1999) 'Historiography for the new millennium: adventures in accounting and management', *Accounting History*, 4: 11–42.

Parker, L.D. (2003) 'Qualitative research in accounting and management: the emerging agenda', *Journal of Accounting and Finance*, forthcoming.

Parker, L.D. and Roffey, B.H. (1997) 'Back to the drawing board: revisiting grounded theory and the everyday accountant's and manager's reality', *Accounting, Auditing and Accountability Journal*, 10 (2): 212–47.

Pentland, B.T. (1999) 'Building process theory with narrative: from description to explanation', *Academy of Management Review*, 24 (4): 711–24.

Reason, P. and Bradbury, H. (2001) 'Introduction: inquiry and participation in search of a world worthy of human aspiration', in P. Reason and H. Bradbury (eds) *Handbook of Action Research: Participative Inquiry and Practice*, London: Sage, pp. 1–14.

Scapens, R.W. (1990) 'Researching management accounting practice: the role of case study methods', *British Accounting Review*, 22 (3): 259–81.

Schultz, A. (1964) *The Problem of Social Reality*, The Hague: Nijhoff.

Schultz, A. (1967a) *Studies in Social Theory*, The Hague: Nijhoff.

Schultz, A. (1967b) *Collected Papers* I, 1, ed. M. Natanson, The Hague: Nijhoff.

Schwandt, T.A. (2000) 'Three epistemological stances for qualitative inquiry: interpretivism, hermeneutics, and social constructionism', in N. K. Denzin and Y. S. Lincoln (eds) *Handbook of Qualitative Research*, 2nd edn, Thousand Oaks CA: Sage, pp. 189–213.

Shank, G.D. (2002) *Qualitative Research: A Personal Skills Approach*, Upper Saddle River NJ: Pearson.

Silverman, D. (1985) *Qualitative Methodology and Sociology: Describing the Social World*, Aldershot: Gower.

Silverman, D. (2000) *Doing Qualitative Research: A Practical Handbook*, London: Sage.

Stake, R.E. (2000) 'Case studies', in N. K. Denzin and Y. S. Lincoln (eds) *Handbook of Qualitative Research*, 2nd edn, Thousand Oaks CA: Sage, pp. 435–54.

Stanford, M. (1998) *An Introduction to the Philosophy of History*, Boston MA: Blackwell.

Strauss, A. (1987) *Qualitative Analysis for Social Scientists*, New York: Cambridge University Press.

Strauss, A.L. and Corbin, J. (1990) *Basics of Qualitative Research: Grounded Theory Procedures and Techniques*, Newbury Park CA: Sage.

Strauss, A.L. and Corbin, J. (1998) *Basics of Qualitative Research: Techniques and Procedures for Developing Grounded Theory*, 2nd edn, Thousand Oaks CA: Sage.

Tosh, J. (1991) *The Pursuit of History: Aims, Methods and New Directions in the Study of Modern History*, 2nd edn, London: Longman.

Wadsworth, Y. (2001) 'The mirror, the magnifying glass, the compass and the map: facilitating participatory action research', in P. Reason and H. Bradbury (eds) *Handbook of Action Research: Participative Inquiry and Practice*, London: Sage, pp. 420–32.

Walker, R. (ed.) (1985) *Applied Qualitative Research*, Aldershot: Gower.

Werner, O. and Schoepfle, G.M. (1987) *Systematic Fieldwork: Foundations of Ethnography and Interviewing*, Newbury Park CA: Sage, vols 1 and 2.

Yin, R.K. (1989) *Case Study Research: Design and Methods*, rev. edn, Newbury Park CA: Sage.

Chapter 12

Writing the thesis

PETER STEANE AND SUZAN BURTON

Writing is not an act of creation; it is an act of correction.

(Anon.)

The prospect of writing a thesis of 80,000 words or more can seem daunting to a research student. Writing any document of such length requires substantial planning, skill and time, and academic writing has particular conventions that present additional challenges, even to experienced writers. In addition, examiners will expect a thesis to conform to certain style conventions and particular standards of prose, structure and coherence. If your thesis falls down in its writing style, an examiner may think that you haven't put in the necessary work in other areas, and may judge your work more harshly. In this chapter we will discuss some of the particular requirements of thesis writing, guidelines for good writing, and strategies to assist you in producing a well written, well structured thesis in the most efficient way.

APPROACHING AND ORGANIZING THE THESIS

The thesis can seem a horrendously big job to undertake. The best advice is to see this big project as a series of smaller ones – not so much 80,000 words as a number of chapters, each containing a series of smaller essays, all contributing to a theme – answering a research question or testing hypotheses. The first step on such a journey begins with one small step, as in the old saying 'How do you eat an elephant? One bite at a time!'

A good way to motivate yourself to write, and to organize the latest drafts of different chapters, is to get a large spiral binder and dividers, and create a section for each planned chapter. You might even start by creating the title page of each section: Chapter 1, Introduction; Chapter 2, Literature review; Chapter 3, Method . . . and so on. Even if you don't know what will go in the chapters, your thesis now has a clear structure. As you complete a draft of each chapter you place it in the relevant section of the spiral folder, and, if necessary, remove previous versions. This method has the advantage that you can see progress (which motivates you) and you can easily refer back to other chapters to check for consistency in your arguments. If you also give a similar folder to your supervisor/s, and progressively give them a copy of each latest chapter version, it demonstrates your progress to them, and also allows them to refer back to previous chapters as they read later work. As the thesis progresses you will have tangible and motivating evidence of your progress as your spiral folder grows thicker and your chapter drafts become more complete and closer to a final version.

A critical, but often overlooked, aspect of organizing your work is ensuring that you make frequent back-ups, in hard and/or electronic versions. At some stage in their thesis most students will have a computer disaster. It may be minor, like a floppy or compact disk not working, so you can't read some of your files. It may be more serious, like a hard disk crash, affecting all files on your computer, or a stolen laptop, or even a fire in your office or home, destroying your papers and written files. If one of these happens to you, the difference between a relatively minor inconvenience and having to start your thesis again will be the extent to which you have backed up your work. Your thesis is too important not to prepare for these problems. Back up! Back up regularly, and keep the back-up files somewhere where they will be safe, even if your office burns down.

CLEAR WRITING

One of the best ways to learn about writing is to write, and to carefully re-read and edit your work. Sometimes a supervisor can seem to be a real pest in exhorting students to 'write it down'. But this is often the best advice. Start by writing your ideas down, and ask yourself whether there is a logical flow of ideas in your writing. There is something about transferring knowledge or information from its mental repository or from some conceptual domain on to a page that tends to clarify thought and build coherence. We also think a couple of basic tools are needed:

- an open mind;
- a dictionary;
- a thesaurus and/or style guide.

With these, you are in a good position to begin.

There are many books and on-line resources which can help you improve your writing, but one stands out for accessibility and readability. Professor Bill Starbuck from New York University is a notable scholar with long links with the Academy of Management. His Internet essay has the long title *Fussy Professor Starbuck's Cookbook of Handy-dandy Prescriptions for Ambitious Academic Writers, or, Why I hate Passive Verbs and love my Word Processor* (www.stern.nyu.edu/_wstarbuc/Writing/

179

Fussy.htm). Although there are many other good writing guides, this is an accessible and free resource with excellent tips on writing for academic purposes.

Starbuck begins with the good advice that your writing will determine whether people will understand what you have to say, and whether they will agree with it and remember it. This brings us to the hard reality of *who* you are writing your thesis for. If you think huge hoards of fellow scholars will be falling over themselves to borrow your thesis from a library – forget it! In reality, probably very few people will read your thesis, but many more will (you hope) read subsequent articles, chapters and/or a book derived from the thesis. Your thesis will usually be carefully read only by your supervisor and your examiners. The examiners, your most important audience, are also likely to read the thesis in a short period of time, and it is this readership and this time frame that you should keep in mind as you write.

Consider this analogy: writing a chapter is like watching the news on television. You turn on the evening news, and what do they tell you? The answer is simple: they tell you the headlines, then they tell the news in detail, then they sum up the highlights. Formal academic writing is much the same: the entire thesis, and each chapter, should contain some form of *introduction*, a *body* and a *conclusion*. The main ideas or argument should be captured within the introduction in order to focus the reader's attention on the main theme and persuade them to continue reading. The various sections comprising the body of the work should then continue a logical flow and linkages that coherently support and expand on the main idea or theme. The conclusion should summarize what has been written, and link this summary with the original argument outlined in the introduction. There should always be a coherent, logical and consistent thread woven through each section, through each chapter and throughout the thesis.

The key to achieving this consistent theme is to constantly re-read and revise your writing. Good writers usually don't just write a section, then move on to the next section. They constantly revise their work to improve the argument, the expression and the readability of each section. Some will revise continually, re-reading each sentence or paragraph after they have written it. Some will write long sections, then carefully edit the whole section. Whichever method suits you, it can be useful to ask yourself some questions as you re-read each paragraph, section or chapter: does this section follow from the preceding section? Is my argument clear? Is it grammatically correct? Do I need to expand on any points? Are there any sections which don't contribute to my argument which should be cut out? By constantly revising your work, cutting out what doesn't contribute, and improving on what you have written, you will achieve a clearer, easier to follow and more persuasive argument.

Similarly, when you come back to writing after a break of a few hours or longer, if you start where you left off it will be hard to keep a consistent theme and flow in your writing. If instead you start again by first reading from the beginning, you achieve two things. You can re-edit your earlier work, and you will find it will become much clearer and easier to follow as you constantly revise it. Second, when you start to write new material, it is much more likely to continue in a clear progression of ideas, because you have reminded yourself of the existing flow. (While this technique is effective, it also creates a danger that material at the beginning of a chapter will have been revised many, many times, and material at the end of the section will be less carefully edited. So if you are happy with the beginning material, you may at some stage begin re-reading half-way through the chapter, so the material at the end receives closer attention.)

Most thesis students use an editor to review their final draft, as discussed later in this chapter. Never assume that this final edit is a substitute for constantly re-reading and editing your work as you develop your arguments. If you do not carefully edit your own work as you write, your thesis will lack coherence and structure, and it is almost impossible for an editor to correct a poor structure (unless you pay them a lot of money, and they also have considerable expertise in the subject area). The better the work you give your supervisor and any final editor, the better the feedback they will be able to give you.

TOPIC SENTENCES

A useful device in structuring your writing is to consciously develop your use of topic sentences at the beginning of each paragraph. A topic (sometimes called a 'focus') sentence summarizes or introduces the main idea of the paragraph, and leads into the following sentences that expand on, or provide evidence to support, the topic sentence. By doing this, the use of topic sentences helps to creates a structured, unifying theme for each paragraph. Each topic sentence should logic-ally follow the paragraph above, creating a coherent flow throughout the whole chapter. The final sentence in a paragraph is often then a concluding sentence or linking sentence that leads the reader on to the next paragraph.

Using topic sentences is also a useful device for checking the relevance and structure of your writing. In each paragraph, the sentences following the topic sentence should relate to the idea introduced by the topic sentence. If your sentences don't relate to the topic sentence, the paragraph may lack structure and flow. You might then need to divide the paragraph into two paragraphs, or write more sentences to develop the link between sentences within a paragraph. Reading the topic sentences for each paragraph in sequence, without reading the other sentences, can check whether you have developed a logical flow of arguments. Because each paragraph should contain one main idea, summarized by each topic sentence, the sequence of topic sentences should summarize the argument of your chapter. If it doesn't, you may need to reorder your paragraphs, or add extra material to obtain a clearer flow.

The basic idea of topic sentences is then 'one paragraph, one idea', with the idea summarized in the first sentence of the paragraph. While this rule is never absolute, and it is possible to find many examples of good writing where there is more than one idea per paragraph, the 'one paragraph, one idea' rule is a very good starting point. It will tend to make your work more readable, and readability is important in conveying to examiners the complex ideas that your thesis will contain. Similarly, in order to increase readability it is a good idea to aim to have only one idea in each sentence. Long, complex sentences containing complex or multiple ideas can break the flow of good writing, and make it harder for the reader to follow your ideas. Breaking complex sentences into two shorter, clearer sentences can avoid this problem, and allow you to make your different points more clearly.

Finally, analysing the length of your topic sentences and of your paragraphs can help to review whether your writing lacks flow, or is too superficial or too dense. You should generally avoid one or two-line paragraphs, or paragraphs that

Box 12.1
TWO SENTENCES BETTER THAN ONE

Example

Product choice has increased from xx models available in 1980 to xx models available in 2003, whilst the market share amongst the domestic producers has reduced as imports have risen.

Suggestion

Product choice has increased from xx models available in 1980 to xx models available in 2003, primarily driven by an increase in imported models. As a consequence, the market share of the domestic producers has decreased sharply.

Analysis

The first example contains several ideas, and sentences like this are generally harder to follow. The suggested sentences address the two issues separately, allowing the two ideas (increasing product choice and decreased domestic market share) to be addressed more clearly. The link between the two ideas is established by the linking phrase 'as a consequence', indicating the writer's suggestion that falling domestic market share is a consequence of increased imports.

contain only a single sentence. Any one or two-line paragraph probably lacks suffi-cient depth: whatever the main thought of the paragraph, it is probably worth expanding. In contrast, if a paragraph takes two-thirds of a page or more, it will not only be dense and difficult to read, but it probably contains several main ideas. The paragraph should be divided into two or more shorter paragraphs, each covering one main idea and summarized by a topic sentence.

GUIDELINES FOR IMPROVING YOUR WRITING

One of the best ways to improve your writing is to learn from good writers. So, read, read and read! Always approach what you are reading with a critical mind, asking yourself, 'What makes this easy/hard to read?' 'Has the author linked their claim to any evidence?' and so on. Reading and thinking critically about what you read is an important part of developing the skills necessary to write a good thesis. If your supervisor or a reviewer criticizes your writing, try and work out what your main problems are. Is it lack of a clear flow? Lack of adequate cita-tion? Inappropriate style? Criticism of your writing, while painful to receive, can be very valuable. Successful academics have generally improved their writing by the often painful process of having journal articles rejected, and by learning how to edit and redraft work in response to criticism.

Another tip is to learn scholarly detachment in reading and writing. Remember, you are a dispassionate investigator. It is the ability to detach your-self from emotion in what you read and write that brings balance, breadth and objectivity to your research. There is occasional reference to the so-called '95 per cent syndrome' in writing (Evans 1995). This means that sometimes you can be so familiar with your area of research and your data that there can be a temptation to leave out crucial background or contextual information because 'it's obvious' or 'everyone knows that'. You have left out that critical '5 per cent'. Remember *who* you are writing for – the examiners. Your examiners may have been chosen because they are experts in one area of your work, but they may not share your deep understanding of other areas. You should ensure that you provide sufficient material and coverage to justify your argument, your methods and your conclusions. Even if your reviewers are experts in the area, providing adequate background and discussion indicates that you have been thorough in your coverage.

In contrast, students often suffer from a tendency to put too much material into the thesis. If a sentence or a paragraph doesn't contribute to your argument in some way (for example, by explaining, supporting or extending the argument) you should think about cutting the superfluous material, or perhaps consigning it to an appendix. Too much material is likely to distract the examiners from your core argument, and perhaps irritate them with your verbosity. Finding the balance between comprehensiveness and information overload is not easy. While simplification in writing is a virtue, oversimplification is not. Again, it comes down to balance, and your supervisor is a good resource to advise you on what approach is appropriate. Choosing what to leave in and what to take out is one of the challenges of good writing, but the essential test of every section is the question you should ask yourself: 'Does this contribute to my argument?'

Writing style is often context-specific. If a thesis involves a quantitative methodology, it is usual to find writing that reflects that paradigm, emphasizing statistical accuracy and formal expression, such as 'it was found . . .' or 'the data suggest . . .'. For a more qualitative or phenomenological methodology, writing often reflects a less formal style, with greater use of quotations from subjects or from other sources. You should investigate the language and style used in other theses, articles and research projects in your area, and ask your supervisor to give you feedback on your style of writing.

Whatever your thesis area, the thesis should be written in an appropriately formal style. This generally means avoiding slang expressions, contractions and jargon. While the style should be formal and the arguments are likely to be complex, this doesn't mean that the thesis should be verbose or hard to read. A complex argument means that you need to pay more attention to a clear structure and flow, to maintain the interest of the reader. It is worth discussing with your supervisor what degree of detail and (abbreviated) jargon is appropriate for the different chapters of the thesis. Some candidates fall into the trap of writing very complex text, trying to convey everything they know, in order to persuade the examiners that they have done a lot of work. This can result in a dense and difficult-to-read thesis, filled with long paragraphs and lengthy sentences, with the result that the reader loses track of the argument. This sort of verbose text is likely to annoy a reader and may even cause them to disagree with your argument. Most research theses involve analysis of complex data and/or issues, drawing on a wide variety of previous research. This naturally produces complexity in both your argument and your analysis. But don't confuse complex arguments with verbosity. Writing a chapter should be done in such a way that it can be easily followed and understood. But while simplification in writing is a virtue, over-simplification is not. Again, it comes down to balance – and your supervisor is a good resource to advise you on whether you are striking an appropriate balance.

HEADINGS

An excellent way to develop and review the structure of your thesis is by the use of headings. Headings signal to the reader the structure and flow of your argument, and a sequence of key ideas. Each heading is a compressed form of the topic sentence, signalling to the reader the content of the sentence and paragraph. The sequence of headings, in turn, establishes the development of the argument throughout the thesis. There are many levels of headings, and there is no hard-and-fast rule for which you should use, but consistency is expected. Generally chapter titles will be 'Heading 1' (perhaps upper-case, bold and centred), the main ideas of each chapter will be 'Heading 2' (perhaps title case, bold and left-aligned) and sub-headings will be 'Heading 3' (perhaps italic and left-aligned). The greatest prominence is given to the most important headings, using combinations of capital letters (upper case), centring and bold type.

When you are working on a chapter of perhaps 10,000 words, it can become difficult to check whether there is an overall consistent flow in what you are writing. For example, material on page 19 might more logically follow material on page 3, but unless you are continually re-reading the whole document (and

Box 12.2
STRATEGIES FOR CLEAR WRITING

- *Stay focused on the point.* It is surprising how often a sentence or paragraph can wander apparently aimlessly. Ask yourself, 'What is this sentence/paragraph about?' and 'What is this trying to say?' Be critical, very critical, of what you write, because your examiners will be!

- *Write in whole sentences* (*except for headings*). Each sentence should be grammatically correct, and justifiable. Perhaps owing to lack of careful editing, many students write much worse than they speak. A good test of whether a sentence is complete and justified is to ask yourself, 'Could I say this to an audience, in a formal lecture?' Statements that are incomplete, emotional or unable to be supported, are usually not suitable for a formal lecture. Similarly, they are unlikely to be appropriate in your thesis.

- *Use linking sentences and paragraphs.* Linking sentences are useful because they build a bridge to the next paragraph and therefore help with coherence and flow. Linking paragraphs are also useful at the end of a chapter, usually after a summary paragraph, inviting the reader to take what has been learned and proceed to the next chapter. Linking sentences such as 'The preceding analysis has demonstrated . . .' can summarize your argument and build a bridge to the next section or chapter.

- *Avoid double negatives.* Not writing sentences with double negatives avoids detracting from the flow of an argument. While the preceding sentence is true, the accumulation of negatives makes the sentence difficult to follow. Positive statements such as 'Avoiding double negatives makes it easier to follow the flow of an argument' are much easier for a reader to understand.

- *Be wary of questions.* Rhetorical questions are often used in writing, but are much less common in theses, where an argument should be clearly stated, not hinted at by means of rhetorical questions. Sometimes, for stylistic purposes, you might choose to pose a question to engage the reader's interest. However, examiners will usually expect you to give your own best answer to your question rather than leave it hanging for them to answer.

- *Be wary of prescriptive language.* This book is written in prescriptive language ('you should'), but your thesis should not be. Junior research students are often tempted to make sweeping judgements ('managers should . . .', 'good researchers must . . .'). Your thesis should include more prudent language such as 'the evidence supports . . .' or 'such a view reinforces . . .' or 'the divergent theories suggest . . .'. Making broad statements only invites a critical examiner to think of occasions when your statement is not true, and then, in consequence, reject an argument that may be true in *most* cases but which, like most arguments, is not true in *all* cases.

- *Use gender-neutral, dispassionate language.* Avoid terms such as 'he' unless you are talking about a specific person. Such terms can usually easily be replaced with gender-neutral language, e.g. 'the manager . . .', 'the researcher . . .'. Similarly, demeaning and dismissive language should always be avoided. For example, be careful of criticizing previous researchers in a dismissive or personal way. If your writing appears to be sexist or arrogant, you may alienate your examiner. Worst of all, your examiner may be a friend of or even the author whose work you criticize, and they are unlikely to look sympathetically on criticism which does not appear to be well founded and objective. This does not mean you should avoid pointing out gaps in previous literature, or failings of previous studies. However, if you suggest that research was poorly done or criticize the author, rather than the work, you are likely to be perceived as arrogant. This can result in an examiner reading your work with a much more critical approach.

- *Always use the spell-check and grammar-check functions.* Spelling and grammar checks are not a substitute for careful editing, but will rapidly identify many problems in your writing. Your instinctive last action before you print any document to give to your supervisor should always be a spell check. Failure to detect and remove misspelt words that would be detected by a spell checker can suggest to your supervisor or examiner that your work is sloppy and poorly done. This is not the impression you want to give!

concentrating carefully) you might miss an overlap or lack of flow. An excellent way to check the flow of a chapter is by using your headings and a very useful and underused feature of word-processing packages called (in Microsoft Word) 'Outline view'. Other word-processing packages are likely to have a similar feature, perhaps with a different name. Outline view is invaluable when you are working on large documents with multiple headings. By designating each of your headings as the appropriate style (Heading 1, 2, etc.) you can view the overall document in any format you want. You can view only the list of first and second headings, to see that there is a logical flow of headings and, as a consequence, hopefully a logical flow of content. You can view all headings, to see that all third-level headings logically follow their second-order headings, and so on. If you decide to move material from page 19 to page 3, you can do so much more easily than in the 'Normal view' format, and then check whether the new position offers a more logical flow of ideas. Take some time to master Outline view, and you are likely to be surprised at the benefits it offers when working with a large document.

COMMON PROBLEMS TO AVOID

Read the following example (First draft) and try to identify any problems in the writing.

First draft

Although loyal consumers are typically satisfied, satisfaction does not always translate into loyalty (Oliver 1999). Previous research has shown that even if customers are satisfied with their current service providers, they may switch to another provider. Service industries present a more difficult setting for understanding customer disloyalty as opposed to manufactured goods industries (Mittal 1998). This study investigates disloyalty in a service industry, hotel chains.

The draft is grammatically correct, without spelling mistakes. Spelling, grammar checks and most professional editors won't detect any errors that must be corrected. However, it is poorly written, revealing a number of common errors in bad academic writing:

- *Oversimplification*. Oliver has been quoted out of context. Few things are 'always true' and to state that satisfaction does not 'always' result in loyalty is a very weak argument. Is a satisfied customer loyal ninety-nine times out of 100? Or ten times out of 100?
- *Inadequate citation*. When previous research is mentioned or implied a citation must always be given.

187

- *More analysis is needed.* Merely repeating statements from previous research (e.g. Mittal's conclusion) rarely adds to the analysis or integration of the argument.
- *Lack of flow.* The connection between the first and second sentences isn't clear.
- *An uncommon, or 'jargon', word,* 'disloyalty', has been introduced without explanation or definition. In addition, the change from discussing 'loyal' customers to 'disloyalty' is likely to confuse the reader. If an unusual word is introduced, it is often a good idea to ensure that the reader knows what you are talking about.

Suggested second draft

Satisfaction has been shown to be a strong and significant predictor of repurchase. However, previous research has shown that even if customers are satisfied with their current service provider, they may still switch to another provider (Oliver 1999). The reasons underlying this 'disloyalty' among satisfied customers are not well understood. Moreover, there are particular problems researching customer choice in service industries, since the basis of consumer choice and continued patronage is less obvious in service firms, compared with manufactured goods industries (Mittal 1998). As a result, this research extends previous work by investigating customer switching, or 'disloyalty', in service industries, analysing the reasons underlying this disloyalty.

The later draft may not be perfect, but it now conveys more information in a clearer, easier-to-read fashion. It uses linking words, 'however,' and 'moreover', to convey a contrast and continuation of ideas. It uses citations to justify a statement, 'since', rather than merely summarizing the work of others. It signals and clarifies the unusual word 'disloyalty' by the use of inverted commas, and by linking it with an understood idea (customer switching). Lastly, it concludes with a sentence that clearly signals the claimed contribution of the research, by showing how it builds on previous gaps in the literature. Lastly, the last sentence provides a link to the next section, paragraph or chapter, which is likely to be a discussion of exactly how the research builds on previous work.

EDITING AND FORMATTING

The discussion above has emphasized the importance of constantly editing and re-editing your work. Features of Microsoft Word which can be particularly useful in formatting a thesis, and which many people are unaware of, are summarized in Table 12.1. Most of these features will also be available in other word processing packages.

188

Table 12.1 *Microsoft Word features to simplify formatting your thesis*

MS Word command	Effect
Insert caption	Automatic numbering and renumbering of figures or tables
Insert cross-reference	Automatic numbering and renumbering of references to figures, tables or page numbers
View outline	Allows viewing a document at different levels of headings or text, and easy movement of large amounts of text
Insert table of contents/figures	If styles are used for headings, allows automatic construction of a table of contents
Keep with next	Ensures headings are not followed by a page break
Keep lines together	Ensures tables are not split by a page break

Your editing should happen both on-screen and off. On-screen editing should include presentation. (Has it been spell-checked? Have I searched for errors that may irritate readers, such as spaces before full stops? Are there formatting problems, such as headings at the end of a page? Tables which have been split by a page break?) Extensive on-screen editing should, of course, also constantly revise the structure and expression. Finally, you should read a hard copy of your thesis from start to finish, rechecking your structure, arguments and looking for grammatical problems. (Some people can edit successfully on screen. However, most people are more accurate in editing a printed copy, and it is the printed copy that your examiners will read, so we recommend using a hard copy for final editing.)

Your last draft should ideally be fully edited by someone else who is unconnected with the research, and who can read the thesis from start to finish, concentrating on spelling, grammar, formatting, expression and presentation. This stage is important for all students in obtaining a final meticulous check, but particularly important if English is not your first language. This final 'editor' may be a friend or family member, or even a professional editor, if you can afford to pay them. It should be a native English-speaker if possible, and should certainly be someone who writes well and who is capable of careful attention to detail.

Most universities have a style guide detailing formatting and presentation requirements for theses (spacing, required sections, maximum length, etc.) which you will need to follow. Getting a copy of this early, and writing all your chapter drafts in the approved style, can save a lot of time later. If you ask your supervisor or other students, you may be able to obtain an electronic file formatted in the required style. If your university has no particular rules for formatting and presentation, then your professional judgement and the rule of consistency should be employed. Read other dissertations in your library and journal articles in order

189

Box 12.3
FORMATTING FIGURES AND TABLES

Most dissertations include figures and tables. The way these are used and positioned can be influenced by the type of thesis and by the methodology. But there are a few general guidelines for figure and table use which help to improve the readability of a thesis:

- Always try to position figures and tables close to the relevant discussion in the text.

- Every figure or table should be preceded by a number and a title/caption which summarizes the point of the figure/table (e.g. 'Figure 13. Summary of hypothesis results'. (Hint: if you are using Microsoft Word, use 'Insert caption' to number and/or renumber any figures and tables automatically.)

- A reference should always be made to any figure or table (e.g. 'See Figure 13 for a summary of the results of hypothesis testing'). It can be very irritating for a reader to come across a figure without any text to explain, even briefly, what it illustrates and why you have included it. (Hint: if you have numbered your captions using the method above, you can update your references automatically by using 'Insert cross-reference'.)

- Avoid too much colouring or complex drawing. Some candidates compensate for lack of confidence in their argument with elaborate coloured figures using arrows and boxes and so forth. Simplicity is the key to a good image and the thesis is not a colouring-in exercise. Colour or shading can highlight and show distinct parts of a diagram, but should not dominate a figure.

to ascertain what general standards apply in your discipline and what structure of headings best helps the clarity of the text. Watch for good and bad examples of the use of bold and italic type, font sizes, and so on.

There are many possible layouts for a final thesis, though most will include a title page, an abstract, acknowledgements, a contents list, a list of tables and/or figures, followed by five to eight chapters, finishing with appendices and references. Any university library will contain copies of previous theses that you can usually look at, but not borrow. Examining the format of several theses in areas similar to yours is a good way to get an idea of what is expected.

190

REFERENCING

Referencing does two things. First, it acknowledges the source of specific material or arguments. Second, it assists the reader to locate the actual source of that material. Very few people are original thinkers. We may like to think so, but we are not. But one of the human traits we all share is our ability to mimic. We read other people's phrases, ideas and conceptual frameworks and build our own ideas and concepts into a woven whole. While sometimes we cannot remember where we heard something or read something, as researchers we need – as best as humanly possible – to provide an 'audit trail' of what we have used to help conceptualize ideas or mount an argument. Plagiarism, or failure to reference material adequately, is one of the most serious academic offences. If an examiner believes that you have taken material from another source without appropriate referencing, it can result in them recommending the failure of your thesis. Correct referencing thus serves to show the breadth of your research, and also protects you from the risk of accusations of plagiarism.

There are two main methods of referencing. The first, more usual in academic circles, is the author-based system. In this approach, a citation includes the author's surname and the year of publication, and full reference details are given in an alphabetical reference list at the end. The second is a number-based system, usually seen in footnoting or endnoting. In this system, citations are indicated by a number, with the source of the material given in a footnote at the bottom of the page or by endnotes at the end of the chapter, where full citation details are recorded in a list in the order of references.

Within each referencing system, different universities and/or departments may request specific styles of references. There are many different methods of referencing, usually marked by minor differences in order, in bold or italic font, commas, full stops and the use of 'and' or '&'. Different referencing methods are known by the organization that specifies them. For example, the Chicago Review and APA (American Psychological Association) methods reference the same book in slightly different ways (Box 12.4).

If you are submitting your work to a journal, it is vital to check which style the journal wants, and format your references that way. Most universities are less specific, and do not require a specific style for thesis submission, so unless your university or department requires a particular style, you should pick a style that is used in one of the main journals in your field of study, and use it consistently.

The tedious task of checking that all references are included in the reference list, and that nothing is included in the reference list which is not cited in the thesis, can be made much easier by the use of referencing software such as Endnote. It is worth acquiring and mastering such software early in your thesis, because its use is likely to save considerable time later. If you submit your work to journals or conferences which require different referencing styles, referencing

Box 12.4
TWO REFERENCING STYLES

Chicago Review

Rust, Roland T, Valarie A Zeithaml, and Katherine N Lemon. *Driving Customer Equity: How Customer Lifetime Value is Reshaping Corporate Strategy*. New York: Free Press, 2000.

American Psychological Association

Rust, R.T., Zeithaml, V.A., & Lemon, K.N. (2000). *Driving customer equity: how customer lifetime value is reshaping corporate strategy*. New York: Free Press.

software can also automate the laborious process of changing the formatting of your references from one style to another.

As a general rule, always include a page reference in the in-text citation when particular details are being referred to, such as a specific phrase, quotation or a particularly important point in your argument. More general ideas should be cited with the author or authors and year of publication. Also, when you have adapted terminology or a schema or figure to your thesis, include the original source and state that it is adapted. Finally, at postgraduate level, it is generally expected that the referencing will be of the primary sources. If a particular scholar or historical source is worth citing, then you should be citing the actual work or original material (if possible) rather than some secondary source, where another writer has summarized or paraphrased the work. This adds greater quality to your writing and avoids the potential problem of the secondary source incorrectly interpreting the primary source. This reinforces the expectation in postgraduate study that the standard of referencing should be very high, and the so-called 'audit trail' clear enough for the reader to identify the source and specific location of any material used.

SUMMARY

This chapter has outlined a range of guidelines to help you develop a well written, well structured thesis. The essential lesson is that you can improve your own writing by constantly reading good writing, but that most people achieve good writing only by substantial editing and multiple revisions. Read from good writers, and think about what makes their work easy to read. If you find something you

Box 12.5
CHECKLIST: IS ALL IN ORDER?

Before you submit the final version of your thesis, you should check:

- Has the last version of the thesis been spell-checked? ☐
- Has the last version of the thesis been grammar-checked? ☐
- Has the final version been checked for minor but annoying errors such as a space followed by a comma or full stop? (Hint: use 'Search/replace' to find and replace these.) ☐
- Has the whole thesis been previewed on screen, one page view at a time, to search for and correct: headings which are followed by a page break; tables split by a page break; large amounts of avoidable white space and/or too little white space (e.g. paragraphs which take up a whole page)? ☐
- Is the thesis formatted to university requirements (spacing, margins, etc.)? ☐
- Have all references been checked to ensure that they are all included in the reference list? ☐
- Has the reference list been checked to ensure that it does not contain references that are not referred to in the thesis? ☐
- Is the reference list complete (e.g. journal volume, issue and page numbers)? ☐
- Are figures, tables and cross-references correct? (Hint: if using Microsoft Word, use 'Insert caption' and/or 'cross-reference' to automatically number and renumber these.) ☐
- Have you carefully edited the thesis, by reading it through from start to finish? ☐
- Has someone else read through the thesis, checking for errors and inconsistencies? ☐
- Have you thanked your supervisor, and anyone else appropriate, in your thesis acknowledgements? (By the time they get to the submission stage, many students are so fed up with their supervisor, for one reason or another, that there can be a temptation not to thank them in print. Trust us, it's not worth upsetting your supervisor over this, even if you don't think that they deserve to be thanked. Most supervisors will look for it, and won't take it kindly if you haven't said something nice about them in the dedication. You still need your supervisor on side, at least until you have formally passed. Do it.) ☐

read hard to read, ask yourself why, and how it could be improved so you don't make the same mistake. Most important, however, is to read and re-read your own work so that you constantly improve it. Your supervisor is also a good source to give you feedback on your writing style, and to advise whether your style of language suits the research area in which you are working. And lastly, don't be too defensive about your writing. Even the best writers in every field have their work criticized, and it is by listening to, and responding to, criticism that you have the best opportunity to improve your writing.

REFERENCES AND FURTHER READING

Dunleavy, P. (2003). *Authoring a Ph.D.* Basingstoke: Palgrave Macmillan.

Evans, D. (1995). *How to Write a Better Thesis or Report.* Melbourne: Melbourne University Press.

Mittal, V., Ross, W.T.J. and Baldasare, P.M. (1998) 'The asymmetric impact of negative and positive attribute-level performance on overall satisfaction and repurchase intentions', *Journal of Marketing* 62 (1), 33–48.

Oliver, R.L. and Burke, R.R. (1999) 'Expectation processes in satisfaction formation: a field study' *Journal of Service Research*, 1 (3), 196–214.

Starbuck, W. *Fussy Professor Starbuck's Cookbook of Handy-dandy Prescriptions for Ambitious Academic Writers, or, Why I hate Passive Verbs and love my Word Processor*, www.stern.nyu.edu/~wstarbuc/Writing/Fussy.htm. Accessed August 2003.

Chapter 13

Common problems and potential solutions

SUZAN BURTON AND PETER STEANE

> Progress has not followed a straight ascending line, but a spiral with rhythms of progress and retrogression, of evolution and dissolution.
>
> (Johann Wolfgang von Goethe)

This chapter identifies problems that students commonly face during a research degree, and discusses some potential solutions. The types of problems that arise during a thesis vary. They range from disagreement between supervisor and student over matters of feedback, shifting expectations and timelines, to matters that relate to the student's own self-esteem, motivation and personal circumstances. The chapter is structured to cover a broad range of these problems, posed as typical student questions, followed by general comments and specific advice. The chapter concludes with advice on how to proceed if your relationship with your supervisor breaks down to the extent that you want to change supervisors. We hope that none of these problems will happen to you, but if they do, the chapter offers suggestions and practical advice.

COMMON PROBLEMS IN THE RELATIONSHIP

While many supervisor/student relationships proceed to a successful thesis completion, problems can occur in any relationship, especially given the financial, emotional and intellectual stresses that exist for most research students. We present below a range of dilemmas that research candidates may find themselves in, and some suggested resolutions.

'My supervisor and I don't agree about the topic/methodology/ content of the thesis/publication order. What can I do?'

Unfortunately, problems can easily arise between supervisor and student, and most students won't get through a thesis without at least a minor disagreement with their supervisor. It may or may not make you feel any better to hear that supervisors can get almost as frustrated with some students as students do with their supervisors. Most minor problems can be worked out by discussion, so that is usually a good first option. You may not always agree with the suggestions or criticisms of your supervisor. However, you have presumably chosen them because they have some expertise, and they may be right, so you should consider their comments very carefully. But they could also be wrong, and their advice or criticisms may be misguided. The further you are into your thesis, the more you should know about the literature in your area and the methodology relevant to your thesis. By the end of your thesis you should generally know as much as, or more than, your supervisor about the specific content area of your thesis. If your disagreement is a matter of content, and after considering their argument, you don't think they are right, you should try to make a case, supported by prior research or other authoritative sources, to convince your supervisor. (See also Chapter 15, 'Responding to criticism'.) Challenges from a supervisor, however, should always be looked on as a valuable guide. If your supervisor has concerns about what you are doing (rightly or wrongly), it is possible that your thesis examiners will also have the same problem. By anticipating and responding to this perceived problem in your thesis, you can protect yourself from later (and more problematic) concerns on the part of examiners.

If the dispute is serious, and you can't resolve it, it is often a good idea to discuss the matter with the academic responsible for your programme (for example, the director of the thesis programme, or the director of research). If you have other academics on your thesis committee, or if you have a good relationship with another academic, you might want to gauge their opinion. Remember, however, that it is generally a good idea to try and frame the problem as a research problem rather than as a personality problem – 'He/she doesn't like me . . .'. Whatever the outcome of the dispute, you will have little to gain, and a lot to lose, by antagonizing your supervisor.

If a serious dispute can't be resolved, you have several options:

- You can drop out, which isn't a good idea if you have invested a considerable amount of time, energy and money, and want to get your degree.
- You may be able to change supervisors. This is a more realistic option early in your thesis, compared with when you are close to completion, but changing supervisors should never be undertaken lightly. If you are thinking about changing supervisors, you should always talk to, and try to involve, a senior academic, such as the director of the thesis programme, who may be able to help you resolve the problem or, if it can't be resolved, can help you to find another supervisor. If you choose to change, you should try to make it an amicable and mutually agreeable arrangement. This presents yourself to other potential supervisors as a

candidate who is clear about what you want, but also capable of discussing matters openly, and ultimately one who is able to address and resolve difficult dilemmas in the research journey. At the end of this chapter we discuss issues involved in changing supervisors in greater detail.

● You can choose to submit your thesis without your supervisor's agreement. This is a high-risk strategy, because a supervisor's support and backing are often crucial at the examination stage, giving you extra weight if you need to address criticisms by examiners. As a consequence, this step should be considered a last option, and only after discussion with senior academics.

Ultimately, if all three options aren't possible, or are unattractive, you may need to consider complying with whatever your supervisor advises, and trust their judgement.

'I don't think I'm up to a thesis. I think my supervisor thinks I'm stupid, and I'm thinking of dropping out . . .'

Most students go through a stage at some point in their thesis where they become depressed at the apparent lack of progress, and wonder whether it is worth continuing. Full-time students, who have generally invested more time and money in choosing full-time study, are particularly likely to become depressed when their thesis isn't progressing, and part-time students often get frustrated with having to balance all the other elements of life: work, study and social demands. Sometimes the supervisor will seem unsupportive under these circumstances, which can be upsetting for the student. However, the supervisor's lack of apparent sympathy will sometimes result from the supervisor being bemused at the candidate's naivety, for example in expecting the whole thesis to move smoothly along without distractions or problems.

Once you have been selected into a research programme, you should always assume that you have the ability to complete a thesis, if you are prepared to put in the work. In the words of one supervisor, 'At this level [that is, once you have been selected] ability makes no difference. It's energy, and what people put into it!' Look around at the other students on your programme. You should assume that you are as competent as them, and as likely to succeed, until proven otherwise. After all, senior academics, who know more about the programme than you, selected you because they thought you could complete a research degree!

The best way to get over depression about lack of progress is to work on your thesis (read Chapter 7 on motivation), and keep working. If you keep working, there may be slow patches and wasted work, but you will slowly, or quickly, make progress, which will, at some stage, re-energize you. It is always worth remembering in research that the journey you start may not be the journey you finish. In almost every thesis there will be periods where the student finds the need to review and redo small or large parts of the work, because things have not proceeded as expected or hoped. Problems like these are depressing, but they are an integral part of good research.

However, if you continue to have serious doubts about your thesis, and/or your ability to complete it, you should probably talk to someone whose opinion, and discretion, you trust. There are two ways to approach this. Some supervisors take on a supportive role as well as an academic role with their students, so if your supervisor is like that, you might make an appointment to see them and explain your doubts, and seek some advice. But other supervisors do not see their role as counselling you or supporting you in times of doubt, and may consider an admission that you are having serious doubts about your thesis to be a sign of lack of ability. If you think your supervisor is like that, it is probably unwise to share self-doubts, in case they lose confidence in you and perhaps unconsciously withdraw some of their effort in guiding you. Instead, you might choose to talk to a student counsellor, or to another student or person whose opinion you trust.

'I have two supervisors and they disagree about what I should do. I've tried to sort it out, but they still disagree'

The first thing to note about this situation is that it may be a healthy indication of the academic debate in the area you are studying. So consider the opportunity it offers you to represent divergent views in your review of the literature and in your analysis. However, it may also be that this disagreement is problematic, and you may wish to resolve the matter. The solution depends first on the stage of your thesis. If the disagreement is about methodology, your supervisors' opinions are likely to reflect some disagreement in how to approach the research area. Early disagreement between supervisors may be an indication of similar views among potential examiners, so your task becomes one of ensuring your thesis accommodates such divergence. When in doubt, always go to the litera-ture to see what other researchers have done. A clear argument based on previous research may convince one or both of your supervisors. If the issue still can't be resolved, and it is significant enough, you may need to go with the opinion of one supervisor, even if it means not continuing with the other supervisor.

If the difference between supervisors concerns your interpretation of results, and the supervisors are arguing for different interpretations, this is again likely to reflect disagreement in the field, which may be shared by your examiners. Your final version of the thesis might then address both points of view, and provide an argument as to why you prefer one interpretation, based on previous research and your own results.

Supervisors will often disagree about the amount of work that is necessary before submission. For example, one supervisor might say that you are ready to submit, and the other argues that you need to do more work. Assuming that this supervisor is making a reasonable argument as to what is necessary, it should usually be taken as good advice. If your supervisor wants more work, it is highly likely that examiners will want more as well. One of the advantages of co-supervision is that you sometimes get more feedback. The down side is that, as a result, you sometimes need to do more work, but should end up with a better thesis as a result.

In the last analysis, it's *your* thesis. In many disciplines a supervisor takes only an advisory role, so crucial decisions on style and what to include and how to interpret results are ultimately your responsibility. It's very common to surpass your supervisor in specific knowledge of your topic. You should then be in a good position to evaluate the advice of your supervisor/s, and decide what action is appropriate.

'My supervisor won't give me enough feedback. What can I do?'

Supervisors vary enormously in the amount of help and feedback they give their students. Some provide constant suggestions and criticisms on multiple early versions of chapters. Others expect to read complete drafts (or even the whole thesis) without having to input into drafts along the way. The second can be ideal if you are an experienced researcher, with good knowledge in your thesis area, but it can also be frustrating if you want more feedback and guidance.

Students can become very frustrated when they and their supervisor have different ideas about the amount of feedback that is appropriate. Discussing this issue with your supervisor early on in the relationship can be useful, so you can identify their expectations. Supervisors can also get very frustrated at being asked to read and re-read chapters which are at an early stage, and/or when a student does not appear to appreciate the time and effort that usually go into giving feedback.

If you find that your supervisor expects to give you less feedback than you would like, it can be helpful to signal the areas where you particularly want feed-back. For example, you might tell them that you are happy with your literature review and results, but you would like them to carefully read your methodology and/or discussion, to give you feedback on those areas. Most supervisors will be much more willing to give you feedback if you direct their attention to the most important areas, and if you respond to previous feedback positively, for example:

> Thank you for your feedback on the discussion section. It was very helpful, and I have made the changes that you suggested, as well as others that I decided made the argument clearer. I think it reads much better as a result. I am still having problems with my discussion of the results of Hypothesis 10 (see pages

xx to xx). I'm not sure if the argument will be clear to the reader/examiner. Could you please have a look at the attached chapter and give me your opinion?

This covering note for a revision indicates to a supervisor that you: (1) have reacted to their suggestions; (2) are also trying to improve the thesis yourself, without just reacting to their suggestions, and (3) focuses their attention on the area where you really want help.

If all else fails, and you still find it difficult to get specific and useful feedback from your supervisor, try and work on something that is directly useful for them. For example, one way to focus the interest of an academic supervisor is to suggest working with them on joint publications based on your thesis work to date. Directing your work to publication has the added benefit of feedback from external journal reviewers, which may give you some indication of how your thesis will be viewed by academics in the field from whom your examiners will be chosen.

'I hand work in to my supervisor and I get the pages back covered with comments. Things which were OK in the previous draft now need changing, and I always have to do one more thing. What can I do?'

This could be considered a problem of too much feedback, and can be very frustrating for a student. However, you should first consider whether it really is a problem. Talk to students with other supervisors, and you may find that they think that you are lucky to get as much feedback as you do. A supervisor who spends so much time to give you feedback is likely to result in a higher-quality thesis, and you are also more likely to pass without problems if your supervisor has given you large amounts of detailed feedback along the way.

It is also very common for a supervisor to comment negatively on something that they did not pick up in a previous draft. No editor will pick everything up the first time, and it may be that, as one section of your work improves, the supervisor will pay more attention to other sections, and as a result criticize work that they had not attended to before.

Sometimes the student can get frustrated because the supervisor appears to keep changing their mind. At one meeting they suggest one method of analysis and at the next meeting, another. If this happens repeatedly, and you can't understand the reason for the change, and the advice seems to be contradictory, you should discuss it with them, adducing evidence (tactfully!) of what has been discussed at previous meetings. It may be that the supervisor's views have changed, and they can explain the apparent change of mind. It may also be that they haven't fully understood your research approach, or it could mean that you have not been clear in defining your research questions. Identifying and discussing apparently contradictory views is a key part of academic debate, and a normal part of developing expertise and ultimately settling on one view. But it takes time. In the supervisor/ student relationship, such disagreements can usually be resolved with open, honest and tactful discussion, with the end result of a clear way forward.

'I'm struggling to exist financially'

Money problems are an unfortunate, but common, feature of research student life, and rarely have simple solutions. However, if financial struggles are impacting seriously on your progress, you should talk to your supervisor, who can sometimes advise what resources the university may be able to provide. Your supervisor may also be in a position to recommend you for a part-time position as a research assistant or for tutoring work within your faculty or the university. At the very least, your supervisor will become aware of any impact of financial difficulties on your progress.

It's also worth investigating any sources of financial support that are available from the university, from scholarships, grants, student loans or part-time work. As a last resort, if you aren't making any progress on your thesis, it may be worth considering suspending your enrolment for a short time to allow you to earn money, then re-enrolling when you can commit more time. However, suspending enrolment to allow full-time work may not be possible if you are studying in another country with a student visa. If this applies to you, check with the international office of the university at which you are studying to find out what options are available.

'I hate my thesis. It's not going anywhere, and I just can't make myself work on it'

Most students suffer from what might be called 'researcher's block' at some time during their thesis, where they seem to be making little progress, and have problems making themselves work on it. Though slumps like this are often temporary, the longer you avoid working on your thesis the harder it is to start again, so achieving some limited progress during periods of researcher's block can be important. Slumps are a good time to do tasks which are time-consuming but not particularly difficult, such as mastering useful software (for example, referencing software like Endnote), or reformatting your thesis to meet university requirements. Other activities include tidying your office, organizing your references, ordering your filing system and doing another library search for relevant references. The important thing is to do *something*. Doing something productive can break a cycle of lack of progress and despair, and the feeling of having achieved something useful can often be sufficiently motivating that you can recommence more critical activity: the path to successful completion of a thesis is momentum.

201

Many people find that physical exercise is a very effective way to address the feeling of despair that can result from apparent lack of progress. If you are like that, it can be worth taking time off for exercise, as long as the exercise itself doesn't become an excuse not to work on the thesis. A weekend or a week away can sometimes be useful to revitalize you if you have been working hard, but if you take days off when you are despairing over your thesis, it often does nothing for the underlying problem. For further discussion of how to maintain and regain motivation, see Chapter 7, 'The motivational journey'.

'I'm taking too long. I'm never going to finish!'

This is a common complaint. You should first think seriously about why you are taking more time than you want to finish the thesis. Sometimes extra time is well spent: if you are taking longer because you are gaining valuable experience, in teaching, consulting and/or publications that will help you to get the job you want when you complete, then it is definitely worth the extra time. Don't get jealous of people who finish in 'record time', especially if they are young. Someone young who finishes a doctorate in record time often doesn't have sufficient work or publication experience to get the first-rate job that they want. For these people, taking an extra year or so to complete can be well worth while if at the same time they are getting experience that will help them to get an excellent first job.

If your thesis appears to be taking longer than you want, however, and you aren't taking the extra time in acquiring useful experience, you may need to think very carefully about why you haven't finished. (We'll assume that you are working on your thesis, but if that is not the case, read Chapter 7, on motivation, and start working!) One question to ask yourself if your thesis is taking too long is whether you are being too ambitious and trying to do too much. Remember: 'A good thesis is a done thesis, but a better thesis is a passed thesis.' Perhaps you need to talk to your supervisor about the quickest route to completion. Lots of students (and supervisors) have a grand plan for a magnificent, prize-winning thesis, and as a result, take longer than necessary to complete the thesis (and still don't win a prize). If you have a complete draft of the thesis, this may be the time to sit down with your supervisor and discuss whether you can tidy the thesis up, and hand it in. Maybe it's not as good as you could get it with more time, but it may be good enough for the examiners. Most often in cases like these, at worst, examiners will identify what needs to be done, which allows you to focus on the essential areas, make the required changes and complete the thesis.

'I've come back to university as a mature-aged research student, and I can't keep up with the energy of my fellow students . . . and besides I've grown out of their interests'

As postgraduate education becomes more common, more older students are enrolling in research programmes. Many of these students are married, or single mothers, or are struggling to meet financial responsibilities beyond those of younger people. These different situations result in different stressors during their study: day care for children, budgeting and finance issues, divorce, pregnancy, caring for elderly parents, and so on. At the same time, different interests may mean that they don't get the same peer and social support that younger students will often give each other.

Most universities have free counselling services available to students, and these centres are very experienced in advising about support services and providing advice on most personal problems. If you think financial, personal or other issues beyond your control will affect your progress, it is usually a good idea to warn your supervisor. Even if they may not be able to assist you directly, your supervisor may be able to support you if financial or personal issues affect the progress of your thesis and university review committees question your progress.

'I can't work with my supervisor any more, and want to change supervisors'

One of the most severe problems that can confront a student is the breakdown of their relationship with their supervisor. The loss of a supervisor's support and/or confidence is always stressful for the student and can seriously hinder the progress of the thesis. If the problem can't be resolved, sometimes the only solution is to change supervisors. Even with an amicable relationship, sometimes the student's and the supervisor's research interests diverge, or changes in the supervisor's circumstances mean that they want to supervise fewer students. Whatever the reason, changing from one supervisor to another is generally a very stressful time for the student, and will nearly always result in lost time, as extra work will usually be required to satisfy the suggestions of a new supervisor. In the worst case, if there is no suitable supervisor willing and able to take on the student, a reluctant supervisor may be appointed, leading to a strained and unproductive relationship, usually to the detriment of the student. The importance of the supervisor/student relationship, the wasted effort in starting with a new supervisor, and the cost of working with an ineffective or reluctant supervisor, mean that changing supervisors should usually be avoided, if at all possible. Unless your relationship with your supervisor has completely broken down, you shouldn't ever begin steps to change supervisors unless you have identified a potential supervisor who you think will be better than your current one, and who you think

203

might be prepared to take you on. This is because you don't want to jeopardize any remaining relationship by alerting the supervisor to the fact that you want to change. However, if it is necessary or desirable to change supervisors, a well thought out and diplomatic approach is likely to maximize your chances of obtaining an acceptable alternative. Changing supervisors isn't common, but it does happen and it is a fact of research life.

If you are seriously thinking about changing supervisors, it is a good idea to first discuss your options with another academic or with someone you can trust to keep the discussion confidential. You don't want your supervisor to hear from anyone that you are discussing changing before you are sure of what you want to do. You may want to talk to a couple of academics and enquire whether they are interested in taking over your supervision. This gives you a good opportunity to gauge your rapport with them. Whatever your reasons for changing, you should be careful not to criticize your supervisor. You should also ask for your discussion to be kept confidential, because you don't want to jeopardize any remaining relationship with your supervisor.

If you have decided to change, then it is best to make an appointment with the university or department director of your research programme. If another academic has expressed willingness to take you on, the change is usually unproblematic, and your main remaining stress is (tactfully) telling your supervisor, in person or by e-mail, that you have decided to work with another academic. Unless your relationship has completely broken down, it's a good idea to do this in person, so you have a better chance of maintaining a relationship with the previous supervisor, who may later become an examiner, a reviewer or a formal or informal referee. While it is a stressful discussion for most students, it usually goes better than they expect. Most academics are somewhat relieved when a student who isn't making progress decides to do something else. Your aim at this discussion should be to end the supervisor relationship on the best possible terms, thanking the supervisor for their work and support.

If you haven't been able to find an academic who might take you on, and you are still keen to change, you should explain your situation to the director of research or other appropriate academic. Be prepared to explain why you think you should change, trying to frame the problem as a research issue rather than a personal problem. Generally, universities are very supportive in such instances, since it is in their interests to accommodate changes with a minimum of fuss, and they will try to match your interests and methodological approach to the most suitable new supervisor to smooth the transition.

In the initial meetings with the new supervisor you should clearly outline why the change was deemed necessary and establish agreement on your direction, your thesis argument, methodological assumptions and research plan, in order to ensure that further change is unlikely to occur.

CONCLUSION

Completing a research thesis is a difficult and stressful time, and most students find that a range of problems arise during their studies. Because of the difficult nature of writing a thesis, and the frequency of negative feedback from the supervisors, at some point in the thesis most students either start to think that they are incapable of completing, or begin to blame their supervisor for their apparent lack of progress. In most cases, neither of these is true: you are almost certainly capable of completing if you have been accepted into a research programme, and your supervisor, while an imperfect human being, undoubtedly wants you to complete a good thesis in a reasonable time.

By identifying problems early, and by discussing them openly and honestly, if appropriate, with your supervisor, most problems during the thesis can be overcome. Completing a thesis is hard. But remember, if it was easy everyone would do it, and your degree wouldn't be nearly as valuable to you if everyone had one!

Part III

Submission and the later stages

Chapter 14

Advice from the examiners

PETER BERGQUIST

> A pessimist sees the difficulty in every opportunity; an optimist sees the opportunity in every difficulty.
>
> (Winston Churchill)

Most books on thesis writing emphasize the mechanical details of what to include and how to include it. There are comprehensive discussions of reading and summarizing the literature, organizing your own research results and putting them in context. To my knowledge, there is little attention paid to advising students on how to make their research attractive to their examiners and how to increase the probability that their thesis will be accepted without modification. The intent of this chapter is to look at the thesis from the other side: that of the examiner, drawn from my own experience as an examiner of theses over several decades, and from many years of sitting on examiners' committees, which make the final decision about a thesis. Many students do good research, but neglect to present it well, so the thesis is viewed much less favourably than the student might like. In presenting your thesis for the examiners, your emphasis should be on clarity, conciseness and economy of language, presenting a document that is easy to read but which shows your talents and skill in a research setting.

THE EXAMINER'S VIEW OF A THESIS

A thesis is a document that reflects the candidate's ability to think clearly, to express logical thought concisely, to discriminate between the significant and the trivial, to display technical competence, to analyse data and to interpret results. The thesis readily reveals faulty thinking, superficiality, inexperience and hasty preparation. How the examiner sees the thesis will depend first on the advice received by the student and second on preparation, long before the results and their interpretation reach the printed page (see preceding chapters), so it is important from the outset to be focused on the big questions implicit in the thesis topic and to be sensitive to the supervisor's comments and criticisms. Perhaps most important, it is necessary to allow sufficient time, not only to write up the thesis, but also to allow it to sit for a while and then to re-read it and edit it appropriately. A colleague of mine who was an outstanding historian in both the academic and popular fields made a habit of writing 3,000 words each day and then putting it away for three months before looking at it again. As a result, he could look at his manuscript with a fresh and critical view, and this was reflected in the incisive clarity of his writing and the great appeal of his monographs both to the public and to professional historians. Most students preparing a thesis will not be able to indulge in such a lengthy process, but it is important to come back and reflect on what is written with a fresh view of the style and arguments. For the student, this process has the benefit of seeing the thesis closer to the manner of the examiners – fresh and without prejudice.

Most universities specify a six weeks' to two months' turn-round time for the examiners' reports to be sent back to the university administration, but it is rare that this time frame is honoured. Examiners, who are experts in the field, are busy people; they have their own teaching, research and administration to attend to, and while they have the best of intentions, thesis examinations tend to be given a lower priority than their day-to-day activities. Most academics don't like being an examiner, because it takes a lot of time to read a thesis and write constructive comments, and it is time that they could be spending on other aspects of their job. Most do it as a favour for a colleague, or out of a sense of responsibility towards the profession. As a result, the assessment process is often done under pressure at the last possible moment, and accordingly, anything that the student can do to make the task easier is greatly appreciated. In particular, the clarity of the text and the appropriateness of the style are critically important. As it used to say in the instructions to authors in the old *Journal of General Microbiology*, 'Easy reading is damned hard writing.'

EXPECTATIONS OF EXAMINERS: WHAT EXAMINERS LOOK FOR

Given the other demands on the time of the examiner, it is likely that s/he will read the abstract three times and the main body of the thesis twice, once to get the overall flavour of the research and once in detail while writing the report, and possibly again while formulating questions, queries or alterations that will be embodied in the report. Accordingly, it is important to get the message of the thesis across as simply and clearly as possible, so the examiner can grasp the points made immediately and not have to deconstruct complex and obtuse grammatical structures to understand the points being made.

The purpose of the thesis

The thesis is a document that is your substantive examination submission of your research, from which the examiners will decide whether or not you have fulfilled the university's criteria for the award. You should be familiar with those criteria for examination, and when writing your thesis, clearly demonstrate that you have fulfilled the criteria. For example, for a PhD, these criteria will usually include evidence of an original and significant contribution to knowledge; a thorough understanding of techniques appropriate to the field; a critical appraisal of published works in the field and appreciation of the relation of the research to the wider field of knowledge. At a master's level, the same general criteria apply, but the contribution of the master's thesis is expected to be at a lower level than that of a PhD thesis.

The introduction and abstract

The introduction to a thesis is one of the hardest parts to write, and one of the most important in terms of impact. Examiners like to see the essence of the thesis captured in an initial sentence that provides focus for all that comes afterwards. The opening sentence should thus capture the essence of your research and make it immediately clear what your work is all about. The same sentence can be repeated whenever it is necessary to drive home the point of your research. It is the point of the whole dissertation, and should keep you focused when you are writing the thesis, and keep the examiner focused when reading it. Clearly, this encapsulating sentence will not arise without considerable thought and revision.

Similarly, the abstract is important and should not be hurriedly composed at the last minute, as often happens. This is an important part of your thesis, as it will be disseminated widely and made available electronically by the Digital Dissertations database. It should be a highly concentrated version of the thesis and should address the problem, the methods used to solve the problem(s) and the results and conclusions. It must be self-contained and give the reader a snapshot of what is to follow. Examiners will read this section first to gain an impression of what follows; some universities send the abstract at the time of inviting the examiner to assess the thesis. The examiner wants a succinct but comprehensive statement of what the thesis is about before tackling the detail that follows.

The introduction is important for both the candidate and the examiner at different stages of the examination process, although the end result is the same. The introduction should contain a succinct account of what is known about the topic. It is important not to overestimate the examiner's knowledge of, and familiarity with, the topic: s/he may be broadly knowledgeable in the field but may not be a specialist in your particular area. The examiner needs sufficient background detail to understand the research problem and the objectives of the thesis, so it is necessary to identify clearly the deficiencies in current knowledge and the significance of their resolution by your research. You must characterize your work as providing a solution to an interesting and manageable problem. The examiner will look for a summary statement of the results and conclusions in the introduction, so that s/he knows the path that the thesis will take and that there will be no surprises.

In many cases, the introduction will include a summarized literature review to paint a broad picture of the field and what is known, and another chapter will contain a more complete literature review or a more specialized review of particularly important papers relevant to that section. The literature review should provide a background as to where the problem came from and what is already known about it. Examiners have little patience for a review of every known paper relating to the field and it is important to demonstrate judgement and understanding by careful selection of the papers reviewed – quality, not quantity, is important. And note that if the examiner is in the same field s/he will not be impressed if his or her papers are not referenced! Further, it is important to read the papers themselves and not provide a review of reviews – this tactic is counterproductive, as the text is generally vague and unconvincing, and the device is obvious to most examiners, who will have read the same reviews. Drawing on reviews, rather than the original source articles, can also perpetuate typographical and bibliographical errors, indicating a sloppy approach. This will not be helpful in creating a favourable attitude by examiners, and may lead to challenging questions if a component of the process is an oral examination.

The methods used

This section will vary significantly from thesis to thesis and will be discipline-specific. In quantitative subjects, it is important to ensure that a competent researcher can reproduce your research by following your description of the methods. Unlike a published paper, in a thesis you have space to provide more detail and have the opportunity of commenting on improvements or alterations to published methods. A thesis is also a valuable resource for the quantitative disciplines, and other postgraduate students and researchers will find it a valuable compendium of methods and procedures. In these cases, the examiner is not likely to repeat your work but will refer to the methods when examining results chapters to confirm that the method was appropriate to the problem. It is also likely that an examiner will go back to an electronic database or an algorithm to check for him/herself as to the nature of the assumptions or the data employed in the results. Accordingly, web sites and other resources that were used should be clearly displayed.

212

The results: the work itself

It is often helpful to include some relevant background to the literature at the beginning of each chapter to focus the examiner's mind on the results that will be presented. It is important to outline the particular line of research that will be addressed and why it is important and interesting. It is also important to set out how the topic was approached, justifying your choice of research method. The results should be discussed – don't assume that graphs, diagrams or photographs are adequate by themselves, and don't just say that a result is interesting – say *why* it is interesting and what conclusions can be drawn from it. Pay attention to describing the content of tables and figures, and only put in the text, tables and graphs that illustrate the story you wish to tell, not the entire history of your research process. Ensure that the sequence is logical, even though the process that generated the data may not have been. Most examiners will appreciate a brief discussion of the significance of the results at the end of each chapter. This action anchors the information in the examiner's mind and means that the final conclusions can be brief and succinct, without the need for recapitulation of earlier material.

The final discussion and conclusions

Examiners generally expect the significance of the results to be clearly explored and their implications and significance discussed. If the results are contrary to those reported in the literature, their significance should be fully explored and explanations for the disparity put forward. Most research leads to more questions than answers and the examiner expects some carefully thought out suggestions as to what are the implications of the research and what should be done next. The conclusion is not the place to discuss problems with methods or results: instead, say clearly what has been done and why it is important. Examiners appreciate an up-front statement of what has been achieved, preferably in dot-point list form, at the start of the final discussion and conclusions chapter. This focuses their attention while reading the chapter, as well as your attention while writing it. You can also use this summary as a framework to structure the discussion.

THINGS TO AVOID: WHAT IRRITATES EXAMINERS

If you want your thesis to be viewed in the best possible light by examiners, it is a good idea to try and make your thesis as clear and easy to read as possible, and reasonable. One way to do that is to avoid particular things that are likely to annoy examiners. Probably one of the most serious irritations for examiners is poor expression, with convoluted and overlong sentences that obscure the meaning of the text. These should not have got past your supervisor's review, but it is not his/her role to teach you basic English grammar or proof-read your work. Examiners are not impressed by the use of incorrect word forms (nouns as adjectives, etc.), typographical errors, the use of discipline-specific jargon and acronyms without explanation and long words where short ones would do. Reference to a style manual (e.g. *Fowler's Modern English Usage*) is helpful in avoiding these mistakes. Use of the active, rather than the passive voice, also assists clear writing.

A close second irritant for examiners would be poor linkage and continuity between the research questions, the methods used and the final results, often also resulting in, or linked with, lack of interpretation of the significance and meaning of the data generated or the hypotheses proposed.

There are a number of discipline-specific conventions that can also cause annoyance if used outside their discipline. For example, footnotes are used widely in the humanities, where it is an accepted practice. In the sciences, footnotes, which may be long and in small print, are a major source of irritation – if it is worth saying and is relevant, why is it not placed in the text?

Other items causing irritation include uncritical listing of references without a careful appraisal of their contribution (if any) to the larger story being told, and, in the references section, papers listed without titles. The full title is important to the examiner, who may wish to look up the original reference; without the title, it may not be easy to do so (and finding the title will certainly be time-wasting for the examiner).

My personal annoyance is those who quote from the classical poets in an attempt to provide justification for what follows: if you do this, you will wince at your choice of quotation when you re-read your thesis in five years' time. Edit it out now and be content that you've shown to yourself that you are a passable classical scholar. Perhaps a more general message is to beware of being highly idiosyncratic in your thesis structure. A thesis is not an exercise in creativity (unless, perhaps, you are studying in the creative arts) and examiners may be irritated by highly individual and unusual aspects in a thesis, which is a formal document. It is almost always good advice to present your thesis in a way that should meet the expectations of the examiners, and to save the creative approach for later, less important, publications, which, in any case, you hope will be read by more people.

UNIVERSITY GUIDELINES FOR EXAMINERS

Most universities send examiners a list of specific points that they ask to be addressed in thesis reports. Clearly, it is an advantage to know the parameters of the thesis examination for your particular university before the thesis is submitted, since this allows you to ensure that the important points to be addressed are covered in the thesis. This information can be found on many universities' web

> ### Box 14.1
> ### UNIVERSITY GUIDELINES FOR EXAMINERS
>
> - Is there evidence of an original investigation or testing of ideas and a significant original contribution to knowledge?
> - Is there a demonstration of a high degree of independence of thought and an independent approach to the research question(s)?
> - Is there a thorough understanding of the appropriate techniques and methodology in the discipline/field?
> - Has there been a critical appraisal of the published literature and research results?
> - Is there an understanding of the particular research theme and its relationship to the wider field of knowledge?
> - Has the capacity to present a well-written work been demonstrated?

sites. Some typical sites from different universities are listed at the end of this chapter, but a search of the Web will reveal many more. Such guidelines generally include some or all of the questions in Box 14.1. There are often more specific sub-sets of these questions which relate to the various sections of the thesis. As well, there may be a request to assess the 'surface' qualities of the thesis (use of conventions, format, readability, etc.) and the 'deep' qualities, including such items as originality, contribution to knowledge, demonstration of the capacity to undertake original research, suitability for publication, etc.

EXAMINATION PROCESSES

For many universities, the examination is solely on the basis of the thesis presented to the examiners and the award of a research degree is then not normally subject to candidates successfully completing an oral examination. This is not the case in some countries, such as the UK, Canada and New Zealand, where the oral examination is an integral part of the examination process, at least for the PhD degree. In some Australian universities (for example, Murdoch and University of Technology–Sydney), candidates may request the inclusion of an oral examination on the basis that it can clarify points of principle or detail in the thesis; and the candidate may benefit from the advice of visiting examiners. An oral examination will sometimes be recommended if it is thought that it will assist in assessing the contribution of the candidate to the content and presentation of the thesis.

After the examiners' reports have been returned, they will be reviewed by the relevant committee of the university, which will make a decision about the result. The most common outcome is that the student should be awarded the degree

215

subject to minor revision to the satisfaction of the internal or the external examiner(s) or both. At some universities, the candidate, and/or their supervisor, has the opportunity before the committee meets to read the examiners' reports and make changes to the thesis in response, and provide a written argument to the committee as to why the thesis should be accepted with or without changes. At other universities, the candidate will not be permitted to read the examiners' reports until they have been viewed by the committee, and a recommendation has been made. In either case, students usually end up making some changes, and then need to justify to the committee why the thesis should now be passed. There is usually a time limit to make these changes, varying from university to university. The timetable should be able to be readily accommodated, as the examiners, and/or the committee, will usually specify very clearly what changes are required.

The next chapter discusses recommended approaches for responding to criticism, whether from examiners or from reviewers. As discussed in that chapter, you do not always need to make a change that has been requested by an examiner or reviewer. You must, however, make an argument as to why changes are not necessary, if you do not wish to make them. Sometimes examiners and reviewers are wrong, or unreasonable, and will suggest changes that are unnecessary. However, in these cases it is up to you, usually with the help of your supervisor, to make a strong case why such changes are not necessary.

Sometimes, if the examiners have raised serious objections to the thesis, the recommendation of the examiners' committee is that the student should be required to revise and resubmit the thesis. In that case, more extensive changes are required. The student essentially has to go back to the beginning, taking into account the particular points raised by the examiners. Additional experimental work may have to be done in the quantitative disciplines, and the results may alter conclusions drawn previously. Accordingly sections may have to be written carefully, taking into account the particular points raised. After resubmission, the examiners will pay particular attention to whether or not the particular issues have been addressed to their satisfaction.

In the worst cases, a thesis may be failed by the examiners, and revision and resubmission may not be allowed. This is rare, but is a devastating result for the student, reflecting poorly on both the student and the supervisor. The best advice to avoid this is that if the thesis work has been well done, well justified, well presented and carefully checked, such a result should not happen.

Oral examination

Depending on the country and the university, an oral examination on the thesis and the broad general area it relates to may be an integral part of the examination process. The oral examination can be a particularly useful method of rapidly resolving uncertainties (compared with requests for revision or resubmission) and can also be valuable for the examiner in determining the calibre of the candidate, as well as possibly giving an introduction to a new and eager potential colleague. Students are generally struck with fear at the thought of the oral examination, but in general it provides an opportunity for the student to show him/herself at their best. The examiners will be experts in their field, but *you* will be *the* expert in this particular field and will be more up to date than your supervisor or examiners. Nevertheless, the oral requires some preparation if you are going to impress the examiners as being confident and knowledgeable about the field.

Before the oral, it is important to prepare by practising presenting, either at a departmental seminar or at a conference. One device used by examiners to put the candidate at ease (they are not out to get you!) is to say, 'Give us a mini-seminar on the field of your thesis and how your work has added to the field,' and you should try to do so in five to ten minutes. This will require you to be thoroughly familiar with the whole argument and the main findings and significance of your work. After this opening, the examiners will ask more pointed questions, usually in areas that interest them, often relating to a particular chapter. So some time before the oral, summarize each chapter and write down possible questions that relate to it. If possible, get a colleague to read parts of the thesis and ask questions on particular aspects of your research that they would like clarified. Think about what you would like to talk about in the oral and see if you can devise ways to steer the discussion in those directions.

In the oral itself, the examiners will expect a robust defence of what you have claimed and concluded, but you should try not to appear arrogant or defensive. Many examiners will want to have a meaningful discussion with you on your results, so don't worry if the examiner seems to be unsympathetic – they probably think that the work is excellent but enjoy the cut-and-thrust of the debate. Take time to think about the questions; say 'That's a good question,' flattering the examiner and suggesting that you have thought about it already, and buying time to think. And don't hesitate to say 'I don't know' (but not too frequently!) rather than be wrong-footed or feel that you have to come up with an obviously contrived response. And take your time over answering questions (but keep to the point): it gives you time to marshal your thoughts and gives the impression of thinking carefully about the answer. Make notes if necessary. In some universities, the oral will also include questions on the field in general; be prepared and not surprised by such a question or questions of this nature, usually at the end of the oral. But finally, keep calm and let the examiner finish the question before you start answering it!

Choosing an examiner: tactics (largely for supervisors)

It is very rare for a candidate to have any say in the final selection of examiners. The student's supervisor will have to make recommendations as to the postgraduate studies committee (or its equivalent) regarding suitable examiners for the thesis. However, it is important for the student to suggest to, and discuss with, the supervisor possible names of suitable examiners. Postgraduate studies committees, or similar committees whose task it is to approve the names of examiners, tend to believe that only people with the title of Professor are sufficiently wise and experienced to act as examiners, since the university's reputation might be seen to be at stake. Generally these people, eminent as they may be in the field, are usually extraordinarily busy. This means that some may only rarely meet deadlines, and the report may be hurried and superficial. A better plan is to discuss with your supervisor the names of up-and-coming younger researchers not at the professorial level, who are likely to devote more time to the assessment, make more useful comments and criticism and tend to report more readily, as they are often flattered by the opportunity, which records the fact that they 'have made it' and they are highly regarded in the field. You may know of these people from your reading as part of the literature review, or you may have been lucky enough to meet them at a conference. Proposing a more junior examiner may cause difficulties with the postgraduate studies committee, but your supervisor should be prepared for it (with your prompting) in providing a strong statement as to why Dr X is preferable to Professor Y as a result of his/her more intimate and recent involvement in the field. If that doesn't work, and Professor Y is known to be tardy in providing a report, then I suggest that you suspend registration and take a paying job until the report finally arrives. It isn't a good idea for you or your supervisor to try to contact a late examiner to speed them up, in case you antagonize the examiner in some way, or are seen to be jeopardizing the neutrality of the process. However, you can sometimes speed up the process if a report is slow, by ensuring that your supervisor rings the relevant administrative section to ensure that reminders to tardy examiners are sent out to encourage them to return their reports. Even very late reports will eventually come in, sometimes after prompting from everyone involved, from the postgraduate administrators to the Deputy or Pro-Vice-Chancellor (Research) or University Vice-President for Research.

CONCLUSION

The most important aspect of thesis presentation from the examiner's point of view is to have the dissertation written simply and clearly. To do so, the important element for the student is time: time to plan, time to write and time to reflect on what has been written. If a thesis has been hurried and hastily written, it is usually obvious to examiners, since it is likely to be full of simple errors, with the resultant risk of irritating the examiners. Get assistance with the writing by asking a colleague or friend to read what has been written, not only for proof-reading but also for sense and logical connections. Reduce acronyms to a minimum (and make sure they are explained). Present only those figures and tables that are necessary to explain the big picture and do not recapitulate the history of your research topic. If an oral examination is a standard procedure, prepare for it carefully with the aid of a student colleague, and regard the oral as a research opportunity, not a threat. In summary, do the work well, and be prepared for at least some criticism from examiners. Few theses get through without any criticism, and an examiner who does not make critical comments is sometimes one who has not taken the time to consider your work in depth. If one aspires to an academic career, robust debate and explanation of one's views will become a way of life.

Box 14.2
WEB LINKS

- www.phys.unsw.edu.au/~jw/thesis.html
  The information on this web site is aimed largely at the physical sciences but there are useful general messages on thesis writing and preparation for postgraduate students in all disciplines. The site does not deal specifically with how the examiner sees the thesis, but has useful advice on how to write a thesis that will appeal to all examiners and is not discipline-specific.

- www.meaning.ca/articles/print/prepare_oral_defense_june02.htm
  A Canadian article on how to prepare for an oral defence of the thesis in a system where it is a standard feature.

- www.ioe.ac.uk/doctoralschool/info-viva.htm
  A useful site from the Institute of Education, London, on how to prepare for an oral examination.

- www.rses.anu.edu.au/gfd/Gfd_user_links/andrew.kiss.directory/
  thesis_writing/thesis_guide.html
  A useful site, originally from Michigan State University, on writing and presenting your thesis.

- http://free.hostdepartment.com/d/deadthesissociety/
  The web site of the Dead Thesis Society. Consult this when the task seems overwhelming. You are not alone. (This site seems to move often, so if you can't find it, search Google under 'Dead Thesis Society'.)

Consult the appropriate web site of your university regarding what is expected of candidates and examiners. For example, Flinders University is very clear about what it expects:

- www.flinders.edu.au/teach/research/postgrad/thesis.htm

Chapter 15

Responding to criticism

JOHN MATHEWS

Life is 10 percent what happens to us and 90 percent how we respond to it.

(Albert M. Wills, Jr)

So, you've put all this hard work into formulating your research question, into gathering your data, analysing it and developing your discussion of the findings, all embedded carefully in the literature. You've written it out beautifully as a coherent and well argued narrative, and submitted it proudly. Your supervisor, after discussing the matter with you, has carefully selected the examiners, and you have tactfully taken care to include a discussion of their work in your literature review. Now you're all set to submit the thesis, and sail to glory. And then back come the examiners' reports: one outright pass, one calling for minor changes to the library copy and one 'revise and resubmit'. Oh, those dreaded words, 'revise and resubmit'!

There are variations on the 'revise and resubmit' theme. It might be intended that you revise and resubmit under your supervisor's guidance, and your supervisor writes a report to the thesis examining committee showing how you've met the criticisms. Or it may be the full force of 'revise and resubmit' where you have to be re-examined – always a tougher one.

The initial response to receiving criticism, by all of us, is defensive. We are outraged at the shortsightedness, the cussedness, the sheer stupidity of the critic who seems blind to the virtues and quality of our work, and wilfully intent only on looking for flaws. In the case of a paper submitted to a journal it is bad enough. But when it is a thesis that stands in the balance in this way, it all just seems so unfair. This is an understandable reaction – but one that is not very helpful in dealing with the criticisms.

Of course, we should concede at the outset that perhaps the examiner is at fault. He or she may have misread the thesis (often done quickly and late at night) or misinterpreted a crucial point, or simply overlooked an important point. The thesis may not have been read as a whole, and connections that were in fact established, not recognized. If the examiner is at fault, then there is a clear proce-dure. It is not up to the student to defend a thesis against a biased or erroneous examiner report. Rather, it is the job of the supervisor. A bad report actually reflects poorly on the supervisor's choice of examiner, and the supervisor should take responsibility for defending a thesis against inaccurate attack to the post-graduate studies committee or its equivalent.

But these are rare cases. From now on, let's assume that the examiner has made some telling points, and that they need to be dealt with. What kinds of criticism are likely to be made, and what should you, the candidate, do about them? In this chapter we will review strategies for dealing with criticisms of your work, whether it is your thesis or an article that you have sent off to a journal for publication, and which is returned with critical comments from reviewers. Most of the discussion will concern criticism of the thesis, and your response to examiners, because this response will be critical in the time it takes to get the thesis accepted. However, keep in mind that a similar systematic approach to crit-ical reviewers is also important in getting your work published, in journal articles or in book chapters. In both cases, a thoughtful, careful and systematic response to criticism is the key to improving your work, and getting it accepted faster, whether for graduation or publication.

THE EXAMINER'S REPORT

A good examiner's report will give you an overall summary of the thesis, seen from the perspective of the examiner, highlighting what are seen as strong points, as well as weaker aspects. This is what we call the global overview. Then there are specific points to be concerned about, such as queries over evidence, or the interpretation of other scholars' work cited, or queries over your findings and how you have interpreted them. And then there are the nitpicking points, such as calling attention to typographical errors, spelling, syntax and all those little points that we could so easily have picked up for ourselves – but for some reason, just neglected to . . .[1]

Don't forget that examiners are working to a formula in responding to your thesis. They have received a letter from the university, requesting that they act in the role of examiner, outlining the shape of the report that is expected of them, and the categories that they can use in evaluating the thesis. The bullet points that they are expected to follow are usually along the lines:

- Does the candidate reveal familiarity with the subject, and with the methods used?
- Does the candidate reveal a critical understanding of the topic?
- Are the methods and techniques applied suitable for the subject studied?
- Is the thesis sufficiently comprehensive for its topic?

221

- Are the hypotheses clearly enunciated?
- Are the results and findings clearly laid out, and are they linked to the hypotheses?
- Is the exposition of sufficient literary quality?
- What, in the end, is the thesis that is defended, and is it defended adequately?

The specific guidelines for examiners for your university should be a valuable guide to you in revising your thesis one last time before submission. Are all the issues dealt with adequately? Can the examiner find clear responses to the points? If there are basically three parts to a good examiner's report, then the way to deal with them is to anticipate such a process. I always advise my students completing a thesis to think in advance of what the likely examiner responses might be, *and to deal with them in the thesis.*

So, to deal with the overall assessment and summary of the argument, the issue for the candidate is: Have you sufficiently clearly spelt this out? Does your abstract rush straight into your methods and your results, without spending a few sentences establishing why these might be of interest in the first place, and what position they might occupy in an established literature? I'm never impressed by the student who tells me that the topic is 'unique' or has 'never before been tackled' – this only suggests that the candidate has not yet identified the relevant literature and set of questions within which to embed the thesis. So help the examiner to work out what the thesis is about, by saying so, in the abstract, in your own words. This is best done at the very end of the process of writing: the last words written will be the first words read. The effort involved will be repaid if you find the examiners using your own words to explain what *they* think the thesis is about.

Then the examiner's report might get down to the questions of substance – the plausibility of the hypotheses, the quality of the evidence submitted, the logical connections and flow, the validity of the findings. Again, it is best to be prepared for these kinds of criticism by anticipating them, and writing into the text hypothetical objections to your argument, and then dealing with such objections – in the text as submitted. Nothing convinces an examiner better that a thesis is well written than evidence that objections and counter-arguments have actually been entertained and dealt with.

And then finally there are the nitpicking suggestions, corrections and pointing to errors of commission or omission. Again, why allow yourself to be the object of such corrections? Why not put the effort into the thesis before submitting it, subjecting it to spell check and syntax check, asking friends and acquaintances to read sections, to ensure that they interpret it as you mean it to be interpreted? Far better that you anticipate corrections before the examiner does so. A well argued thesis that is full of careless misspellings is unlikely to be passed first time by any examiner.

Let us assume then that you have checked all these things. You have antici-pated counter-arguments. You have spell-checked and hunted for syntax errors until you feel you are going blind. And when the examiners' reports come back, you find you have a 'revise and resubmit' and that it is accurately and fairly formu-lated. What now do you do?

This is where some candidates feel like throwing in the towel. No one likes to receive criticism – *particularly criticism that is telling, and that is justified.* I well remember receiving my first negative reviewer reports. I was outraged, and blamed the editor of the journal for allowing such disreputable and unworthy comment to be released. But of course, later, after I had adapted the paper to accommodate the criticisms, I was able to acknowledge that it was a stronger piece of work. In its final form, it could withstand criticism of the kind launched by the reviewer.

This is the way to adjust your mind set to the criticisms. Think of them in a wider sense as a contribution to scholarship, as a way of maintaining scholarly integrity. They're unpleasant when we are on the receiving end of them – but then, we wouldn't want unworthy theses to be accepted, because that would devalue the worth of our own efforts. So it is best to knuckle under and see how to respond to such criticisms.

Think of parasitism in the biological world. Parasites have a bad name; we call people who sponge off others 'parasites' and we view them with distaste when we come across their life histories in biological texts. Yet parasites play an important role in the greater scheme of things. By preying on a species and attacking its weaker members, parasites actually keep the species fit and well adapted to its changing environment. Without the pressure of the parasite, the members of the species would grow flabby, and possibly succumb to an unexpected threat. Indeed, in the rarefied world of artificial life, where computer programs iterate their oper-ations millions of times over, and capture in a few milliseconds the equivalent of a few thousand years of biological evolution, parasitism emerges as a surprising property of healthy programs. The point of this extended analogy is to argue that critics, reviewers and examiners play a role similar to that of parasites. They keep the scholarship healthy, and fit, and alert to criticisms.

I tell my students that the way to think of your tough examiners' responses is to treat them as suggestions for making your thesis better and stronger. So you might respond by imagining that you are writing a letter to the examiner. 'Dear examiner, I want to thank you for taking the trouble to read my piece of work, and for making some suggestions to make it better and stronger.' This is a way of starting to think differently about the criticisms, of seeing them in a positive light as well as being cussed and negative. (I hasten to add that I do not mean by this that the candidate should actually send a letter to the examiner. In most juris-dictions this is against the rules of thesis examination. However, by changing your attitude to the criticism you can begin to respond more positively to it.)

223

A CASE STUDY

A thesis is a structure that has to be built and defended. There are conventions dating back in some cases hundreds of years governing how it is to be built and defended. A good thesis has a certain style, and a form, that is appealing and aesthetically pleasing. It has an introduction that sets the scene skilfully, setting out the problem to be addressed and giving an overview of previous approaches, all of which have their limitations and all of which can be seen as leading up to this moment, this triumphal entry, of the thesis being presented. It then poses its research questions in a skilful way, not as open-ended questions such as 'What is the significance of phenomenon X?' or 'Is phenomenon X increasing in importance or decreasing?' but more along the lines 'Phenomenon X is expected to be more prevalent in situations Y and Z than in situation S or T, and the likely reasons are A and B rather than C or D.'

Take as an example the case of a thesis in international business, one which looks, for example, at economic development of a country (say, Malaysia) and is concerned with the respective roles of three kinds of companies in this developmental process, namely foreign multinationals, domestic large firms, and domestic small and medium-size firms. The process might also involve the contribution of public sector research institutes. So here we have the ingredients of an interesting investigation, one that already has a rich literature, and where the questions to be asked have some immediate, practical import.

Now one way of tackling it is to pose the research questions in an open-ended way, along the lines of 'What have been the principal sources of development in Malaysia?' or 'To what extent have foreign multinationals contributed to the development of Malaysia?' The problem with such open-ended questions is that they do not lead to clear answers, and invite digressions and incongruities in the arguments constructed by the thesis. They also invite examiners to query whether you have adequately answered the question – and there will always be room for doubt and argument over your response to such open-ended questions.

So the way to deal with them in advance is to pose the research questions in a more nuanced fashion, in such a way as to allow a clearer answer. The problem might be posed as 'Foreign multinationals are proposed to have retarded the emergence of local small and medium-size firms in Malaysia' or indeed as its opposite, 'Foreign multinationals are proposed to have created the economic space in Malaysia that local small and medium-size firms have been able to capture.' The advantage of such a 'question as proposition' is that it enables you to interpret your evidence so as to give a clear yes-or-no response.

This in turn gives your examiners something meaty to deal with. Unless you have badly bungled the process, they are unlikely to dismiss your answer. They are more likely to highlight some aspect of the evidence you have cited, or query the way you have interpreted the evidence – which in turn gives you the opportunity of engaging with this criticism, to defend your interpretation, or bowing to the wisdom of the examiner and acknowledging the point.

I frequently have to deal with research students who are passionate about their subject – such as the role of foreign multinationals in robbing a country of its resources, or the policy errors introduced to deal with major social issues like pensions and superannuation – and are bitterly disappointed when they find that instead of writing with gusto, with the cut-and-thrust of political debate, they are expected to deal with the arguments, and even – horror of horrors – deal reasonably with opposing arguments. The danger is that such students end up losing interest in the subject, or losing touch with the passions that fired them in the first place.

This does not have to happen. The way round it that I advise is to keep the larger picture very much in mind, in the way that a series of research questions are posed. The more pointed and specific the questions, the greater can be the scope of reference of the research, as developed in the introduction and the conclusion. So, to revert to our case of development in Malaysia, the passionate novice is full of hot-blooded concern over, say, the role of foreign multinationals in exploiting low-cost labour in the country, and poses an open-ended question like 'Are foreign multinationals exploiting Malaysian workers?' – to which the answer can only be 'Yes or no – it depends on your point of view.' More to the point in the present context, it invites an examiner to answer yes or no – and if the student's answer is yes, and the examiner's answer is no, then it makes it very hard to retrieve the thesis.

A more promising approach is to pose a question precisely, such as 'Has the contribution of foreign multinationals to GDP in Malaysia increased or decreased over the ten years 1980 to 1990?' or even better to turn it into a proposition to be tested, such as 'The contribution of foreign multinationals in Malaysia to GDP has increased over the decade 1980 to 1990.' The point is that in gathering the evidence to test such a proposition, and in testing it on the evidence gathered, the very real issues that motivated the thesis are actually being put to the test, are being refined and are feeding the work. And they invite a reasoned response from the examiners, who can discuss, say, the adequacy of the evidence collected, or offer an alternative interpretation of the evidence collected, or an alternative interpretation of the data sources and their significance. The point is that any one of these responses invites a reasoned response from the candidate, with the result that the thesis overall is strengthened.

Let's say that you find that the contribution of foreign multinationals to GDP has increased. This fuels the passion – or, maybe, it invites reflection as to whether the Malaysian economy is being upgraded, and made more internationally competitive, by this contribution of foreign multinationals. Or you demonstrate the converse, namely that the contribution of foreign multinationals declined over the decade 1980 to 1990. This then calls for some explanation and

225

interpretation. Let's say that you demonstrate that the contribution of foreign multinationals actually declined over the course of the ten years, and you discuss this in terms of the competitiveness of local firms. The examiner might then comment that the explanation appears to be plausible, but that there are alternative explanations, namely that the government stepped in and set limits on their involvement. Or alternatively, that the multinationals themselves simply grew tired of the frustrations they encountered in Malaysia, and looked to do business elsewhere. Your first response might be anger that such suggestions play down the heroic importance of the domestic small firm sector. But then, on reflection, you concede that they may have some plausibility, and that they at least warrant some further investigation. So here the examiner has highlighted a potential weakness in the argument, or a rush to judgement on your part. To meet the examiner's point calls for some more investigation on your part, and some more argument to deal with these alternative explanations. Whether you end up agreeing that it was the state stepping in that caused the decline in foreign involvement, or some other factor, your final thesis is richer for the discussion of these various sources of explanation. You are forced to deal with the alternatives before you settle on one particular line of explanation.

DEALING WITH THE EXAMINER'S POINTS

Most examiners want you to succeed. Their comments are not designed to make it impossible for you to succeed, unless they are actually motivated – very rarely – by pure malice. In the thesis on Malaysian development, for example, the examiner might contest your claim that local domestic firms have entered the space created by the withdrawal of foreign firms, arguing instead that scholar X found that local firms were not up to the mark. Now you may know that scholar X did her work on Malaysia in the 1970s, whereas your data are referring to the 1990s, and so you consider this to be sufficient grounds for challenging the continuing validity of scholar X's claims. (Note that you are not saying that scholar X is wrong, or that scholar X is a bad person; you are simply querying whether the claims that refer to the 1970s are still valid in the 1990s.) Now this would be a perfectly reasonable line to argue, and that any reasonable examiner might concede, when it is pointed out. So you do not just agree with everything the examiner says, willy-nilly; on some points you argue the case, and by doing so in a scholarly and reasoned tone you *enhance your own standing* in the eyes of the examiner.

Your response to the examiner would then involve a detailed listing of the points made by the examiner, and your response to each point, and a reference to any changes made in the thesis in response to each point (including page references to the final version). This response is something that you would first give to your supervisor, and if they are satisfied that you have covered all necessary points, it would typically be submitted to the university committee responsible for making a decision on your thesis. A detailed response like this is evidence that you have taken each point carefully and given it sufficient consideration.

What you do *not* do is utter a sweeping statement like 'Having considered the examiner's points carefully, I decided to make no changes.' This supplies no evidence that you considered any of the points in any detail. It smacks of arrogance, or carelessness – both capital crimes in the world of thesis examination.

What are the kinds of points made by examiners? One frequent cause of comment is failure to make a sufficiently tight link between the literature review and the findings of the thesis. So, in our Malaysian case study, you might have provided a literature review of economic development, of foreign direct investment and of state involvement in the economy – all prepared at an early stage of your thesis work. Once your thesis argument is well developed, and written down, you have to go back over your literature review, to ensure that the points highlighted are absolutely relevant to your theme. So you might have had a long segment on foreign direct investment (FDI), thinking at the time that it would be an important theme, but in your final revision of the thesis this segment has to be cut, or drastically scaled back, because in the end your argument does not engage directly with FDI. But if you neglect to do so, the examiner is likely to pick up the point. If and when this is done, the only thing you can do is acknowledge the point, and amend the literature review accordingly.

Another frequent cause of comment is lack of logical flow, or connection between the chapters. To continue with our Malaysian example, you might have prepared two conference papers along the way, one on FDI in Malaysia compared with other South East Asian countries, the other on foreign multinationals in Malaysia and the government's policy towards them. On your supervisor's advice you include both contributions, which have been refereed separately, as separate chapters of your thesis. This is good practice. But having done so, you have to make a connection between the chapters, in terms of an overall argument, that connects an analysis of FDI in Malaysia with the experience of foreign multinationals and with the government's policy towards them. Again, if you neglect to make these connections the examiner will highlight the point, and ask you to make them. Better to make the connections yourself, in the first place.

A third common issue picked up by examiners is multiple citations, or multiple mentions of a single literature source, without connecting them coherently with your final argument. Examiners are quick to pick up two disparate footnotes, one referring to the work of, say, Jones *et al.* (1968) on FDI in Malaysia in your literature review, in a context where you say the study discussed the negative impact of FDI on local firms, and again in chapter 5, when you again refer to Jones *et al.* (1968) but this time say that the study concerned the linkages between foreign firms and local suppliers. The examiner will be quick to point out that there is inconsistency in your citation practice and that you need to be clearer about what and why you are sourcing. Jones *et al.* may indeed have covered both the issues you mentioned, but to cite the same study twice, summarizing it differently on each occasion, suggests that you have not identified the main point of the article.

This raises the wider issue of citations, and what they are for. This is one of the issues most frequently raised by examiners. As a work of scholarship your thesis stands or falls on its argument, which needs to be plausible, well supported by evidence, secured either from the data you present (suitably manipulated and analysed) or from the literature. If your evidence is from the literature, you might cite a particular authority, for example the work of Jones *et al.* (1968), in support of your claim or your argument. It is like a prop helping to hold up a tottering wall. The more props you can find, the stronger the wall will be. So the citation needs to be (1) relevant, (2) soundly interpreted and (3) accurately referenced. Failure on any one of these fronts will invite a critical comment from the examiner.

Finally, be reasonable. When an examiner makes reasonable points, agree to them. There is no point in standing your ground and arguing every point. That just makes it harder still to get through, because you are inviting the examiner (when you resubmit) to contest your counter-claims, and thus delay the eventual award of the degree. If at all possible, agree with the examiner's points, and act on them. You do so by:

- considering the examiner's point and fleshing it out;
- acting on the point, by inserting some change in your argument, or your citation;
- inserting any relevant follow-on points, such as changes in another part of the argument depending on this point;
- writing up a response on that point, explaining how you have interpreted the examiner's point, what you have done in response, and giving page references so that the examiners can easily check what you have done in the new version of the thesis.

You do this in detail for every substantive point raised by the examiner. You do it initially for your supervisor, so that the supervisor knows that you have indeed considered each point carefully, and have responded. (You do this even if, after careful consideration, you reject the examiner's point, except that your response, on this point, instead of outlining changes, argues coherently why you feel no changes are necessary.) There is no better advice to be offered than to carefully respond to every point made by the examiner, treating each on its merits, and indicating exactly how you have dealt with the point.

Similarly, if you have submitted a paper for publication in an academic journal, it is very rare for it to come back without at least some, often substantial, criticism from reviewers. Journal reviews are often so negative that some academics will get the reviews, read them, then put them away for a week or a month, to give their irritation and frustration with the reviewing practice time to subside. But if you want to get your work published in a journal you will need to respond to journal reviewers in a similar, systematic way. Frequently the reviewers will make valuable suggestions, and though few people want to do extra work on something after they think it is finished, you may need to do the work to get the paper published. Alternatively, you may be able to make an argument as to why the changes are not necessary. Overall, however, an excellent response to a journal's reviewer will be similar to a response to thesis examiners: a detailed, point-by-point response to each criticism or suggestion, showing what changes have been made, perhaps arguing why some changes are not necessary, and giving page references so the editor or reviewers can easily check that you have made the claimed changes. A considered response like this will undoubtedly improve your work, and is likely to result in a much higher chance of getting the paper published.

COMPLETING THE EXAMINATION PROCESS

In most Western countries outside North America the thesis examination process is conducted through written external examination. In most universities, you agree with your supervisor on a list of external examiners, and these are passed to your university's postgraduate studies committee, or equivalent, which settles on a short list of three examiners and sends the thesis to them. The examiners prepare written reports, and make a judgement as to whether the thesis should be passed outright, should be passed with minor corrections, should be revised and resubmitted (for judgement by the committee) or, in the usual worst case, should be revised, resubmitted and re-examined. Then there is outright failure. In the rare cases where this happens it is naturally devastating for the student, but in some universities there may still be fall-back options such as a Master's of Research, so the result may not be as catastrophic as it sounds.

In other countries the thesis examination process is an oral affair, and there is an opportunity for you to display your learning, and to engage with points made by the examiners on the spot. Oral examinations are dealt with in Chapter 14, 'Advice from the examiners', so won't be covered here.

Let's think about these three thesis examiners for a moment. No one will read your thesis more closely than these three people. In fact, if your thesis is written for anybody, it's written for your supervisor and the three examiners – for four people! Perhaps no one else will ever read the work. Certainly no one else will ever read it so closely. So treat the examiners' reports as extremely valuable; they are the fruit of a close reading that you couldn't buy in any market. They are an inestimable source of wisdom and insight that you should treasure – rather than dismiss with contempt.

I advise my students to think in very personal terms about the examiners as they revise and prepare their thesis for submission. Think of these people paying close attention to your work. What is going to stand out for them? If you know who your examiners are, or who they are likely to be, have you ensured that you discuss their own contributions – without engaging in obvious flattery, but with due recognition? Nothing grates on an examiner more than reading a thesis in a field where the examiner has made an important contribution, only to find that contribution ignored. It's not grounds for failing – but it certainly feeds a desire to find fault. Have you ensured that issues that they have signalled in their earlier work as being important, in their eyes, are also seen as important in your thesis? Have you treated data that they have dealt with in a sympathetic way?

Remember that a thesis is a highly artificial construction. It is a prolonged meditation on a single issue, using all the devices of scholarship to illuminate and clarify the nature and causes of the issue under discussion. The difference between a thesis and a literary work is that a thesis is a statement as to the nature of objective reality, interpreted through the lens of a set of concepts and questions. It is a set of statements that 'Such and such is the case' or 'is not the case' or is something else altogether. This is different from a literary work, where the emphasis is on how you feel about something, or how you respond to some event, or how you strategize to get your own way in some set of circumstances. None of these issues applies to a thesis, which seeks to establish that the phenomenon X actually happened or did not, and for reasons Y and Z rather than reasons P or Q. Thinking about the thesis in these broad terms not only enables you to pose research questions in an intelligent way, but also gives clues as to how to respond to examiners' points.

It still pays to think about the examiners as individuals who are paying you the compliment of reading your work closely. They are the gatekeepers who have the key to letting you through – or not. Think about their role from their perspective. It will help you get through the gate.

And now, after all the tears, the anguish, the waiting – you get the letter that tells you that your thesis has been examined, and that the university has decided to award you the degree of PhD (or DBA or Master . . .). Hallelujah! Now you really have something to celebrate. But think for a moment about what you are celebrating. You are celebrating because you have been deemed worthy to enter a very select circle. You have produced scholarship that your scholarly peers have judged and found to be worthy. This is what the agony is all about. It is the price to be paid for entry into the select circle that signals your achievement through the award of your degree or the title 'Doctor'.

When people at some social gathering ask me what kind of doctor I am, and whether I can give them advice on some ailment, I tell them that I'm sorry, I'm a real doctor – a doctor of philosophy. I'm not a bachelor of medicine or of surgery. A doctor of philosophy is a mark of distinction in terms of philosophy, or the love of knowledge (from the Greek *philein*, love, and *sophia*, wisdom). It is a badge of honour. You achieve this distinction because three examiners have read your work closely and judged it fit to join the world of scholarship. You are thereby judged fit to join the community of scholars. There is no greater honour. Treasure it – and work hard at it.

NOTE

1 There is some empirical investigation of examiners' reports in surveys reported in the literature, reinforcing these points. See, for example, Johnston (1997) and, in the Australian context, Holbrook *et al.* (2001).

REFERENCES

Holbrook, A., Bourke, S., Farley, P. and Carmichael, K. (2001) 'Analysing PhD examination reports and the links between PhD candidate history and examination outcomes: a methodology', *Research and Development in Higher Education* 24, proceedings of the twenty-fourth International HERDSA conference, pp. 51–61.
Johnston, S. (1997) 'Examining the examiners: an analysis of examiners' reports on doctoral theses', *Studies in Higher Education*, 22 (3): 333–47.

Chapter 16

From thesis to publication

JAMES GUTHRIE, LEE PARKER AND ROB GRAY

> The greatest problem with communication is the illusion that it has been accomplished once and for all.
>
> (George Bernard Shaw)

You've completed your thesis, and now the tantalizing question arises: 'What next?' While the bound volume on your bookshelf gives you a warm glow, the graduation photos swell you with pride and the extra letters to your name convey some feelings of status and self-worth, your research findings are likely to languish in the shadows unless you take further action. It is very likely that, with just a little more effort in revising it into an acceptable format, the standard of research you have produced will qualify you for publication in one form or another. In doing so you have the opportunity to make a significant contribution to your discipline's wider stock of *accessible* knowledge, and as a by-product enhance your own profile and credibility in your chosen field.

In this chapter we aim to help you to go that extra mile, giving you some inside tips on how to get results from your thesis published. With our combined seventy years of experience as scholars – reviewers, authors, journal editors, editorial board members and PhD supervisors – we have learnt about research and publishing the hard way: through a process of submission, rejection, trial and error, that is, by actually writing! We hope that what we share can be of use to young scholars.

Researching and publishing are the two main activities that distinguish the scholar from the teacher, manager, businessperson or consultant. Scholarship is much more than teaching – it is the pursuit of learning and understanding through formal research, reading, reflection, discussion and writing. The value of such scholarship is then tested and confirmed as it is disseminated by means such as teaching, workshops, conversations, conferences and, of course, publication. To put it more starkly, we would dare to say that scholarly research findings and insights that are never disseminated cannot be called true scholarship, on the grounds that they are not accessible to others and so they don't add anything new to humanity's stock of knowledge. This observation applies to your thesis on the bookshelf with its attendant risk of gathering dust! If you don't publish the results of your thesis in some form, you will certainly limit any career as an academic, but you will also lose the chance to have the results of your hard-won degree recognized by the resulting publications.

In this chapter we will guide you through the various forms of publication, and provide some tips on how to write and keep writing. We end with words of encouragement: don't give up! The excitement of new discovery and continuous self-improvement will, we hope, keep you going through the difficult and often frustrating process of publication.

PUBLICATIONS, YES, BUT WHAT KIND?

So you have decided to try and get your thesis published, but in what type of publication? In Box 16.1 we list the types of publication available to the scholar. The list is intentionally alphabetical, so as not to imply that one publication type

Box 16.1
TYPES OF SCHOLARLY PUBLICATION

- Academic journals in the discipline
- Academic journals outside the discipline
- Book reviews
- Books
- Chapters in texts
- Conference papers and conference proceedings
- Consultants' reports
- Discussion papers
- Edited texts
- Internet
- Newspapers/videos
- Other (non-new-research) monographs
- Other non-academic/popular journals
- Professional journals in the discipline
- Professional journals outside the discipline
- Research monographs
- Submissions to government/regulators
- Textbooks (basic/conventional teaching or new approaches/research synthesis)

Source: Adapted from Gray *et al.* (2002)

necessarily has priority over others. Each publication type has its own appeal, purpose and advantage and we hope in this section to provide you with information to help you select the channel that is most suitable for your work.

It's often hard to know which type of publication to read, let alone which to publish in. On the whole, despite the variety of publications on offer, in most academic disciplines the refereed research journals are generally regarded as the primary, and most desirable, source of research output. The process of 'refereeing' is central to scholarly publication and peer assessment. The term refers to the process whereby an article or other piece of work is sent by the editor or by whoever is overseeing the eventual publication to recognized experts in the field for comment. However, our experience suggests that focusing exclusively on refereed academic journals neglects other important channels of knowledge input and distribution. To help you decide which type(s) of publication provide the best avenue for your research work, we will now comment on some of the forms of publication listed in Box 16.1.

Refereed journal articles

Refereed research journal articles have traditionally been viewed by most academic disciplines as the most authoritative source of research material and the most sought-after channel of scholarly publication. The distinguishing characteristic of academic journals is that all articles will have been refereed, subjecting each paper to an independent review, which hopefully results in higher-quality publications. Reports from referees, particularly for the higher-quality journals, will often be critical of aspects of your work, so submitting your work for independent review can be a depressing process. However, the reports will also typically provide detailed and useful suggestions to improve the work before the article can be published. Whilst we are trying not to enforce a hierarchy of publication types, there's no denying that articles in the better journals require a high standard of research rigour, and that the data analysis, communication, argument, critique and theorization must all be of a high standard. Writing for publication in a refereed research journal is challenging and hard work, but the results are worth it. As a result, journal publications are a common and very popular publication method for thesis writers, many of whom manage to publish two, three or more refereed journal articles on different issues from the one thesis.

Journals also vary enormously in quality. Publishing an article in one of the best journals can establish an academic reputation, but the best journals accept only a small percentage of the articles submitted to them, and even if it is eventually accepted there may be multiple revisions and a substantial delay before your article is accepted for publication, and again before it is actually published. Less prestigious journals will often have a much higher acceptance rate, and will publish articles faster. The decision as to which journal you should target is discussed in greater depth later in this chapter (see 'Choosing a journal for publication').

Books

Books can be further divided into three main categories: textbooks, research books and edited books. All books, regardless of the type, generally involve substantially more time and personal commitment than shorter forms of publication. As a result, there will generally be a substantial delay before a book is published, and new academics, in particular, often find that they will have pressure put on them to achieve early publication. As a result, books are often a more feasible and attractive publication option later in an academic career.

Textbooks

These are the primary source material for students, and are constantly revised in the light of current theories, teaching styles and events. For the scholar seeking to publish, textbooks represent a major commitment of time and effort as authors become committed to subsequent revisions, new editions, associated teacher guides, manuals for students, case studies, short-answer questions, multiple-choice test banks and so on. Your thesis is likely to represent only background data for some parts of any textbook (e.g. possibly a chapter). Because textbooks are recommended by academics, and used by students, who will remember the name of the person who wrote the textbook, textbooks can be an effective way to establish a reputation if your textbook is widely used. However, textbooks are generally given relatively little value by university committees hiring staff or deciding tenure or promotion, so the decision to devote substantial amounts of time to writing a textbook should not be taken lightly.

Research books

These are more focused than textbooks, being typically orientated towards leading-edge thinking and research in a highly specific subject area. In terms of publishing, such books are less likely to require authors to engage in subsequent revised versions or new editions. Some students may have the opportunity to submit their entire thesis (or a revised version of it) for publication as a research book, and this can be an excellent way of getting the broadest audience for your findings. Again, research books will often be viewed less favourably than journal articles by universities, but publishing a book based on your thesis can be an effective way to demonstrate your expertise in a particular area, and to make a name for yourself. If you don't intend to pursue a career as an academic, publishing a book based on the findings of your thesis can be an ideal strategy. Publishing a research book can also allow a two-pronged strategy; publishing a detailed discussion in a book, and publishing shorter, more focused sections as journal articles. This can be a very successful way to ensure the widest dissemination of your research, while also developing a scholarly reputation.

Edited books

These books bring together a spectrum of often diverse views and perspectives on a given topic area. In terms of publishing, edited books often involve the editors doing little less than personally writing the entire book themselves. Their role as an editor sees them chasing up the contributors and trying to compile and edit the chapters into a unified whole. The contribution that edited books make to knowledge can vary dramatically, depending on such factors as who the editor is, and who the fellow contributors are.

Book chapters

Book editors will often request chapters from particular individuals with a known reputation, or will announce the project and invite submissions from people who are interested in submitting work. A chapter in a book, particularly an edited book of readings, can consist of a critical review, a theoretical treatise or a report of an empirical study. It provides a succinct account of, or argument on, a given topic. The book chapter can also allow greater flexibility in subject, format and length than a journal article. An invitation to contribute a chapter to an edited book can open up one of the easiest forms of publication, because the invited book chapter, though usually of lower prestige than a journal article, offers a higher likelihood of publication, often with less work. New academics, who do not usually have an established reputation, are less likely to be invited to submit a chapter. However, a recent thesis, with the resultant deep knowledge of the literature in one area, can be ideal preparation for providing a review chapter. You should therefore be alert for publication opportunities by book chapters, while at the same time working to publish your main thesis findings in other formats.

Commissioned reports

Reports commissioned by governments, businesses, professional bodies and other parties provide an interesting insight into public policy thinking, and also into the debates surrounding such policy. If there is a government inquiry into some issue with which your thesis has also dealt, you may have the opportunity to provide a written submission to that inquiry, and some of it may be incorporated in that inquiry's ultimate report. Contributing to a commissioned report makes for an interesting form of research, often providing access to otherwise confidential information and to the thoughts and perspectives of policy makers and their critics. In addition, contributing to a government report can sometimes result in a substantial public profile if your submission is seen as a crucial input. The drawback to such reports is that generally the academic has to work under rather strict guidelines and there is a potential loss of academic independence.

Research monograph

A research monograph is normally a shorter, privately published book or booklet that reviews and reports on a commissioned and/or funded piece of research. Research monographs typically provide in-depth insights into the debates surrounding public policy, and allow broader exploration of a research topic than would typically be the case in a journal article. For scholars seeking an avenue for publication, research monographs have some particular advantages: they often involve the acquirement of a research grant, they may be commissioned, thus resulting in high probability of publication, or the academic may make a bid for a subject area which interests them. As they are frequently refereed by independent experts, research monographs can also be perceived to have a respectable scholarly quality. Your thesis may provide an excellent foundation for a research monograph, although you are likely to be asked to substantially edit its length and to ensure that the monograph concludes with clear recommendations for policy and/or practice.

Professional journal articles

Professional journals provide a bridge between the world of the academic and the practitioner. In the current higher education environment, where collaboration between scholars and professionals is encouraged, such journals are playing an increasingly important role in the communication of research findings to the relevant professional audience. They provide an important alternative to the refereed journal. This type of publication is used less by thesis writers, but there is certainly merit in taking some key thesis observations and findings and translating them into brief, simply worded professional and business journal articles for a practitioner audience.

Conference papers

Conference papers are akin to discussion papers – since they are usually not the final version of a research publication, they provide the reader with stimulating ideas that can be challenged and debated. Generally, the conference paper represents a partly, though substantially, finished piece of work, fit for public display, but still requiring critical comment and improvement to make it acceptable for publication in a refereed journal. For the publishing scholar the conference paper is rarely an end in itself, but it is frequently published to a limited audience as part of the conference proceedings, and thus holds some limited weight in a portfolio of publications. For someone who intends to have a career as an academic, the ultimate aim of every conference paper should be publication as a journal article or a book chapter. Conference papers can be a valuable interim method of publication, particularly for postgraduate students and recent graduates, to first present ideas and findings and expose them for critical comment, in order to obtain feedback and thereby improve the ultimate publication.

THE ART OF WRITING A RESEARCH PAPER

If you are reading widely and engaging with a variety of publication types, the natural outcome is to want to produce research publications of your own! At the foundation of good research output is strong research input. However, writing is an art form, regardless of the nature of the research being undertaken, and the way you express your research, thoughts and ideas in writing will influence your success in publishing your work. This section offers some suggestions on how to write a research paper, though most of the insights will also apply to writing for other publishing media.

Writing up your work

The most effective and efficient writers plan and structure their paper in advance. Even before laying down a structure of the paper, you may elect to try the technique of 'brainstorming' which involves simply writing down whatever comes to mind on the topic, based on your prior reading and research on the topic area, and looking for clear themes in what you have written. This process can help you to identify the most important issues for the paper to address. You then need to sift through these brainstormed ideas in order to identify key, perhaps recurring, themes, issues and observations that will give your paper focus. 'Mind maps', flow charts and other visual aids can also help you move from a collection of ideas to a set of linked, logically ordered themes that relate to your focus, a supporting logical argument, a clearly expressed methodology and a set of meaningful and significant conclusions. The aim at this stage is to establish a basic foundation and flow of ideas for the draft paper.

In developing the structure for your paper, chapter or book, you will need to devise a series of sections and section headings, and supplement these with brief notes outlining possible substantive content and the key points to be included in each section. Charts and flow diagrams can also be helpful when trying to clearly

Box 16.2
THE STRUCTURE OF AN ACADEMIC PAPER

- An *abstract* that summarizes the primary objective of the study, the research methods used and the major finding or findings. Many authors appear to write the abstract last, without a lot of thought, and the abstract becomes a replication of the introduction and/or conclusion of the article. However, the abstract is probably the most important section of an article, because readers will look at the abstract first and on that basis, decide whether to keep reading or not. As a result, the abstract should be very carefully written and reviewed, to ensure that it does justice to the contents of the article. The abstract should clearly and succinctly answer a number of questions. What research was done? How, when and where was the research done? Why was it done? What was discovered or concluded? And, importantly, why does it matter?

- An *introduction* that sets out the subject area, the central objective and supporting research questions, a brief statement of the methodology employed, a brief guide to the key issues to be addressed, and a brief plan of the article.

- A *review* of the background literature in which you summarize and critique prior research in the subject area. This section should also include the literature's relevance to the focal questions of the research project, and argue the significance of the research being reported from your own study.

- A *rationale* for and description of the research method, in which you outline the theoretical and methodological perspective(s) you are using and the specific steps you took during data collection and analysis.

- The research *findings*, clearly and succinctly outlined, focusing on material specifically related to the central objectives or research questions of the paper. This section will vary in structure and length depending on the nature of the project (e.g. survey, field research, historical study).

- An *analysis* and interpretation of the findings, their significance, relation to findings in prior studies, and implications for further research and/or for contemporary practice or policy.

- A *summary*, providing conclusions and directions for further research.

structure your work. In general, journal articles and most forms of academic paper will follow a similar structure, shown in Box 16.2. Of course every paper (or chapter) will have its own unique structural model. Our suggested structure is a general guide, outlining the components that are generally expected to be incorporated within your paper's uniquely designed structure. Most important, however, your structure must conform to the requirements outlined by the editors of your paper's intended destination. This means that you should choose your target journal *before* you start writing the article. (See the later section on 'Choosing a journal for publication'.) You should then check the journal's 'instructions for authors' section, which will be contained on its web site, and read a few articles from previous issues to allow you to follow the general style used in that journal. Matching your article closely to the style and requirements of a particular journal means it is more likely to be viewed favourably by the editor of the journal, and will avoid the need to restructure the paper at a later date.

Upon finishing the draft of a paper, your next step will be to review its contents and ensure that you have an effective synthesis of the various components. The most effective way to do this is to juxtapose the first sentence of the introduction, literature review, summary, conclusion and abstract. Doing this will help you determine whether the paper has been successful in achieving the objectives you set out for it in the introduction, and whether:

- you have actually addressed all the questions/issues you raised in the introduction;
- your conclusion has actually concluded something rather than simply repeating your summary of findings;
- your findings have augmented, filled a gap in, challenged or even overturned prior published research in the field;
- you have actually concluded anything significant!

The following questions can be used as a guide during this process:

- Are the research objectives or questions posed in the introduction addressed and answered in the summary and conclusion?
- Are the limitations of the study spelled out in the discussion or in the research method(ology) sections? (*Methods* are the means whereby one collects and analyses data. *Methodology* refers to the philosophical issues which underlie those methods. The terms, therefore, mean very different things – but journals vary in the extent to which they differentiate between the two terms.)
- Has the significance of the subject, indicated in the introduction, been reinforced with an explanation of the significance of the findings later in the paper?

Once you have done all this, you will probably be convinced that it is your finest work and that you have made a breakthrough contribution to your field's knowledge base! This is the point where you need to take a break from your manuscript. Go to the movies, go for a walk, go cycling, do the shopping, or whatever turns you on, because the most challenging part is yet to come! When you return to your paper for critical evaluation, you will find that you can read it in a clearer, more dispassionate light. To assist your own critical re-read, you might want to consider such questions as:

- Does the writing communicate clearly and with an economy of words?
- Does the language suit the target audience?
- Are the conclusions fully supported by the evidence?
- Does the paper meet the 'so what?' test? Why is the paper important?
- Does the paper tell a complete and credible story?
- Does the paper develop its theme(s) in a coherent manner?
- Are there further implications and theorizations that can still be developed in the paper's concluding discussion?

By subjecting yourself to this rigorous self-evaluation, you are guaranteed to find areas to improve the first draft. Once you have incorporated these ideas into a second draft, ask one or two colleagues to critique the second draft. Then revise it again, addressing the concerns and questions that they raise. *Then*, depending on its intended destination, your paper can move to its next stage. If it is intended for a professional or business audience, you should do one last proof-read, a final check that it conforms to the requirements of your target publication, and then you can send it off and wait for feedback. If it is intended for a refereed research journal, you would be wise to expose it to presentation at a research seminar at your, or another, university or at a research conference. By doing so you are likely to obtain further valuable comments and criticisms that will enable you to finally polish the paper before submitting it to your target journal's editor. Now let us go back and look at this process in a little more detail.

Knowing your target

In writing up your work, it's important to be clear about the following:

- Who is your audience? Is the paper for students, for practitioners, for fellow researchers and postgraduate students, or for some other audience?
- The answer to the first question will help you determine the answer to the next question: what type of publication is best suited to your paper:

a refereed journal, book, professional journal or other? Being clear on this point will make it easier for you to determine what the content should be, the length and structure, the language employed, and the style and extent of referencing.

- In summary, you need to decide at the outset which *specific* publication you would like to publish in, as each publication has a unique set of editorial board members, previous literature and academic style, all of which should influence the style and content of your paper.

This process can be presented as in Figure 16.1:

Figure 16.1 *External factors determining paper style and content*

Particularly in the case of journals, it is vital to ensure that your paper's subject matter, length, structure and bibliographic style are appropriate for the journal to which you intend to submit. If not, the editor(s) may assume that the paper has been rejected by another journal, or that you are unfamiliar with their journal and view it less favourably. You can avoid this problem by carefully examining, and complying with, the journal's style guide. It is also helpful to become familiar with work already published in the target journal that may be directly relevant to your paper, and to include reference to this work in your literature review. We would also generally advise including in the literature review a cross-section of relevant prior publications, thereby demonstrating that you are familiar with the ground-breaking work, leading authors, latest developments and international sources in your topic area.

Fine-tuning for publication

If you think your first draft will turn out to be the final version of a paper, then think again! High-quality journal articles are usually the product of many rounds of revision. Less experienced authors have been known to submit first draft work to journal editors in the hope of avoiding the redrafting process. This strategy is risky because it risks alienating the editor of the journal and giving you a reputation as someone who does poor work. As highly experienced scholars themselves, the referees will usually detect a first draft submission and may return the work, recommending against its reconsideration by the target journal. Similarly, the submission of an incompletely proofed paper (e.g. incomplete bibliography, poor grammar and paragraph cohesion, etc.) is likely to antagonize referees and editors, quickly earning the author a bad reputation.

242

In our experience, you can enhance your paper's chances of being accepted for publication by submitting drafts to colleagues for comments, by presenting it at research seminars in your own university and/or other universities and by presenting your work widely at conferences. We also recommend publishing your draft work in a widely circulated discussion paper series or on specialist web sites as an intermediate step towards submission to a journal. This exposure will benefit you as the author, identifying errors, alternative perspectives, ideas for further improvement, methodological issues, findings requiring further research and areas requiring improved explanation. The more work that you put into the paper and its dissemination prior to its final submission the greater will be the chance of a favourable reception by reviewers.

Choosing a journal for publication

When trying to choose a journal for publication you may find yourself asking the question: 'Where is the "quality" research published?' This is a hard question to answer, because there is no clear agreement in any field, and the answer often depends on someone's personal perspective. Academics often talk about journals in terms of 'quality' or 'tiers', but these terms usually reflect the perceived status of the journal, and not always the actual significance or impact of the work it publishes. A large part of the problem is that the concept of 'quality' is not well defined and is interpreted in a variety of often inadequately articulated ways (Tinker and Puxty 1995).

This explains why there is often a wide variation in rankings of journals between the different ranking schemes. Journals' rankings, and their reputation, are often based on surveys, where academics rate the importance that they believe that such journals have for other academics. Journal rankings can then become a self-perpetuating system, where journals are rated as important because people think that other people think they are important, irrespective of the journal's readership or citation rate.

Whether you agree or not with the published rankings of journals, there is no doubt that publishing in journals that are seen as high-prestige can be beneficial for academics seeking jobs, tenure and promotion. Different universities vary in the importance that they attach to the 'quality' of journal publications in hiring or promoting staff. However, if you can publish in a journal that is ranked as one of the best in your field, your career is certainly likely to benefit.

While publishing in one of the best journals has undoubted advantages for an academic reputation, if your aim is to reach as wide an audience as possible, or to publish quickly, then the highest prestige journals, which typically have high rejection rates, long lead times and low professional readership, may not be your best target. In choosing whether to target a particular journal, the most important factor should be the fit between your research and the journal's aims. Every journal, on its web site, will give a description of the sort of research it publishes. If the journal specifies that it prefers a particular sort of research, and your research does not fit into that category, you probably have little chance of being published in that journal, and submitting to it is likely to lead only to extended delay before rejection. By ensuring that the subject of your research is compatible with the material that the journal publishes, you will increase your chance of acceptance. This may sound obvious, but many authors target journals on the basis of the perceived quality of the journal and, as a result, tend to suffer from an extended and depressing series of rejections.

In Box 16.3 we list factors that may influence one's judgement of the value of a particular journal. Clearly Box 16.3 is by no means exhaustive. However, such a list clearly shows that an assessment of journal quality is often subjective and may reflect only the scholar's admiration for the journal, the personal influence of the journal on the scholar and/or the reputation of the journal as perceived by the scholar. These qualities may in fact have no relation to any objective factors that might in reality ascertain a journal's intrinsic quality, such as the rigour of its refereeing system, its citation in the discipline, or its readership. In other words, such categorizations are inevitably value-laden and subjective, and it is therefore important for the individual academic to avoid excessive reliance upon journal rankings. The most important way to decide where to publish is to think about *why* you are publishing. If you are publishing to advance your academic career, and your university, or a university where you hope to work, values particular journals, then if you think your work has a chance of being published in those journals it can be worth targeting them. If you want your work to be more widely read by academics, it is sometimes worth publishing in less prestigious journals, if you know they have a wider readership and higher citation rate. And lastly, if you want your work to be read by professionals, you should publish a less technical, often condensed, version of your work in professional journals. Even if your university does not value professional journals for promotion purposes, such publications can be a valuable way of establishing a professional reputation and of making valuable contacts.

JUGGLING THE BALLS AND STAYING IN THE RACE

Experienced authors rarely put all their eggs in one basket. That is to say, whilst a research student may well spend three years or so on a single research project to obtain a doctorate, once the PhD is completed we do not advise spending similar amounts of time working exclusively on a research project with the aim of targeting a top-tier publication. Particularly for a younger researcher working on one of his or her first major (postdoctoral) research projects, concentrating

244

Box 16.3
ASSESSING JOURNAL QUALITY

- How often do you read an article in the journal?
- How often do you browse the journal?
- How often do you consult the journal?
- Do you subscribe to the journal?
- Does your university subscribe to it?
- What databases carry the journal?
- Is the journal indexed by relevant citation sources?
- What is its actual rejection rate?
- What is its perceived rejection rate?
- What are your views of how others perceive the journal?
- How have previous ranking/reputation studies rated it?
- What is its subject/method/ideological orientation?
- What is the purpose of the journal (e.g., to influence practice, teaching etc.)?
- What has been your experience as a referee/editor for it?
- How often do you cite it?
- How often is it recommended reading for students?

Source: adapted from Gray *et al.* (2002)

on one research project, to target a journal known to have an extremely high rejection rate (e.g. often 80–90 per cent for some journals) is a very high risk indeed. If the paper is unsuccessful in getting published in that journal, resubmission to another journal with further consequent revisions will significantly delay eventual publication.

In the early stages of one's publishing career it is therefore advisable to have a number of research projects with multiple targets, and to target some journals in which there is a greater chance of (ultimate) acceptance. In any case, working on a sequential project-by-project basis can be boring, and is likely to involve long fallow periods between successful publications. Experienced researchers and authors typically run four to five (or even more) research projects concurrently. This is not as difficult as it may sound, since each project is at various stages in the process of publication. For example, one project may be at the conceptual design stage, another may be at the literature review stage and another at the revision stage. This strategy is made easier by co-researching and co-writing some projects with others, which also allows the author to maintain a variety of research that is both enlivening and that permits cross-fertilization of ideas. It also ensures a steady stream of published research over time. Of course if you are aiming to produce a number of papers or book chapters from your thesis, then you automatically have a head start in terms of drafting, revising, presenting and submitting a number of papers to various journal outlets.

Another aspect of managing a research strategy is maintaining diversity of publication type. Some academics write only research articles, others write only books. Still others write only professional articles. There are even some academics who write only research articles for one or two selected journals. We believe that the best long-term approach is to develop an 'all-rounder' profile – that is, a personal publishing profile that includes theoretical and applied research, empirical and critical review studies, professional and research publications, in journals and in book chapters. This, it seems to us, will provide you with variety as well as with the chance to develop a range of empirical and theoretical skills and topic areas (through academic journals, books and conferences), in addition to the chance to engage with practical and policy issues (through professional journals, reports, and so on).

Identifying your next research topic

After completing your thesis, your first publications will generally be focused on identifying and summarizing the results from your thesis research, in one or more journal articles. Sometimes further research flows naturally from that work, and the thesis is the beginning of a long stream of successful publications. Sometimes, for a variety of reasons, after publishing work based on the thesis, a new academic wants to develop a different research area. This can be a frustrating period, trying to choose an interesting and topical area that can be the source of future publications. It is similar to the frustration that many PhD students go through in selecting their thesis topic, except the new academic may be working by themselves, without the guidance of a supervisor, which can be very threatening. As an aspiring scholar it is often hard to know what a fruitful topic for research work and writing may be. Some of the best ways to identify potential areas of research interest are discussions with colleagues, debates at conferences, observations made by presenters and commentators at seminars, and contemporary discourses in the professional and business communities.

However, the most common source of ideas lies in the prior literature. If you are seeking a new research area, our advice is to read the existing professional and research literature relating to your area of intended specialization, keeping a special eye open for:

- questions addressed but not yet satisfactorily resolved;
- questions not yet addressed;
- questions partly resolved but worth further investigation;
- questions raised in 'further research' sections at the end of research articles;

- issues being debated in the business and professional media;
- theories that require testing or offer new perspectives;
- practices about which we know little in terms of sources, rationale or longer-term impacts;
- phenomena or practices that, as yet, remain largely unexplained or inadequately theorized.

CONCLUSION

As researchers and publishers we find ourselves driven by a passion to make a lasting, if incremental, contribution to our academic discipline, to continue to build a network of collegial scholars around the globe, to discover new knowledge, and to contribute to theoretical understandings, strategic policy and practical processes in our fields of research. To develop a successful research and publishing career and to maintain momentum, it is vital for you as an emerging scholar to develop your own rationale as to why you are engaged in research, and target your research efforts and publications accordingly.

Many researchers and publishers continue to pursue research regardless of the sometimes limited rewards and despite the personal costs in time, effort, energy and sacrifice. Why? It is because these researchers are energized by the investigation of the new and unfamiliar, enjoy the cut-and-thrust of academic and professional debate, and gain immense satisfaction from their contribution to society through the power of the printed word. We encourage you to make the world of research your world, and invite you to join us in broadening the knowledge base accessible to scholars, policy makers and practitioners. We wish you the best of luck on your exciting path towards becoming a published scholar.

ACKNOWLEDGEMENTS

We draw extensively from a prior research project undertaken by the authors and, in particular, owe a great deal to two papers: Parker *et al.* (1998) and Gray *et al.* (2002).

REFERENCES

Gray, R., Parker, L. and Guthrie, J. (2002) 'Rites of passage and the self-immolation of academic accounting labour: an essay exploring exclusivity versus mutuality in accounting', *Accounting Forum*, 26 (1), 1–30.

Parker, L., Guthrie, J. and Gray, R. (1998) 'Accounting and Management Research: Passwords From the Gatekeepers', *Accounting, Auditing and Accountability Journal*, 11 (4), 371–402.

Tinker, T. and Puxty, T. (1995), *Policing Accounting Knowledge*, London: Paul Chapman.

247

Index